Business Organ D1766655

THE M. & E. HANDBOOK SERIES

BUSINESS ORGANISATION

RONALD R. PITFIELD
A.C.I.S., M.B.I.M.
Formerly Principal Lecturer, Polytechnic of North London.

SECOND EDITION

MACDONALD AND EVANS

Macdonald & Evans Ltd
Estover, Plymouth PL6 7PZ

First published 1977
Reprinted in this format 1978
Second edition 1982
Reprinted 1984

© Macdonald & Evans Ltd
1982

0 7121 0295 7

*Printed in Great Britain by Richard Clay (The Chaucer Press) Ltd,
Bungay, Suffolk*

PREFACE TO THE SECOND EDITION

This HANDBOOK is designed to be an aid to those studying for various examinations in the business field. It will be particularly relevant to those working for the Higher National Diploma (or Certificate) in Business Studies offered under sundry schemes approved by the Business Education Council. It has also been planned to assist those studying for the following professional examinations:

>The Institute of Chartered Secretaries and Administrators
>>Management Techniques and Services
>>Management: Principles and Policy;
>The Association of Certified Accountants
>>Organisation and Management;
>The Institute of Cost and Management Accountants
>>Organisation and Production
>>Organisation and Marketing Management
>>Corporate Planning and Control;
>The Institute of Administrative Accounting
>>Business Organisation for Accounting Staff;
>The Association of International Accountants
>>Business Administration;
>The Society of Company and Commercial Accountants
>>Business Administration.

The selection of material for the book has been aimed to include not only the major aspects of the subject but also those areas which frequently feature in examination questions.

The first part provides a survey of the framework within which business operates. The second, and major, part deals with the organisational features and managerial practices relevant to business in general and to broad functional areas.

The book has been deliberately planned as a learning aid. This has been achieved by providing a "framework" for each area of study, within which facts are presented in a logical sequence. Headings and sub-headings are used to confine facts within strict bounds so that all and only the relevant information is given, thus giving the benefits of objectivity. The result should be that, firstly, progressive reading would facilitate learning in a programmed sequence; and, secondly, selective reading would provide an economical method of revision.

The Progress Tests should be used as a form of self-checking and as an aid to revision (the numerical references are to the relevant paragraphs in the chapter). The examination questions should be studied so as to become familiar with the style of the questions as well as the subject areas. Grateful acknowledgment is given to those bodies whose past examination questions are quoted.

The necessity to produce this edition has made it possible to take account of recent changes in legislation and to comment on new practices and business attitudes.

(June) 1982   R.R.P.

CONTENTS

Part Two: ORGANISATION WITHIN THE BUSINESS

LIST OF ILLUSTRATIONS

PART ONE

THE STRUCTURE OF THE BUSINESS COMMUNITY

CHAPTER I

THE COMPLEX OF COMMERCE

BUSINESS INTER-RELATIONSHIPS

1. The trading chain. No business can operate in isolation. Any trading business must stand in a direct relationship with those from whom it buys and those to whom it sells. A business unit must therefore be a link in a chain and perform the function of passing the object along the chain. In so doing it may *transform the object* (that is, by processing it or altering it so as to increase its value) or *perform a service* in expediting the movement. As such transforming or servicing must have had a reason to justify its performance, the work undertaken by the link must be paid for. This would be the source of the profit attributable to that link.

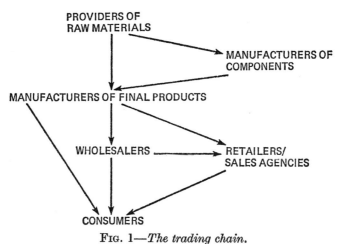

FIG. 1—*The trading chain.*

1

In Fig. 1 it will be seen that the manufacturer of the final product and the manufacturers of the components of the final product *convert* that product. The other units *perform services* in moving the product towards the ultimate consumer.

2. Functional units. In addition to the units directly involved in trading as shown in Fig. 1, there are many others providing services which are related to the traders. Some of these will be specific to any one trader; others will have a general application to all businesses. One method of categorising the functional units in a business community, therefore, is as follows:

(*a*) Trading businesses;
(*b*) Direct services;
(*c*) General services.

3. Inter-relationships of unit types. An outline of the mutual dependence and interlocking relationships of the above categories is as follows:

(*a*) *Trading businesses.* A business directly involved in trading (i.e. the making, buying and selling of goods) will be positioned within the framework illustrated in **1** above. In some instances it will perform the functions of more than one position. For example, a manufacturer may sell to a retailer or, even, directly to the consumers, thereby assuming the role of wholesaler and, in the second instance, the retailer also (*see* V, **11**(*a*)). The manufacturer may provide his own components or have control of some of his raw materials.

A single unit may therefore have more than one function.

(*b*) *Service businesses.* A business may not be directly concerned with buying and selling, but may operate as the provider of specialist services to other concerns. These could range from window cleaners to financial advisers; from suppliers of stationery to owners of computer bureaux.

(*c*) *All businesses will have relationships with the following*:

(*i*) banks;
(*ii*) Government departments, such as the Department of Health and Social Security, the Inland Revenue, the Department of Trade etc.;
(*iii*) auditors;
(*iv*) the law. This will include legislation specific to one

type of organisation (e.g. the Companies Acts) and legislation applicable to all businesses (e.g. the *Employment Protection Act* 1975);

(*v*) the Stock Exchange, if they are companies whose shares are listed;

(*vi*) any trade association applicable to the industry;

(*vii*) trade unions, directly at local level and indirectly at national level;

(*viii*) consumer protection organisations, where applicable;

(*ix*) local authorities (rating, planning permission, local bye-laws etc.).

4. Specialisation. The concept of specialisation in any form is that concentration on a narrow field results in increased efficiency. This is because, firstly, such focusing will take place where the circumstances are especially favourable (e.g. localisation of industry in geographical areas with marked advantages over other areas; occupations undertaken by those with a particularly relevant expertise) and, secondly, because knowledge and experience can be increased if the area is confined.

In business, specialisation can take the following forms:

(*a*) *Within industries.* The firm can be a specialist in one area of an industry, e.g. a motor manufacturer producing only sports cars; an electrical manufacturer confined to the domestic market.

(*b*) *Of industries.* The majority of business units are confined to one broad category of industry.

(*c*) *Of functions.* A manufacturer, for example, may have no function other than that of producing goods, leaving distribution to other firms.

(*d*) *Of labour.* By aptitude, or perhaps because of trade union demands, a worker may be restricted to one type of work. In ship-building, for instance, the work-scope of boiler-makers and fitters are strictly segregated, although in some areas the work is very similar. The specialisation may also be because of the method of planning work. Thus, a worker on an assembly line would have a very narrow range of activity.

(*e*) *Of location.* Historically, industry congregated close to sources of supplies and energy, but the development of transport reduced the tendency.

5. Over-specialisation. In spite of the advantages of specialisation, the principle can be extended to the point of being
detrimental to efficiency. The following are examples of some
of the dangers.

(*a*) *Undue reliance upon a market.* A business concentrat-
ing on one market will suffer in the event of a decline in that
area. Lack of demand for sports cars in the example in **4**(*a*),
would adversely affect such a manufacturer, whereas one
engaged in motor production generally would not be so
placed.

(*b*) *Complete dependence upon an industry.* A business
engaged entirely in one industry would have its fate linked
to that of the industry. A business operating in several
industries, however, would thereby diversify the risk (*see*
V, **11**(*c*)). Reliance upon one industry to provide business
can also be dangerous. Thus, a manufacturer specialising in
motor car instruments would suffer if the motor industry was
depressed.

(*c*) *Single function.* The advantages of a business having
more than one function can be considerable. A manufacturer
may derive benefits by, for example, owning his suppliers or
his retail outlets.

(*d*) *Labour demarcation.* The confining of a worker to
strict limits of what he may do can adversely affect production and the worker himself. Time can be lost in passing a
job between different workers, when it could quite reasonably
be done by one worker; bottle-necks can result from an
imbalance between those engaged on the sub-stages of a
process. A worker has less expertise to offer where his scope
of work has been restricted and this may reduce his employment prospects elsewhere.

(*e*) *Intense localisation.* A concentration of similar industries in one area will result in widespread unemployment in
the event of depression, because of the lack of alternative
employment for a labour force which is specialised. There
would also be a cumulative effect on the dependent local
businesses.

6. Collective terms. Generally accepted terms concerning
classifications of business groups are necessary. These may be
as follows:

(a) *Establishments*. These relate to physical units—factories, warehouses, shops, offices, etc. The Government's Census of Population regards them as "the whole of the premises under one management at a particular address". Thus, if one manufacturer has a factory in Birmingham and another in Glasgow there are *two* establishments.

(b) *Firms*. This refers to a collection of business resources unified within the framework of a single business organisation. Thus, the example in (a) above would be of a single firm if there was overall management.

A difficulty may arise if each factory was autonomous, as they may be if each factory was engaged in different types of production. In such a case it may be more indicative to refer to an *industrial group* rather than to a firm. If each establishment operated completely independently, but each was jointly owned by a controlling body (such as in a conglomerate, *see* V, 11(c), it would be usual to refer to it as a *financial group*.

(c) *Industries*. A broad division would be between:

(*i*) extractive (mining, agriculture, fishing etc.);

(*ii*) manufacturing (making and assembling of components, processing);

(*iii*) construction (building);

(*iv*) tertiary (services).

The allocation of any business to a specific industry can be complex. Many businesses would come within more than one industry; some are marginally involved outside their major industry; new industries come into being, often as sub-divisions of existing ones; firms move from one industry to another as a matter of business strategy.

7. The influence of the economic climate. The prevailing economic climate will influence the direction of business both generally and specifically.

(a) *General influences*. In periods of optimism there will be an inclination to expand existing areas of business and to enter new areas. Prospects of increased sales generally will encourage investment in new plant, etc., with beneficial effects on providers of equipment, services, etc. The consequent increase in employment and personal incomes will encourage the production of consumer goods.

(b) *Specific influences.* Separate types of businesses may be affected differently by the same economic condition. For example, in periods of high spending-power, encouragement will be given to the "leisure industries" (entertainment, gambling, etc.) and those producing consumer "luxuries"; those in the export trade will benefit from general world prosperity, particularly in those areas where they have an advantage; the willingness of the Government to spend as an effort to reflate the economy will obviously affect some businesses more than others.

BUSINESS ATTITUDES

8. Business objectives.

(a) *Maximising of profits.* This may be regarded as the major objective of business, but, even accepting that concept, some refinement of it is necessary.

(i) The period of measuring profit must be considered. A business, because of the nature of its industry, may expect to make no profit in its early years (e.g. the builder of a dam will receive no return for some years). It may be the type which can expect extreme fluctuations of profit (e.g. nickel mining). It may be politic to keep profits deliberately low, in order to capture a market by charging competitive prices. It may be decided to "plough back" a larger than usual proportion of income for future development. In all these cases it would be unrealistic to accept the profit of any one year as a yardstick.

(ii) A business may decide to avoid over-trading by being satisfied if it achieves the "norm" of profit relevant to the industry generally.

Other attitudes may be discerned:

(b) *Shareholders.* The objectives of shareholders are security of capital and net gain. Security may be endangered if the company embarks on projects which produce exceptional profits but with a consequent increased risk. It must also be borne in mind that the amount of dividend payable is decided by the directors and may not be directly related to the size of the profits (*see* VI, 8(a)). Shareholders are concerned with overall return; that is, income in the form of dividends *and* capital growth.

Thus, the profit rate may not be the major factor to be considered.

(c) *Employees*. Staff whose remuneration is partly dependent upon sales will be mainly concerned with the amount of sales. These can be high whilst profits are low, because of a narrow profit-margin per unit of sale. Staff generally will be concerned with job-stability and prospects. Thus, they will be satisfied if the firm is making such modest profits as will allow them to continue in rewarding employment.

(d) *"Empire-building"*. This is an expression relevant to love of power. It may be the characteristic of a dominating personality in the business, or it may be a corporate philosophy. It is a desire for power for its own sake and may reduce profit-maximisation to a lesser role (*see* V, 4(*f*)).

(e) *Sociological concepts*. Profit may have a lesser importance if the dominating attitude is to produce worthwhile goods, provide good conditions of employment, demonstrate "industrial democracy" by schemes of worker-participation, contribute to the national economy, etc.

9. Social responsibilities. These are the obligations devolving upon a firm beyond the financial objectives of the business. They are brought into being by the constantly developing attitudes of society generally. In many cases, the responsibilities of firms may be enforced by legislation, but such regulations can only result as an expression of public opinion. The responsibilities will include the following:

(a) *Wage standards*. The somewhat harsh laws of supply and demand for labour are tempered by recognition that there must be socially acceptable levels of remuneration. A high proportion of wage rates are determined by-agreement with trade unions.

(b) *Working conditions*. In addition to the legal compulsions to maintain standards of safety, health, facilities, etc., employers generally recognise their responsibility to provide acceptable working conditions.

(c) *Staff welfare*. Businesses are expected to have some concern for their employees beyond the strict confines of the work situation. This is expressed in such facilities as payment during sickness, pension schemes, recreational facilities, etc.

(*d*) *Trade Union co-operation*. There is general acceptance of the necessity to recognise and work with trade unions in their representation of the work force. This would include recognition of officials and the provision of facilities to enable them to carry out their duties. It may or may not include machinery for participation in different levels of management, but certainly the concept of consultation is now accepted.

(*e*) *The environment*. A business has a responsibility to the community at large to prevent perils to the public and to protect the standard of life. "Environment pollution" is recognised as a modern disease and includes despoiling the landscape, the emission of toxic wastes, the erection of unacceptable buildings, the creation of noise and dirt, etc.

(*f*) *Fair dealing*. This denotes a code of behaviour in relation to the buying public. The supplying of impure or dangerous goods is obviously undesirable, but other transgressions are possible. Advertising, for example, should not be deceitful, or calculated to play on the natural fears of people; prices should be fair and clearly stated; artificial shortages should not be created or monopolies unfairly exploited.

(*g*) *Codes of conduct*. Agreed standards of conduct exist within trade associations; listed companies are subject to rules imposed by the Stock Exchange; financial bodies subscribe to the City Code concerning take-over bids, etc.

(*h*) *Consumer protection*. In recent years there has been a considerable increase in legislation to ensure that consumers have rights against those from whom they buy goods and services. For example, irrespective of whether an article is "guaranteed" or not, a buyer can claim against the seller (who need not necessarily be the manufacturer) if an article is faulty, does not conform to its description or does not serve its intended purpose. There is also protection against buyers entering into credit transactions (including hire purchase) before they have had time to fully appreciate what they are committing themselves to.

PROGRESS TEST 1

1. Explain direct connections and indirect connections between commercial units. (1–3)

2. What forms of specialisation exist in the commercial world? (**4**)

3. Give examples of excessive specialisation. (**5**)

4. Distinguish between the accepted definitions of establishments, firms and industries. What are "industrial groups" and "financial groups"? (**6**)

5. Give examples of general effects and specialised effects of a change in economic conditions. (**7**)

6. What could be the objectives of a business besides that of making profits? (**8**)

7. Give examples of the "social responsibilities" of industry. (**9**)

8. What is meant by "consumer protection" and why is it necessary? (**9**)

CHAPTER II

PRIVATE BUSINESS UNITS

TYPES OF UNITS

1. Basic types. The basic types of units in the private sector of business are:

(*a*) sole traders;
(*b*) partnerships;
(*c*) limited companies.

SOLE TRADERS

2. Characteristics. The distinguishing features of sole traders are as follows:

(*a*) *Ownership* is by one person.
(*b*) *Management.* Day-to-day management is usually by the owner, but not necessarily so. In larger concerns, some element of delegation is essential and in a few cases the owner may delegate management entirely but retain overall control of policy.
(*c*) *Finance.* This may be provided entirely by the owner but frequently part is in the form of borrowed funds.
(*d*) *Size.* The business of a sole trader is usually small, but is not necessarily so. The features of small-scale trading, therefore, may or may not apply.

3. Advantages. The advantages of trading as a sole trader may be as follows:

(*a*) *Managerial freedom.* Decision-making can be effected quickly because it may not be necessary to consult anyone else. Any consequences of action are the sole responsibility of the owner.
(*b*) *Business personality.* The personality of the owner can

be imprinted on the business because of his control of policy.

(c) *Simple management structure.* The unit is probably small enough to make small-scale management possible. The difficulties of management often met in larger organisations (*see* V, 4(a)) are thus avoided.

4. Disadvantages. The disadvantages will include the following:

(a) *Unlimited liability.* In the event of the insolvency of the business, the owner will be solely responsible for making good the deficiency from his personal estate.

(b) *Responsibility for decisions.* The benefits of consultation with fellow-owners are absent. In a large concern, the advice of managers, etc., may be sought, but any decisions must be the sole responsibility of the owner.

(c) *Difficulties of outside finance.* It may be impossible to obtain further finance without surrendering personal control by admitting a new partner. Lenders may be reluctant to provide additional finance because they could resort to only one person in the event of financial failure.

(d) *Indispensability of the owner.* Undue absence of the owner will result in loss of personal direction during that time.

(e) *Problems upon dissolution.* There would be no assurance of continuity if the owner died or retired. Thus, if it was necessary to sell the business there would be no saleable goodwill if it could not be sold as a "going concern".

(f) *Limitations on expertise.* The owner may not possess all the attributes required to run a business. An expert engineer, for instance, may have little financial acumen.

PARTNERSHIPS

5. Definition. "Partnership is the relationship which subsists between persons carrying on a business in common with a view to profit".

6. The partnership agreement. The joining of two or more persons in business to trade as a partnership will entail the following agreements, which should be embodied in a Partnership Deed.

(a) The amount of capital subscribed by each partner.

(b) The division of distributable profits and the determination of the amount to be distributed.

(c) The extent to which each partner will participate in daily management (a *sleeping partner* will undertake no management).

(d) The amount of salary (if any) payable to each partner.

(e) The extent of any right to make personal drawings against entitlements to profits.

(f) The method of making and recording decisions.

(g) The terms and conditions applicable in the event of dissolution of the partnership.

7. Legal status of a partnership. *A partnership is not a legal entity (except in Scotland)*, that is, it is not recognised as a person in law but is regarded as an association of individuals. This has the following consequences.

(a) The firm cannot sue or be sued in its own name. Any legal action must be taken by or against any or all of the partners.

(b) It cannot contract in its own name.

(c) On the withdrawal of any partner, voluntarily or upon death, or upon the bankruptcy of any partner, the partnership is terminated.

(d) In the event of insolvency of the business, any or all of the partners can be held liable to contribute to the deficiency from his private estate.

(e) Any partner acting within an apparent authority as a representative of the business, binds each of his partners.

(f) A partner may not transfer his share of the business without the consent of his fellow-partners.

(g) In the event of insolvency of a partnership, a partner may not prove against the firm in competition with outside creditors.

8. Legislation. The following statutory provisions apply to partnerships.

(a) No partnership consisting of more than twenty persons may be formed for the carrying on of any business which has for its objects the acquisition of gain (*Companies Act* 1948).

(*b*) Where the liability of a partner is decreed to be limited, there must be at least one general partner (that is, one with unlimited liability) (*Limited Partnerships Act* 1907). Such associations are very rare.

(*c*) As from 26th February 1982, partnerships (and all other businesses) which trade under a name other than that of their owners were no longer required to supply details to the Registry of Business Names, which was abolished. From this date, such businesses are required to display the names and addresses of their owners at their business premises and on their business stationery.

9. Advantages. The advantages of trading as a partnership may include the following:

(*a*) *Division of responsibilities.* The work-load can be spread and some flexibility may be possible.

(*b*) *Specialisation of duties.* Each partner may specialise in his duties by employing any particular expertise he may have.

(*c*) *Joint consultation.* Decisions may be made by taking account of viewpoints of others (but *see* **10**(*f*) below).

(*d*) *Finance.* Additional finance may be provided by introducing another partner (but *see* **10**(*c*) below).

(*e*) *Sharing of losses.* In the event of insolvency, losses would be shared between the partners.

10. Disadvantages. These may be summarised as follows:

(*a*) *Agency.* A partner may bind his fellows to a contract without their knowledge or consent (*see* **7**(*e*) above).

(*b*) *Dissolution problems.* Withdrawal of a partner will result in dissolution of the partnership, with a liability to repay capital and accrued profits to the partner or his executor.

(*c*) *Problems of disturbing the partnership.* The introduction of a new partner may disturb the previously-existing personal relationships (*e.g.* where the partnership was a "family business").

(*d*) *Personal liability for loans.* Any loans to the business would, in practice, be made to the partners as individuals.

(*e*) *Unlimited liability.* Each partner has a potential unlimited liability for the debts of the business.

(*f*) *Problems of joint decision-making.* Joint decision-making is often difficult and time-consuming. Inaction may result from personal differences between the partners.

LIMITED COMPANIES

11. Basic characteristics. The fundamentals specific to the limited company method of trading are as follows.

(*a*) *Limited liability.* A member's liability is limited to any amount unpaid on his shares. Thus in the event of the insolvency of the company his financial loss will be restricted to the amount he has paid or is due to pay on his shares. The consequent important advantage of trading by this method is that in the event of financial failure his private estate cannot be distrained upon to satisfy the company's debts.

(*b*) *Legal entity.* A company is a legal entity (a "person" in law), separate from its constituent members. Thus a company may contract in its own name; it may sue a member and vice versa; a shareholder may be a creditor of his own company.

(*c*) *Continuity.* The existence of a company is not affected by any change in its membership. No matter how much its ownership changes by the transfer of shares the company remains unaltered.

12. Types.

(*a*) *Statutory companies.* These are those formed under Acts of Parliament specific to each company.

(*b*) *Chartered companies.* These are those granted a charter by the Crown. Such companies are still occasionally formed in respect of charitable bodies, etc.

(*c*) *Registered companies.* These are those formed in accordance with the Companies Acts and constitute the major proportion of companies.

Companies may also be categorised as public companies and private companies (*see* **13**).

13. Public companies and private companies. There are two types of companies limited by shares—public companies and private companies.

(a) *Any* company must have at least two members. There is no maximum number.

(b) A *public* company must state in its Memorandum of Association (*see* **16**(*a*)) that it is a public company and it must be registered as such.

(c) A *private* company is a company which is not a public company.

(d) A *public* company may invite the public to subscribe for its shares and debentures; a *private* company may not.

(e) The shares of a *public* company are freely transferable; a shareholder in a *private* company may have to have the agreement of the other members.

(f) A *public* company must end its name with the words "public limited company" or the abbreviation "PLC".

(g) A *public* company must have the "authorised minimum of allotted share capital" (currently £50,000).

(h) A *private* company may commence trading immediately it is registered; a *public* company must first have a "trading certificate" after it has proved that the authorised minimum share capital has been issued.

14. The separation of investment and management. In a limited company the only investors who may engage in management are the directors. These are those shareholders to whom the power of management has been delegated by the body of shareholders. (The unique position of company directors is explained in VIII, **29–33**.)

15. The members.

(a) *Acquisition of membership.* Membership may be obtained by various methods—applying for a new issue of shares; purchasing from a present holder; accepting a gift or bequest, etc.—but it must be a voluntary action. A person may not be a member against his will and a person whose name appears in a company's register of members without his consent may take action to have it removed.

(b) *Subject to company regulations.* Having acquired membership a person is bound by the regulations of the company (*see* **16**(*b*)). Application to be registered as the holder of shares includes a commitment to be so bound.

(c) *Voting power.* Shareholding may give a member the right to vote at company meetings but there is no automatic legal right to a vote. The extent of any voting power (usually one vote per share) is specified in the terms of issue and in the company's regulations.

16. Internal and external regulations. Regulations concerning the company and its members are mainly contained in the following.

(a) *The Memorandum of Association.* This establishes the legal identity of the company and determines and limits its objects. Any activity of the company or its directors beyond the scope of the objects is *ultra vires.*

(b) *The Articles of Association.* These are the internal rules for governing the conduct of the company. They will include regulations establishing the powers, rights and obligations of members and of directors. They may be altered, within the bounds of the law, with the agreement of the holders of 75 per cent of the voting shares.

(c) *The Companies Acts 1948 to 1981.* These comprise extensive legislation, supported by a considerable amount of case law.

(d) *Stock Exchange regulations.* Shares in public companies may be dealt in on the Stock Exchange only if they have been "admitted to listing". The "permission to deal", granted by the Stock Exchange, imposes on a company and its directors regulations stricter than those required by law. The main purpose of this is to give additional protection to shareholders and investors generally (*see* VI, **13**).

17. Ownership and control. Because of the characteristics specific to companies and the regulations to which they are subject, it can be said that a company is:

(a) *owned* by its shareholders;

(b) *managed* by its directors; and

(c) *controlled* by those holding a majority of the voting shares, because those members can determine who are to be the directors (*see* VI, **18**).

18. Public disclosure of company affairs. All companies are required by law to make returns to the Registrar of Companies. Any member of the public may inspect the documents upon payment of a fee. The information to be lodged is extensive and includes the annual accounts (set out in the form and containing the information specified by law). Details have to be given about the directors and the secretary; the personal holdings of directors and any changes thereof; directors' emoluments and service agreements, etc. Any alterations to the Articles of Association, changes in the board of directors, etc., must be notified immediately.

If the company's shares are listed the Stock Exchange requires to be published any proposed alteration in the nature of the company's business, news concerning proposed mergers, summaries of half-year trading figures and any dividends, etc.

19. Companies trading under a name other than that of their owner. From 26th February 1982, all businesses (whether owned by individuals, partnerships or registered companies) which trade under a name other than that of their owners no longer have to supply details to the Registry of Business Names which was abolished. Instead, they are required to display the names and addresses of their owners at their business premises, on their business stationery, and to customers and suppliers on request.

PROGRESS TEST 2

1. Relate the position of a sole trader with that of a partner in a firm with three partners, as regards (a) possible liability for trading debts; and (b) management. (2–10)

2. What are the consequences of a partnership not being a legal entity? (7)

3. To what extent is it advantageous for a partner to be able to consult with other partners? (9, 10)

4. Explain the importance of limited liability to shareholders. (11)

5. A company is a "legal entity" and has "continuity". Explain the effect of these characteristics as compared with the position of a sole trader. (11)

6. What is the difference between a public company and a private company as regards (a) the size of its capital; (b) the number of members; (c) its name; and (d) when it may commence trading? (13)

7. What are the implications of being a member of a company? (15)

8. Distinguish between the Memorandum of Association and the Articles of Association. (16)

9. To what extent are shareholders and the general public made aware of the affairs of a company? (18)

CHAPTER III

FUNCTIONS IN THE TRADING CHAIN

1. The extent of specialisation of functions. The complete pattern of trading, as discussed in Chapter I, must include the provision of raw materials and the functions of manufacturer, wholesaler and retailer. Ancillary to those will be servicing units. In discussing the stages from producer to consumer in this chapter, it will be seen that although each *function* has its own characteristics, there need not necessarily be one trading unit specific to each function. For example, some manufacturers sell direct to the public by owning the retail outlets; in other cases the connection may be direct to the consumer; the manufacturer may own or control his suppliers.

THE MANUFACTURER

2. Definition. A manufacturer is a producer in the business sense (as opposed to the economists' definition which includes the provision of services as well as of goods) in that he converts raw materials or components into finished or intermediate goods. Thus, one manufacturer may complete the whole chain from the acquisition of raw materials to producing marketable goods. Because of specialisation, however, most will be responsible for only part of the chain, their products going to (and sometimes deriving from) other manufacturers.

3. Operational essentials. A manufacturer must be satisfactorily situated as regards the following:

(*a*) *Supplies.* The availability of regular supplies of raw materials and/or components.

(*b*) *Capital.* A sufficiency of capital to meet the costs of establishing the business and to meet all running costs and expenses until the point of profitability is reached. The extent of the period from establishment to profit-making will vary as between types of production. A manufacturer engaged on a large single project, for example, would obviously require to be financed over a long period until the "pay back" stage was reached.

(c) *Credit.* The availability of credit from lenders (including, perhaps, the right to extend loans or overdrafts at a later stage) and from suppliers.

(d) *Research and development facilities.*

(e) *Market outlets.*

(f) *Management expertise.* This could be in the form of personnel and techniques.

(g) *Managerial services.* These services include such things as statistical aids, etc., for assessing costs, sales incomes, etc.

(h) *Accounting expertise.* Expertise for recording, budgeting, etc.

(i) *Labour.* A pool of labour of the required types. For example, the work may require a high proportion of female labour, some of it part-time.

(j) *Labour disputes.* Negotiating machinery for dealing with labour problems.

4. Aids external to the firm. In addition to the expertise within the business, a considerable amount of assistance could be available from outside it. Some of the facilities are as follows:

(a) *Statistics and information.* Some of these would be provided by Government agencies (such as the Central Statistical Office) and could include "guide lines" and explanations of official directives. Similar types of information would be provided by the relevant trade association and trade journals.

(b) *Employees.* The Department of Employment would assist in providing labour and, if circumstances made it necessary, would provide conciliation facilities in labour disputes. The Department and the Department of Health and Social Security would also provide interpretations of the many regulations appertaining to employment. Staff agencies could provide specialist staff when recruitment is necessary.

(c) *Exports.* The Export Credits Guarantee Department may provide insurance for acceptable risks specific to exporting. Information concerning market conditions, etc., abroad could also be given and similar intelligence may be available from banks and any overseas agents the manufacturer may have.

(d) *Management.* Particular problems of management which require an unbiased "outside view" could be given to firms of management consultants. Such firms could also offer management training schemes for staff.

(e) *Sales.* Market surveys beyond the scope of the firm's periodic surveys could be conducted by market research organisations. It is also sometimes possible for them to provide data about such matters as population-spread, etc., without making a special survey.

(f) *Financial.* A sizeable company would retain a merchant banker as adviser concerning problems of capitalisation, etc., and, where necessary, mergers. Advice would also be available from the same source about the investment of company funds. In this respect, further assistance could be provided by the company's brokers. Expert advice and service in respect of the company's pension fund could be provided by outside specialists. An insurance broker should be retained for all matters of insurance.

(g) *Legal.* A lawyer should be retained for dealing with any matters beyond the scope of the company's legal department (if any).

THE WHOLESALER

5. Traditional functions. As the link between manufacturer and retailer, the historic services afforded by the wholesaler are to:

(a) *provide storage facilities.* Storage is expensive as regards rent and wages. By using the wholesaler as a warehouse, the manufacturer can rid himself of produced goods in a short time; the retailer need store only sufficient to meet his immediate needs. This is especially important where the method of storing is particularly expensive, e.g. refrigeration chambers;

(b) *even out irregular flows.* The production rate of goods may be uneven over a period. This may be because the raw materials are available on a seasonal basis or because it may be more economic for the manufacturer to concentrate on certain products for limited periods. Similarly, the demand by retailers may fluctuate while production is at a uniform rate. In any of these instances, the wholesaler could store goods as they became available and release them as the retailers demand;

(c) *break bulk.* Produced goods could be packed and transported in bulk with a consequent cost-saving and the wholesaler would re-pack in marketable quantities;

(d) *reduce marketing risks.* Where the trade is such that the type of consumer demand has to be estimated and the goods have to be manufactured ahead of the demand being expressed, the manufacturer passes to the wholesaler the risk of the estimate being proved to be incorrect;

(e) *assist cash liquidity.* By buying from the manufacturer, the wholesaler ensures that the former is paid more regularly and at an earlier date than would be the case if goods went directly to retailers.

6. Wholesaling as an essential function. In spite of the considerable reduction in the number of independent wholesalers in recent years, the *function* of wholesaling remains essential. The existence of fewer units specialising in wholesaling means that wholesaling, as a function, must be carried out by someone else in conjunction with other functions.

The independent wholesaler is now restricted almost entirely to businesses where the manufacturers and/or the retailers are small. The reduced number of independent wholesalers is therefore largely due to the advantages of large-scale trading, because large concerns can:

(a) bear the costs of warehousing and direct distributing;

(b) provide the efficient organisation needed for quick turnover, stock control, transport, etc.;

(c) communicate consumer demands rapidly to the production unit (particularly where one business combines the functions of retailer and producer).

The extent to which retailers have assumed the functions of wholesalers is indicated in **8, 9** below. It will also be seen that some retailers are also the manufacturers.

7. Wholesaler units. Those operating solely as wholesalers may be broadly categorised as follows:

(*a*) *General wholesalers.* These are large concerns dealing in a wide range of non-perishable goods. Retailers can inspect samples in showrooms or give orders to representatives who call on them.

(*b*) *Specialist wholesalers.* These cover a narrower range of goods, but with a wider choice, e.g. fabrics.

(*c*) *"Cash-and-carry" wholesalers.* These enable retailers to buy, collect and pay for the goods from the wholesaler's premises. Prices can be reduced because of the elimination of costs of transport to the retailer and the practice of giving no credit.

THE RETAILER

8. Functions. Retailers provide the final point of sale to the consumer.

(*a*) *The traditional functions* derive from the personal relationship with the consumer, the emphasis being on service. Thus the customer has the advantages of:

(*i*) wider choice of goods. An attraction would be the provision of ranges of goods not available generally;

(*ii*) individual packing and grading where appropriate (e.g. tea blenders);

(*iii*) advice from the retailer. Such a retailer would be knowledgeable about his goods and the customer would have the benefit of his experience (e.g. sports shops);

(*iv*) delivery. This is an expensive service and a grocer, for example, who provided it would charge more for his goods;

(*v*) credit facilities. This could be a selling advantage but is expensive to provide and, in general, would derive from some relationship with the customer.

Such services are not now generally available, except from small food stores and retailers selling specialised goods with a restricted market.

(*b*) *The current methods* of retailing provide fewer services but cheaper goods in most instances. This is due to:

(*i*) operating on a large scale and so deriving the benefits of reduced overheads per unit of sale;

(*ii*) buying in bulk;

(*iii*) reducing the choice of goods. By limiting the range of goods, savings can be effected by the retailer in buying, packaging and displaying;

(*iv*) pre-packing. Grocer's "dry goods" will be stored in the packaging provided by the producer. Large stores will cut, pack and price meat before it is put on display. There would thus be a saving of labour and of storage space at the point of sale;

(*v*) overall improved efficiency. A large retailer can justify the cost of sophisticated methods and equipment, e.g. ordering and stock control by the use of computers.

9. Types.

(*a*) *Independents.* These are single shops or small groups of shops and will have the characteristics outlined in **8**(*a*) above. In general, their volume of sales will be low with comparatively high profit margins per unit of sale.

(*b*) *Departmental stores.* These aimed to make shopping a "social activity" by offering in one building a very wide selection of goods, classified into departments. This philosophy was extended by the provision of services such as hairdressing, restaurants, travel agencies, etc. They prospered in a period of a rising middle-class, but have suffered some decline because of the lack of flexibility in inter-departmental policies. The method can also be somewhat wasteful in the use of floor space because of the ambition to create "atmosphere". Such stores have buying departments which purchase on a large scale direct from manufacturers, thus assuming the role of the wholesaler.

(*c*) *Multiple stores.* These are chains of stores selling a range of goods within a specialised field, e.g. pharmaceuticals (Boots); suits (Burtons); shoes (Dolcis). The keynote is standardisation—of shop-fitting style, of goods, of methods. Besides operating as their own wholesalers, most manufacture many of the goods they sell.

(*d*) *Variety chain stores.* Similar principles of standardisation and bulk buying apply to such stores as they do to multiples, but the range of goods is wider. Supplies are often made to the retailer's specification (e.g. Marks and Spencer). Many have extended their range of goods considerably in recent years. Woolworth, for example, has developed to include expensive items such as furniture.

A feature of many stores in the above categories is the system of *own-branding*. Because of their immense buying-power, they can induce manufacturers to make goods under the name of the store at reduced prices. The manufacturer benefits in having a large and certain market without the expenses of sales promotions.

(e) *Supermarket.* Supermarket is a term applied to any store selling a wide variety of goods and which usually operates as a self-service store.

(f) *Hypermarkets.* These are extensions of the super-market principle, on the American style. The term relates to a very large store with a selling area of at least 2,500 square metres. The target is the motorist-shopper and the store would be situated on the outskirts of a town with ample parking space. Development has been slow because of the reluctance to give planning permission for projects which draw trade away from town centres.

(g) *Co-operative societies.* These were founded as a form of political and social expression by establishing shops which belong to the customers. The principle is the dividing of the profits amongst the members in proportion to the purchases made by each. The local retail Societies (which are now being reduced in number and amalgamated as a form of rationalisation) buy from the Co-operative Whole-sale Society which, in turn, pays its profits proportionately to the member-Societies. The C.W.S., besides being a wholesaler, is also in the field of production (e.g. tea and footwear). In addition, it provides a banking service.

Management often had an atmosphere of "amateurism" about it and the business suffered because of competition by large, more-efficient stores and also because of the relaxing of political commitment by many members. The Societies are now modernising under more expert management.

(h) *Mail-order houses.* The growth of such organisations has been exceptional. By direct mail approach, or by agents, customers are offered goods for delivery by post. Credit is usually given. Because of the need to gain by buying in large quantities, the choice of goods is limited, but this also means that buying on a mis-judged assessment of the market demand could be costly. Another danger is that prices must be decided well in advance of catalogues being printed.

The cost of publicity material and postage is high. The managerial essentials are precise planning, efficient stock control and sound office organisation.

(*i*) *Discount houses.* These are based on the "stripped price" principle; that is, the selling of standard goods at prices "stripped" of all customer service. Neither credit nor delivery is provided, the selling areas are starkly functional and no after-sales services are available.

(*j*) *Voluntary chains.* This is a combination of one wholesaler and a large number of retailers—usually sole traders. The retailers obtain the benefits of bulk-buying by the wholesaler as well as other advantages provided by him. These include promotion aids, managerial and financial advice and, sometimes, financial help in modernising the shop. The retailer agrees to a minimum amount of purchases and undertakes to maintain set standards of hygiene etc., and to trade under the group "label". The wholesaler benefits in having a guaranteed turnover.

(*k*) *Franchise units.* These are those which have concessions to sell or use products of the grantor of the franchise. In return, the retailers must restrict their buying to the other party and, in respect of shops, conform to some uniformity of style. The vendor of the franchise provides technical and management training, the goodwill of a well-known name and publicity. Examples are hamburger bars and launderettes.

(*l*) *Automatic vending.* Selling by slot machines (which may operate as a form of franchise) has obvious advantages in the saving of labour costs and the fact that the unit is always "open for business".

10. The changing pattern of retailing. Recent years have seen significant changes in the retail trade, other than those mentioned above. The following are some examples:

(*a*) *Increased uniformity of goods.* Manufacturers have tended to produce larger amounts of goods within a narrower range. The variety of articles with the same function has been reduced to obtain the benefits of simpler and larger batches of production. To the consumer, the result is that the same goods, limited in range, can be found in almost every shop retailing that type of goods.

(*b*) *Reduced specialisation by retailers.* The larger shops no longer confine themselves to their original selling ranges. Grocers sell clothing, wine, etc.; chemists sell cameras and fancy goods; bookshops sell records, typewriters, etc.

To some extent, therefore, chain stores are reverting to the principle of the departmental store. Their aims are to persuade customers to buy more than one type of article once they are in the shop and to reduce financial risk by diversification.

(*c*) *Extension of packaging.* For the convenience of shops with any element of self-service, manufacturers produce many articles already packed which previously would have been supplied loose. An example is the extensive range of such items as screws, metal fittings, etc., encased in plastic "blisters" which can be found in hardware shops.

PROGRESS TEST 3

1. What external services are available to a firm in its position as employer? (**4**)

2. What advantages accrue to a manufacturer and a retailer because of the services of a wholesaler? (**5**)

3. Why does the wholesaling function continue to exist? (**6**)

4. Distinguish between (*a*) cash-and-carry firms and discount houses; (*b*) departmental stores, multiple shops and variety chains. (**7, 9**)

5. What sort of retail organisation is likely to be small? (**8**)

6. What are the characteristics specific to voluntary retail chains? (**9**)

CHAPTER IV

OTHER UNITS OF COMMERCE

PUBLIC SECTOR UNITS

Public sector units are publicly-owned units operating in the business field and may be broadly classified as follows:

(*a*) nationalised industries;
(*b*) Government financed companies;
(*c*) municipal undertakings.

1. Nationalised industries. These are industries directly engaged in commerce but organised as publicly-owned corporations. As commercial units, they operate within the same confines as do privately-owned businesses with regard to capital costs, markets, organisation, etc. Certain important differences do apply to State undertakings, however, some of which are as follows:

(*a*) *Non-commercial objectives.* Policy decisions may be made in which the national interest (which must, in practice, be interpreted with a political bias) is given priority over purely commercial principles. On the grounds of national security, for example, it may be desirable to maintain an industry which is making losses.

(*b*) *Pricing.* A publicly-owned corporation is expected not to suffer losses over a period. Unlike private monopolies, however, there is no restriction by law on the prices it may charge in an attempt to be profitable. A State corporation cannot become insolvent in the usual commercial meaning of the word; where any further price increase was beyond public acceptability, additional advances would come from the Treasury.

(*c*) *Policy control.* As with companies, a public corporation Board has responsibility for the day-to-day running of the concern within expressed limitations. The Act which gives those powers to the Board of a nationalised industry, however, also allows the Minister concerned to give directions to the Board. Accordingly, such a Board has less freedom than a company Board of Directors in that it may have policies imposed upon it by the Government.

(*d*) *Magnitude of the project.* Apart from political considerations, some industries are state-owned because no private concern could raise the amount of capital required and because, due to the nature of the enterprise, no return could be expected for a long time. One reason for establishing the Atomic Energy Commission, for example, was the enormous capital outlay required, the experimental nature of the industry (and the consequent impossibility of estimating costs) and the uncertainty of the return.

2. State participation in companies. The Government has substantial holdings in many limited companies. Examples are British Petroleum Ltd. and I.C.I. Ltd.

3. Political attitudes. The extent of state participation is largely decided as an expression of political philosophy. Those against state-owned and state-aided concerns maintain they are inefficient because:

(*a*) there is insufficient inducement for them to make a profit;

(*b*) they have no direct competition; and

(*c*) their policies are often determined on a political basis.

It is contended that this leads to unduly high charges and/or a drain on the Exchequer when losses are sustained.

4. Municipal undertakings. Local authorities provide a number of services which may be regarded as commercial. These include such essentials as street lighting, water supplies and, frequently, local transport. All these were previously provided by private enterprise. Some authorities provide services specific to the nature of their own area, e.g. entertainment facilities by Blackpool and Bournemouth Corporations.

In addition to local rates and rate support grants from the Government, local authorities obtain finance (subject to

Ministry approval) by issuing bonds direct to the public and issuing stock on the Stock Exchange.

COLLECTIVE ORGANISATIONS

5. Objectives. Collective organisations consist of persons or units which have an interest in common. Membership is usually voluntary but, in practice, most of those who would qualify for membership *are* members. The general objectives of such bodies are as follows:

(*a*) *Provision of information.* To pool and disseminate information specific to the common interest.

(*b*) *Imposition of standards.* To establish standards of conduct; of products and services; of objectives, etc.

(*c*) *Joint representation.* To reach decisions which can be put forward to other bodies as the views of the organisation.

(*d*) *Investigations.* To conduct investigations, surveys, etc., and to produce reports on aspects of their common interests.

6. Trade associations. These consist of members of one type of trade and their functions may be summarised as follows:

(*a*) *Information.* To collect and distribute, by means of circulars, journals, meetings, etc., information about proposed and present legislation, market opportunities, trade marks and patents, economic conditions, etc.

(*b*) *Standards.* To establish and control standards of conduct, contracts and specifications, conditions of sale, etc.

(*c*) *Technical advances.* To organise exhibitions, establish training schemes, institute technical investigations, etc.

(*d*) *Representation.* To represent the organisation on committees of other bodies.

(*e*) *Lobbying.* To take concerted action by making representations to Government departments, etc., on behalf of the members.

(*f*) *Trading policies.* To establish trading policies concerning output, prices, etc.

7. Professional bodies. These are composed of persons who are members of the same profession. Their functions usually include the following:

(*a*) *Qualifications.* To establish qualifications for membership, which may include examinations.

(*b*) *Code of conduct.* To establish and maintain a professional code of conduct, with provisions for disciplinary action in the event of any breach.

(*c*) *Information.* To collect and distribute information relevant to the profession.

(*d*) *Representation.* To represent the profession on committees of other bodies.

(*e*) *Lobbying.* To act on behalf of members in the furtherance of or opposition to any course of action affecting the profession.

(*f*) *Education.* To provide educational facilities for its members.

8. Trade unions. These are organisations for labour. They may be formed according to the type of work (craft unions), but the larger unions are more generalised in their membership. For example, the Transport and General Workers Union has a membership covering many industries and trades.

Organisation is, firstly, into local branches, with officers elected by the local members. Such officers may represent the branch at the next tier of the organisation, such as district or area councils. Direct contact with employers is usually first established by an employee acting as a shop steward. At the head of the organisation structure would be the union executive, some of whom will be employed full-time. A system of voting operates for the appointment of officials at every level.

9. Trades Union Congress. 90 per cent of total union membership is affiliated to the Trades Union Congress, the national body. Affiliated unions send delegates to the annual meeting of the T.U.C. where membership of the General Council is decided, the Council being the effective policy-making body of the movement.

The T.U.C. has a powerful voice in expressing its views to the Government about matters of policy. It will be consulted by the Government on any matters relevant to labour.

The T.U.C. will not interfere in any industrial action by a union unless requested to do so. It can exercise some discipline over member-unions in its insistence that they conform to

General Council policies and it will intervene in inter-union disputes.

10. The Confederation of British Industry. This is representative of management in industry, aiming to promote the prosperity of British industry. Its regional and national structure permits the pooling of views which can then be expressed as the attitude of the management sector. It advises and is consulted by the Government and, as with the T.U.C., can make powerful representations.

11. Chambers of Commerce. These are local autonomous bodies and include members of every type of business in the area. They are thus able to be represented in discussions with local authorities and other bodies on such matters as town planning, public transport, etc.

Various services are available to members, many of them at national level, such as the provision of information and assistance concerning exporting and importing; legislation and other regulations; agencies and specialist firms, etc.

12. Advantages of collective organisations.

(a) *Lobbying.* The expression by a representative body of the views of its members allows more pressure to be applied in putting those views to other bodies in the form of a "lobby".

(b) *Sharing of costs.* The cost of the services provided could often only be met from the pooled resources of a collection of people.

(c) *Uneconomic services.* Many of the services would not otherwise be undertaken because to do so would not produce profits. Thus the cost of some research by one member may be unrewarding, but if it is to benefit all the members it could be undertaken by the organisation.

13. Disadvantages of collective organisations.

(a) *Conflicts of interest.* Conflicts of interest between the members may result in no firm policy being established. Thus an action beneficial to most may not be fully implemented because it may be disadvantageous to some.

(b) *Power of the majority.* The organisation may be dominated by the larger members acting in a manner which ignores the interests of other members.

(c) *"Politicising"*. Manoeuvring and manipulation in its various forms may not lead to the expression of the true attitudes of the members.

(d) *Procedural delays*. The impetus of action may be lost by the requirement to be concerned with such procedural matters as committees, reports, etc.

PROGRESS TEST 4

1. Give examples of non-commercial objectives in the public sector of industry. (1)

2. How are the policies of a nationalised industry decided and implemented? (1)

3. What are the sources of a local authority's income? (4)

4. Define collective organisations. (5)

5. Compare the objectives of trade associations with those of professional bodies. (6, 7)

6. How may collective organisations exercise pressure on other bodies? (6–12)

7. Explain the structure within a trade union and its relationship with the T.U.C. (8, 9)

8. What is the C.B.I.? (10)

9. List the possible advantages and disadvantages of collective organisations. (12, 13)

CHAPTER V

BUSINESS EXPANSION

THE SIZE OF BUSINESS UNITS

1. Determinants of growth. The physical size of a business is not necessarily relevant to financial size, although in manufacturing firms it will almost certainly be. A staff employment agency, for example, may grow physically without the necessity for considerable financial growth.

The principal factors which determine physical growth are as follows:

(*a*) *The nature of the industry.* Where the nature of an industry is one requiring a large outlay of capital, the key firms will be large. Examples are construction engineering, oil refining, motor manufacturing, etc. This is the case if reference is being made to the basic members of an industry, but other concerns which, although having a peripheral relationship to the leaders are nevertheless *within* the industry, may be very much smaller. A motor manufacturer, as such, is largely concerned with the assembly of components; some of those components may be supplied by small firms.

(*b*) *The availability of capital.* This, firstly, will depend upon general economic conditions, because these will influence the amount of funds which can be released for investment and the general prospects of any such funds producing a satisfactory return. Secondly, there are the factors relevant to the firm itself. Basically, a business seeking funds must show a good record of profitability. Thus, a new business could have no such record and must therefore rely largely on resources from outside the capital market. There must also be, in both instances, satisfactory evidence of profit potential. Other factors will include the standard of management, the history of labour relations, etc.

(c) *Policy of the firm.* Most businesses start in a small way. The ultimate size of the firm will partly depend upon its attitude to growth. The general tendency is to expand but it may be the policy of a particular firm not to do so, either because of the personal wishes of the owners or because they recognise the firm has reached the optimum size.

(d) *Market size.* A vital factor is the size of the market. The product may be one with a small appeal or even an ephemeral one. Thus a business may provide a very specialist product with a limited market or it may produce something which has no lasting appeal; that is, it may be something with a short period of popularity, such as a game or a fashion "gimmick".

(e) *Availability of labour.* Size may be limited by the insufficient availability of labour *generally*, because of full employment in the area of operation or because of the comparative remoteness of the area. Alternatively, the limiting factor may be the shortage of *specialist* labour. Thus the demand may be for a type in short supply in the area, such as unskilled female labour, technicians of certain types, etc.

(f) *Potential for large-scale economies.* A business with methods which lend themselves to the economies of large scale must be of a certain size before those economies will materialise (*see* **3** below).

2. The tendency to growth. The general inclination has been to increase the size of firms, the reasons for which may be summarised as follows:

(a) *Economies of large scale.* To reap the benefits of trading on a large scale (*see* **3** below).

(b) *Enlarged consumer markets.* To meet the demands of consumer markets which, because of the increase in the standard of living, has intensified demand generally and which has also extended demand in what were previously "luxury" or "near-luxury" markets (e.g. the demand for home-freezers). To meet such demands, large-scale production is necessary.

(c) *Ambitions of the owners.* The type of person with the initiative and energy to start a business may not be satisfied once he has established it on a firm footing. Having experienced a sense of achievement, his inclination will be to expand.

(d) *The limited company system.* The reduced risk of investing in limited companies has lead to a greater willingness to participate actively in business (*see* II, 14). Also, established companies can draw on the resources of the public for finance so that owners may expand by using capital provided by others.

(e) *Production techniques.* The use of sophisticated techniques increases production, but such systems as assembly lines, automation, etc., are economic only if used extensively.

(f) *Reduction of risks.* In general, the more a business can dominate an industry or a market the safer it will be. Overall risk can also be reduced by diversifying into several types of industry or integrating within an industry (*see* 11 below).

(g) *Reluctant expansion.* The owner of a small business may be compelled to surrender the satisfaction of "being his own boss". To meet the competition from larger firms benefiting from the economies of scale, he may have to expand in order to obtain similar benefits.

3. The advantages of large scale. The advantages of operating on a large scale can include the following:

(a) *Reduction of unit costs.* A substantial increase in output would result in a considerably smaller increase in total overhead costs. With the spreading of such costs over more units of production, the unit cost must fall.

(b) *Administration costs.* When a business is very small, organisation would be only part of the owner's functions and would therefore tend to be inefficient. At a certain stage of development, management would become a separate function and the business would have what may be regarded as a conventional administration. Such an administration structure could cope with subsequent increases in size with comparatively little added to total administration costs.

(c) *Division of labour.* The concept of division of labour and the consequent specialisation within narrower fields can be demonstrated only where there is a large labour force. Specialisation can be increased by the introduction of additional machinery, which can be economically justified only when output is high.

(d) *Specialists.* A large concern could afford specialists of various kinds, such as those in different branches of management, financial experts, technical advisers, etc.

(e) *Research.* Research is expensive and, by its very nature, some of it may be unsuccessful. Only a large concern could bear expense of that magnitude.

(f) *Integration.* A large business could accept opportunities to integrate vertically and/or horizontally or become a conglomerate.

(g) *Supplies.* The ability to buy in large quantities will reduce costs of raw materials and components. Control over the supplier will be increased where it is agreed to buy all or a large proportion of the output of a supplier because of that supplier's consequent complete dependence. The buyer may own his suppliers.

(h) *Marketing.* The unit cost of marketing will reduce when sales exceed a certain figure. Also, better marketing expertise could be afforded. A manufacturer of sufficient size may own his retail outlets.

(i) *Financial.* A large business may have reserves within the business on which to draw for development or which could be used to provide stability. One with a good financial and management record would be able to obtain additional funds by issuing shares to the public and borrowing from the financial sector.

(j) *Staffing.* A large business would be better able to offer positions which are financially rewarding and with prospects of promotion than would most smaller businesses. The standard of staff should therefore be higher.

4. The disadvantages of large scale. There must be an optimum size for any business. After a certain size has been reached, dis-economies may emerge, evidenced by diminishing returns. These can be as follows:

(a) *Unwieldy management.* Beyond a certain stage, management becomes too complex. There are more managers to manage; co-ordination of departments becomes difficult; and managers, because of their specialisation, become too narrow in outlook.

(b) *Bureaucracy.* Every business must have procedures, but as a firm increases in size the procedures tend to become more extensive and rigid. Events must be dealt with according to stipulated rules, resulting in delays and loss of initiative. The process of delegation and specialisation results in an increasing number of executives, many of them with little managerial ability. Executives may create "little empires" for themselves and attempt to justify their positions by inventing additional duties.

(c) *Decision-making.* Decisions are often reached only after going through various officials and committees. The result is often a compromise of conflicting views which may have had to take account of the "vested interests" or prejudices of some members, resulting in a decision insufficiently positive. Slowness in reaching decisions can often be dangerous in business.

(d) *Mistakes.* A miscalculation or error of judgment in a large organisation can be more disastrous than one made in a small one. More people within the firm are liable to be affected; concerns outside the business, but dependent upon it, would also suffer; the failure of one business in a complex can have a "domino" effect.

(e) *Morale.* A very large business can be impersonal so far as those employed by it are concerned. There is a feeling of increased remoteness between workers and management, indicated by the increased likelihood of industrial disputes in large concerns. With increased staff and more formalised structures, the tendency to indulge in "office politics" increases.

(f) *"Power complexes".* Some businesses have grown beyond a viable size because of the love of power of those controlling them. Power for its own sake can become an addiction and failures have resulted from such attitudes.

5. Attitudes to large concerns. Following a period of a considerable increase in the average size of businesses, very large units have become increasingly out of favour in recent years.

(a) *Within business.* More recognition of the optimum size concept is now prevalent in the business world. Many businesses have experienced difficulty because of the impossibility of efficiently managing a concern beyond a certain size. Some have been saved by splitting them into smaller units—a complete reversal of the practice for many years.

(b) *External to business.* Some organisations have such a complicated interlocking of companies that even financial experts may have difficulty in disentangling them; certainly, investors are frequently unaware of the extent of the ramifications of their companies. The collapse of one unit in a complex has lead to financial disasters.

Concern has often been expressed about the political power of large organisations, particularly when multinational companies exercise influence on foreign governments. The dangers of monopoly are greater where there are large concerns (*see* **14** below).

6. The small firm. In spite of the advantages of large scale, a high proportion of firms are small. The reasons for this will include the following:

(a) *Personal service.* The types of business which are largely dependent upon the personal nature of the service offered must remain small in order to retain that advantage. This largely accounts for the continuing survival of the small grocer. The personal nature of the service may take the form of expert advice, such as that provided by art dealers, interior decorators, etc.

(b) *Individuality of the product.* A business whose main advantage is the unique character of the product must remain small because any increase in output would destroy the individuality of the product. This would include such businesses as jewellery designers and most other forms of artistic work.

(c) *Craftsmanship.* Some businesses cannot expand because the product cannot be produced by mechanical means and, therefore, the benefits of large-scale production would not apply. Examples are basket weavers, harness makers, etc.

(d) *Limited demand.* Where the market is small, a firm must also be small if it is limited to that market.

(e) *Transient firms.* Many small businesses have a short life, meeting failure before they can expand. These will include builders and building tradesmen, such as plumbers, electricians, etc.

(*f*) *Infant firms.* At any one time there must be a number of small firms in the stage of development.

7. Change in traditionally small firms. Some types of business which have traditionally been small are, in fact, increasing in size. Accountants in private practice were usually small firms because of the necessity for close contact between an accountant and his clients. Because of the increasing complexity of accountancy work, however, the tendency now is for larger firms so that partners may specialise in different areas. Another example is that of stockbrokers and jobbers. For some time the Stock Exchange has been encouraging the formation of larger partnerships in the interests of financial stability.

BUSINESS GROWTH

8. Methods of growth. These may be summarised as:

(*a*) by internal development;
(*b*) by vertical merger;
(*c*) by horizontal merger;
(*d*) by becoming a conglomerate.

9. Internal development. This is a method of expanding by using reserves of profit within the business, or by borrowing or issuing more shares. It has the following features:

(*a*) *Orderliness.* Expansion is a smooth progression with no violent changes within the business.

(*b*) *Management.* The specialists required will already be on the staff except for any new areas the company may be entering. It is possible, however, that the existing management may not be sufficiently expert to cope with an enlarged organisation. Also, if the old management is to continue, there would be no encouragement to bring in new ideas, as there would be if "new blood" was introduced.

(*c*) *Organisation structure.* If the expansion is to be largely within the present scope of operations, little disturbance of the organisation's structure would be required.

10. Methods of merger. Mergers are the result of joining with, or taking over, other businesses. The methods of merger relevant to companies are as follows:

(a) The undertaking of one company is purchased by another, the former being dissolved.

(b) Two companies wind up and form a new company containing the combined undertakings. The shareholders of the two companies would receive shares in the new company in exchange for their old ones.

(c) One company buys the shares of another from the present holders. *This is a take-over bid* and results in the continuation of both companies (thereby preserving the public goodwill of each), but one would be a subsidiary of the other.

11. Forms of merger.

(a) *Vertical integration.* This is the merging with other units operating at different points in the same chain of production. Thus a manufacturer can make certain of his supplies by purchasing or merging with his suppliers or securing his market by acquiring retail outlets. This also has the effect of adding to the profit-making areas. Examples are motor manufacturers owning car body-making firms and clothing manufacturers owning shops.

(b) *Horizontal integration.* This involves combining with those at the same level of production. It may be in order to remove a competitor or to enter a sub-division at the same level. An example of the latter would be an electrical manufacturer supplying large production units to power stations, etc., wishing to also supply the domestic appliance market.

(c) *Conglomerate.* This applies where a company enters an area completely unrelated to its present one. The intention would be the diversification of risk by not being entirely dependent upon the fate of one industry. Thus a property company owns a well-known shipping line; a shoe manufacturer owns department stores and turf accountants; one business manufactures detergents and frozen foods and owns a chain of retail stores.

A danger with conglomerates is that one company within the complex may be guilty of unfair competition by reducing its prices to an uneconomic level. This may be possible because the overall profit of the conglomerate would sustain the low profits (or even losses) of the one company until it had captured its market.

12. Problems of merging. A merger results in *instant* growth. It is therefore quicker than internal expansion, but this in itself creates problems.

Any form of integration must involve a degree of rationalisation—that is, the now existing components must be reorganised into a new structure. This may require the closing or reduction of some areas with a consequent effect on employment (including the management sphere) and the creation of discord between executives with changed responsibilities. The restructuring of management will mean that managers will strive to retain their old powers and work with their old methods. To enforce conformity to the new pattern, overall management would have to dominate and this in turn would create more human problems.

The new management (particularly in a conglomerate) will have to control areas of business of which it has little or no experience. Even if it allows a degree of freedom to the old managers because of their experience, there will be occasions when the new management must enforce unwelcome decisions concerning those areas in order to comply with the corporate strategy.

Even if some top executives and directors are not removed, the allocation of new duties and the changes in the management hierarchy may lead to resentment and even resignations.

Many mergers have been at least partly unsuccessful because of the problems of "digesting".

MONOPOLISTIC ORGANISATIONS

13. Public monopolies. State-owned and State-controlled industries operate generally in conditions of monopoly, although there is an element of competition between fuel suppliers (coal, gas, oil and electricity) and in transport (rail, road and air). One of the reasons for State ownership can be the prevention of private monopoly. The only machinery for protecting the public from the effects of such monopolies are the various "consumers" boards.

14. Private monopolies. These can be monopolies of supplies and/or of markets. They can be achieved by various forms of merger and by price agreements between individual concerns.

In general, the attitude to any such proposed control

is that monopolies are undesirable to the extent they are "against the public interest".

Monopolist powers properly used can result in lower unit costs being extended to lower prices; the extensive resources of a "protected" business could be used for research which could not otherwise be afforded. On the other hand, because of the lack of competition a monopoly has less incentive to be efficient. There could be less inclination to reduce costs and to innovate and there may be a reluctance to study the requirements of its customers.

Abuses of monopoly are reduced by the powers of the Monopolies Commission to forbid an organisation reaching the stage of being an unacceptable monopoly and by Government control on prices. The threats presented by monopolies include those of misused power by large organisations (*see* 5(*b*) above), which may or may not be monopolies.

MULTI-NATIONALS

15. Objectives. Multi-nationals are large organisations operating across national boundaries. This can enable such companies to manufacture near their markets and to take advantage of differentials of national wage rates. It can also avoid any national restriction on overseas trade, such as tariffs, by producing and selling within the same country.

The policy may be to establish subsidiary companies abroad with local directors or to operate foreign divisions of the home company; to grant licences to foreign companies; to merge companies of different nationalities.

PROGRESS TEST 5

1. What is the relationship between physical growth of a business and financial size? (1)

2. What factors may determine the growth of a business? (1)

3. Why has the general tendency been to larger organisations? (2)

4. What advantages may accrue from trading on a large scale? (3)

5. What can be the disadvantages of large-scale trading? (4)

6. How do you account for the element of disillusionment concerning large concerns? (5)

7. Why do small firms continue to exist? (6)

8. By what methods may businesses increase in size? (8)

9. What are the characteristics of internal development? **(9)**

10. What are the available methods of merger? **(10)**

11. Compare: (*a*) vertical integration; (*b*) horizontal integration; (*c*) conglomerates. **(11)**

12. What difficulties may follow a merger? **(12)**

13. Compare the protection available in the case of State monopolies with that relevant to private monopolies. **(13, 14)**

14. What are the characteristics of multi-nationals? **(15)**

CHAPTER VI

THE FINANCING OF BUSINESS

CAPITAL

1. Sources of finance. The available sources of finance will be determined, firstly, by the type of business. The following broad distinctions can be made:

(*a*) *Sole traders.* Most, if not all, of the finance will be provided by the owner, because:

(*i*) the amount required will be small; and
(*ii*) loans will be difficult to obtain because of the risk of lending to one person in a small way of business.

A bank would not normally lend unless the business was well established and security could be given, although overdraft facilities may be made available. The owner may be able to obtain private loans from friends.

(*b*) *Partnerships.* The initial capital would be provided by the partners, so the number of partners will, to a large extent, determine the total capital. Problems could arise later if additional finance was required because a private lender may demand a partnership (*see* II, **11**(*c*)). Bank finance may be available.

(*c*) *Private limited companies.* Capital could be provided in the form of shares and loans but no invitation could be made to the public to subscribe for them.

(*d*) *Public limited companies.* These may invite the public to take up shares and debentures. Loans could also be obtained from banks and other lenders.

2. The effect of borrowing. The capital of most businesses contains an element of borrowing. Certain principles can be stated about the consequences of capital being partly in the form of loans, but the *particular* effect will depend upon the

44

financial stability of the firm and the relationship between the amount borrowed and the total capital. The following general provisions apply:

(a) *The positive liability in borrowing.* The interest on a loan *must* be paid when due and the loan *must* be repaid on the agreed date. There is thus a positive commitment, whereas the amount of income from which the loan is to be paid is unknown at the time of borrowing. Failure to meet any commitment may result in the business being forced into liquidation. This would be particularly unfortunate if the inability to pay was only temporary and the business did, in fact, have good prospects. Dividends, on the other hand, do not have to be paid if the company cannot afford to do so.

(b) *The yield on owners' funds.* If the rate of profit to overall capital exceeds the net cost of the loan, the difference will accrue to the benefit of the owners (*see* **3** below).

(c) *Tax allowance on loan interest.* Interest on loans is a business expense and allowable for tax against profits. If a business is taxed at the rate of 50 per cent and 10 per cent interest is payable on a loan, for example, the net cost of the interest is 5 per cent. The sharing of the profits amongst the owners of the business (the sole trader, the partners or the shareholders, as the case may be) is a *distribution* and is not allowable for tax.

(d) *Security for loans.* If security has to be given for a loan, the securing asset will be constrained. In other words, although the borrower retains ownership of it, he may not dispose of the asset and may also be subjected to restrictions on its use.

(e) *Control.* Some company shares carry voting rights, whereas a lender to a company has no voting power in company meetings. Provided the terms of a loan are complied with, a lender has no authority to interfere with the management of a company.

(f) *Credit rating.* The ability to obtain credit is adversely affected if it is seen that a business has a heavy loan commitment.

(g) *Provision for redemption.* Arrangements must be made for the ultimate discharge of a loan. If annual allocations are made to a reserve to provide for redemption, the amount of available profit is thereby reduced.

3. The yield on owner's funds. The amount of the return to the owner can be expressed as the relationship between the amount of profit due to him and the amount of his investment. Expressed as a percentage, this is known as the yield. If part of the capital is in the form of a loan, the owner's yield will be affected by the rate of interest on the loan and the fact that the interest is allowable for tax. This is demonstrated in the following example.

EXAMPLE

Business *A* has a capital of £20,000, provided entirely by the owners.

Business *B* has a capital of £20,000, of which £5,000 has been borrowed at 10 per cent.

Tax is at the rate of 40 per cent.

Calculations are made on a profit of £4,000 and a profit of £1,800 (both before interest and tax).

It will be seen that when the profit is high, the yield improves if there is a loan but that the reverse applies when profits are below a certain level.

	Business *A*		Business *B*	
Profit	£4,000	£1,800	£4,000	£1,800
Interest	nil	nil	500	500
Taxable	4,000	1,800	3,500	1,300
Tax	1,600	720	1,400	520
Return	2,400	1,080	2,100	780
Yield	12%	5·4%	14%	5·2%

ESTABLISHING A BUSINESS

4. The initial capital. The amount of capital required to establish a business will be far more than the sum necessary to purchase an existing business or to "set up" a new one. When a business is fully established on a profitable basis, the income will be sufficient to pay for outgoings as they become due. Costs and overhead expenses, however, must be paid *before* the relevant income materialises. This means that in the early life of the business, outgoings will exceed income and can be met only from capital. The length of time before the point of balance is reached will depend upon the volume of sales and the rate at which the income from them accrues—which latter will be affected by the credit terms given to customers.

The amount of capital must be sufficient to cover the following outgoings during that critical period:

(a) The cost of purchasing the business (including goodwill), if the owner is taking-over another firm.

(b) The cost of stock, raw materials, etc.

(c) The cost of machinery, equipment, premises, etc.

(d) Operating costs, such as wages, etc.

(e) Overheads, such as lighting and heating, rates, insurance, etc.

(f) Salaries and fees, including any amount (if any) payable to the owner(s).

5. Budgeting for cash requirements. A very real problem in determining the required amount of capital is assessing the length of time during which cash outgoings will exceed cash income. The amount of *sales* is of lesser importance at this stage; the vital factor will be the amount of *cash* coming in from sales. Conversely, the burden of cash demand will be reduced to the extent that credit may be available to the business (for raw materials, etc.) and because some expenses are paid in arrear (such as tax). Certain expenses must be paid immediately, however (such as wages and state insurance), and some are usually paid in advance (such as insurance premiums and rent).

A cash schedule can be compiled to show the expected cash incomes and outgoings throughout the period. A simplified version is shown in the following example.

EXAMPLE

	Jan.	Feb.	Mar.	April
Income from sales	£800	£800	£1,200	£1,500
Outgoings:				
Materials	500	400	400	500
Production expenses	400	400	500	400
Overheads	200	100	200	200
	1,100	900	1,100	1,100
Operating differences	−300	−100	+100	+400
Opening cash balance	5,000	4,700	4,600	4,700
Closing cash balance	4,700	4,600	4,700	5,100

6. Under-capitalisation. The figures in the cash schedule can, of course, only be conjectured. If estimates are not realised, the business may fail because of cash shortage. This often happens with small businesses, even where the business is shown to be profitable or, at least, with the prospect of being profitable.

Even short of insolvency, however, a business may suffer because of insufficient capital. The dangers would include the following:

(a) *Cost of credit.* If the business tries to preserve cash liquidity by paying for its supplies as late as possible, those costs will be increased by the loss of any discount available for prompt payment. Undue delay in paying may result in further supplies being refused.

(b) *Credit rating reduced.* A business known to be short of cash will have difficulty in getting further credit.

(c) *Cost of granting discounts.* In an effort to induce an earlier flow of cash from sales, the business may improve the credit terms offered to its customers. This will reduce the amount of cash received because of the higher discount offered, but many customers will prefer to forgo the discount in order to preserve their own liquidity.

(d) *Loss of opportunities.* Because of the restricted availability of cash, the owner may not be able to accept business opportunities which would otherwise be open to him. For example, he may have the chance of a lucrative contract or a purchase of goods on favourable terms, either of which would require the immediate outlay of cash.

COMPANY FINANCE

7. Capital and its suppliers. The capital of a company may be broadly divided into two categories, which also serve to distinguish the two main classes of investor.

(a) *Share capital.* This is that part of the capital subscribed in the form of shares.

(i) Shareholders are *members* of the company and its *owners*.

(ii) Their rights and obligations are those contained in the company's Articles of Association (*see* II, **16**(b)) and such provisions of law as are applicable.

(*iii*) With the exception of Redeemable Preference shares (*see* **8**(*e*)), shares cannot be repaid except in rare circumstances and with the permission of the Court.

(*b*) *Loan capital.* This consists of debentures and other types of loan.

(*i*) Lenders are not members; they are *creditors*.

(*ii*) Their rights are set out in the document containing the terms of issue. Any relevant legislation is mainly contained in that appertaining to the winding up of companies.

(*iii*) Loan capital is not permanent but, except with the agreement of lender and borrower, it cannot be made repayable before the fixed or ascertainable date of redemption.

8. Types of shares. The classes of shares in issue may be itemised as shown below. Concerning the dividends, these can be paid only from profits as it is illegal to pay them from capital. A share with a fixed rate of dividend, therefore, carries no guarantee that that dividend will be paid.

(*a*) *Ordinary shares.* The holders of these shares (which are generally known as *equities*) are the true risk-bearers. They are entitled to share in the profits only after other classes of shareholder have received their dividends.

The rate of the dividend is not fixed because, of course, it will largely depend upon the amount of profit available after payment of priority shareholders. The proportion of that amount which will actually be paid as a dividend is determined by the directors because they have the responsibility of deciding the sum which, in the interests of the company, must be placed to reserve.

In times of prosperity, therefore, the Ordinary shareholders will be entitled to high dividends. Conversely, when low profits are made, there may be little or even no dividend paid. The effects of the profit level on the dividend rate can be distorted by the gearing of the capital (*see* **10**). Ordinary shares usually carry voting rights but not necessarily so.

(*b*) *Preference shares.* These carry a fixed rate of dividend, which is payable in priority of Ordinary shares. Any arrears of dividend must be paid before the Ordinary shares may participate. Such shares can be of more than one class, there being a degree of priority between them.

(*c*) *Non-cumulative Preference shares.* The dividend on these shares can be paid only from current profits—any amounts not previously paid because of the absence of profits are forgone. Such shares are now rare. (All Preference shares are cumulative unless otherwise so titled.)

(d) *Participating Preference shares.* These carry the right to a fixed dividend, plus a share of the profits, after the Ordinary shares have been paid a certain rate. Thus, the entitlement may first be to 8 per cent; if there is sufficient profit to pay the Ordinary shareholders, say, 25 per cent, the excess of profit beyond the cost of that rate would be divided between the two classes at an agreed ratio.

(e) *Redeemable Preference shares.* This is the only type of non-permanent share. The terms include the undertaking to redeem the shares at a fixed or determinable time, often at a premium.

9. Debentures. Although there is no legal definition of the word, it is generally recognised as referring to loans to companies. It can also refer to the document evidencing the loan. Debentures may or may not contain security for the loan, and take the following forms:

(a) *Registered debentures.* These are those registered in the name of a single lender, such as a bank.

(b) *Debenture stock.* This refers to an issue of debentures to the public. The debenture is registered in the name of trustees who look after the interests of the lenders.

(c) *Loan stock.* This term generally refers to unsecured debentures.

(d) *Convertible debentures.* These, as for all debentures, carry a fixed guaranteed rate of interest, but with the additional right to later convert the holding into Ordinary shares. The terms of issue will set out the holder's *option* to convert to Ordinary shares at a fixed ratio, e.g. to convert £100 stock into Ordinary shares with a nominal value of £45, at certain specified times in the future. If at any of those times the Ordinary shares are very much more valuable than that of the debentures to be exchanged, it may be advantageous to convert. Against this must be set the risk of forgoing a security with a guaranteed rate of interest. If more than one option date is given, the exchange rate may be reduced for the later dates; for example, the above option may be reduced to shares valued £44 and £43 on the second and third dates respectively. As there is no compulsion to convert, the holder may decide to not exercise his option, in which case the debenture will continue until the maturity date.

10. Capital gearing (or leverage). The capital structure of a company may consist of various types of shares and loans. The effect on the amount available to Ordinary shareholders at different levels of profit is influenced by the relationship between the types of security. If priority capital represents a sizeable proportion of the total capital, the gearing is said to be "high". The effect of such a gearing would be for the profits to affect more than proportionately the amount available to Ordinary shareholders.

This is shown in the following example. When the profits of the highly-geared company doubled, the potential Ordinary dividend rate increased six times, but a doubling of the profits of the other company increased the possible rate only two-and-a-half times.

EXAMPLE

	Company A (high geared)	Company B (low geared)
Capital:		
8% Preference shares	£100,000	£40,000
Ordinary shares	40,000	100,000
	140,000	140,000
Profit	10,000	10,000
less Preference dividend	8,000	3,200
Available to Ordinary shares	2,000	6,800
=	5% =	6·8%
Profit	20,000	20,000
less Preference dividend	8,000	3,200
Available to Ordinary shares	12,000	16,800
=	30% =	16·8%

THE FINANCIAL SECTOR

11. The channelling of savings. Investment can arise only from an excess of income over expenditure and all investment must derive ultimately from the general public. Even a company which invests its own reserves in another company must have obtained the funds giving rise to those reserves from the public, even though the intervening period may have been long and many units of commerce involved.

This position arises because the many methods by which people save result in huge sums of money being concentrated and then invested by certain bodies. By this means, sums which are too small to be invested directly are merged with a considerable number of similar small savings to provide large funds which can be channelled into investment. The consequent incomes from such investments are thereby available for the benefit of the small savers who provided them.

12. The Institutions. This is a general term for those bodies which invest large sums of money provided by other people and which is used, partially at least, for the benefit of those providers. Examples are as follows:

(a) *The clearing banks.* Customers place money with banks for safety, convenience and, to a limited degree, interest. Because banks are able to estimate the amount likely to be demanded by its customers at any one time, it can plan the investment of the remainder. Most of the money is invested "short term" (that is, it can recover the investment quickly if there is an exceptional demand from its customers), but some is placed in more permanent investments (such as subsidiary finance companies).

(b) *Assurance companies.* Such companies have a steady income of premiums which can be estimated for the future, because of the long-term commitments of its policy-holders. By means of actuarial tables, they can estimate fairly accurately their liabilities for policy maturities and liabilities in respect of deaths before maturity. The balance is invested and the enormous sums thus available provide income and capital profits. A large proportion of that sum will accrue to the benefit of policy-holders in that it will enable the company to quote advantageous terms for its policies. Those holders with "With Profits" policies will also directly benefit by the amount of "bonuses" added to the capital value of their policies.

(c) *Superannuation funds.* Pensions schemes for employees are either run in conjunction with assurance companies or are self-financed. Whichever method is used, the result is the creation of some of the largest investors in the City. The profit on the investments goes towards the cost of the pensions.

(d) *Unit trusts.* This is a method whereby small investors buy units which, in turn, are invested in bulk by the managers of the trust. The total income less management expenses is made available to the unit holders.

(e) *Trade unions, Church Commissioners, charities, etc.* The very large accumulations of small contributions are invested for the benefit of the organisation and its members.

In all the above instances, the institutions are able to use the expertise of market analysts, economists, financial specialists, etc., and, in general, obtain the other benefits of operating on a large scale.

13. The Stock Exchange. This is a market place for the exchange of transferable securities. Shares in public companies can be dealt in on the Exchange only if they have been "admitted to listing"—that is, accepted by the Exchange. A company wishing its shares to be listed must first satisfy very stringent regulations concerning the prospectus, the rights of members, the duties of the directors, etc. It must also agree to abide by the rules of the Stock Exchange about many aspects of its conduct and these are far more demanding than those of the law.

The functions of the Stock Exchange may be regarded as being as follows:

(a) *To provide a workplace for its members.* Stockbrokers and jobbers who work in the Stock Exchange are provided with all the resources for carrying out their duties.

(b) *To provide a market.* The organisation of the Stock Exchange provides for the complicated work of enabling the public, through the offices of brokers, to buy and sell securities already in issue.

(c) *To provide a pricing system.* The Exchange makes possible the determination, at any one time, of the effect of supply and demand on price. The very sensitive pricing mechanism and the constant quoting of market prices allows investors to always be aware of values. This in turn also enables the production of various indexes which indicate trends, etc.

(d) *To provide protection for investors.* The Stock Exchange's chief concern is to ensure that investors are provided with all the information necessary for them to make a fair judgment of a security and that directors disclose all material facts to their shareholders. Anything likely to create a "false market" (that is, one in which favoured persons are in possession of information not generally available) will result in action by the Exchange, such as "suspending dealings". It also operates a Compensation Fund which is available to investors suffering loss as a result of the financial failure of a member.

(e) *To facilitate the issue of new securities.* Proposed new issues are "vetted" before being approved and the Stock Exchange exercises strict control over the procedures.

(f) *To discipline its members.* Members of the Stock Exchange are subjected to a strict set of rules designed to protect the public and fellow-members.

(g) *To establish a code of conduct in the City.* The power of the Stock Exchange is available to take action against those who resort to unacceptable practices. In particular, the Stock Exchange was instrumental in establishing the City Code, which lays down strict rules concerning the conducting of take-over bids.

14. Other financial institutions.

(a) *Issuing houses.* These undertake the complicated work of issuing securities to the public on behalf of companies. This will include negotiations with the Stock Exchange, the publishing of the prospectus, etc. Instead of the company issuing a prospectus, the house may make an *offer for sale.* This is an indication to the public that the house has purchased the securities in the new issue and is now offering them to the public. By this method, the company runs no risk that the issue will not be fully taken up by the public.

(b) *Underwriters.* These are financial organisations which insure against a public issue being a "flop". In the event of not all the securities being subscribed by the public, they undertake to take up the deficiency.

(c) *New issue departments.* The large banks have departments organised to handle all the administration connected with new issues of securities, including receipt of applications monies from the public, "rationing" an over-subscription, etc.

(d) *Merchant banks.* These are large organisations which, amongst other activities, may act as issuing houses and underwriters. They also provide finance where appropriate, act as financial advisers to companies, accept bills of exchange (known as *accepting houses*) and act on the foreign exchange and gold market, etc.

CONTROL AND OWNERSHIP

15. The separation of functions. Ownership is not necessarily synonymous with control. The following three factors may exist in relation to a firm:

(a) ownership;
(b) management;
(c) external influences.

The predominance of one over the others will vary from business to business, but broad tendencies can be seen between types of businesses.

16. The sole trader. In most cases, he will have control of management and the determination of policy will be his concern alone. He will also be the legal owner but he will be subject to a reduction in his *effective* ownership to the extent that he has borrowed capital.

As a member of a voluntary retail chain or the owner of a franchise he may surrender some freedom in policy-making and may have financial obligations which limit his effective ownership.

17. Partnerships. Diminutions in control and ownership may apply to these as they may to sole traders. Ownership will be shared between the partners, of course, as determined by the amount of capital of each partner. Day to day management will depend upon the duties as agreed between them, but *control* may depend upon voting strength. One partner of three is likely to be out-voted at any time but a powerful weapon is the threat of a partner to withdraw. The relationship must be a very personal one and not subject to the rigid voting rules which operate within a company.

18. Limited companies. The owners are the shareholders but, except in a small company, they have effectively little control of their company. The authority delegated to directors is extensive and shareholders are powerless to prevent any action by the Board within its authority. The only scope for changing the control is the concentration of over 50 per cent of the votes to remove any or all the directors. This is difficult to achieve when members are comparatively small holders and there is no procedure enabling them to act in concert.

Shareholder power *is* possible, however, when a high proportion of voting shares is held by one or a few large shareholders, such as another company or an institution. They may have sufficient voting power to dictate the composition of the Board. Again, this leaves the small shareholders (and all holders of shares with no votes) with ineffective control.

The existence of large lenders will influence the action of the directors and thereby provide control at arm's length. A company will hesitate to take action which may upset a large lender, particularly one (such as a bank) with the right to demand an early redemption of a loan.

PROGRESS TEST 6

1. How does the scope for financing differ as between: (a) sole traders; (b) partnerships; (c) private limited companies; and (d) public limited companies? (1)
2. What factors will influence the amount of capital which should be borrowed? (2)
3. Define and explain the significance of the "yield on owners' funds". (3)
4. What costs must the initial capital be expected to cover? (4)
5. What is the purpose of a cash schedule or budget? (5)
6. What could be the dangers of under-capitalisation? (6)
7. What are the differences between share capital and other capital of a company? (7)
8. Explain the differences between Ordinary shares and Preference shares. (8)
9. What are: (a) Participating Preference shares; and (b) Redeemable Preference shares? (8)
10. List the various types of debentures. (9)
11. Define and explain the significance of capital gearing. (10)
12. What are "the institutions"? Explain their significance. (12)
13. What are the functions of the Stock Exchange? (13)
14. Define: (a) issuing houses; (b) underwriters; (c) new issue departments; (d) merchant banks. (14)
15. Compare the control of a business with its ownership as regards (a) sole traders; (b) partnerships; (c) limited companies. (15)

PART TWO

ORGANISATION WITHIN THE BUSINESS

CHAPTER VII

MANAGEMENT PRINCIPLES

THE NATURE OF MANAGEMENT

1. Defining "management". "Management" can have various meanings in different contexts and it has been defined from a number of viewpoints, but a generally accepted definition must be that by E. F. L. Brech (*The Principles and Practice of Management*, ed. E. F. L. Brech, Longman, 1975), who described it as:

"A social process entailing responsibility for the effective and economic planning and regulating of the operations of an exercise, in fulfilment of a given purpose, such responsibility involving

(a) judgment and decision in determining plans, and the development of data procedures to assist control of performance and progress against plans; and

(b) the guidance, integration, motivation and supervision of the personnel composing the enterprise and carrying out its operations".

This definition can be analysed to allow a preliminary examination of the elements in the function of management.

(a) *"social process"*. This phrase recognises that successful management is wholly dependent upon the skilful handling of people. Every aspect of management entails human co-operation and the eliciting of the necessary response is essential.

(b) *"responsibility"*. This refers to the structures in all forms of management whereby there are defined areas of responsibility for the *"planning"* and the *"fulfilment"* of objectives.

(c) *"effective and economic"*. The prime purpose of management is to ensure that the objectives are actually achieved and by the most economic methods.

(d) *"judgment and decision"*. This relates to the demand for the use of a high standard of managerial skill.

(e) *"control of performance and progress against plans"*. An essential in any management scheme is a system of constant checking of actual performance against the pattern of the plan.

(f) *"guidance . . . of the personnel"*. This relates to administration in action in organising the personnel to carry out the operations necessary to achieve the objective.

2. Defining "administration". There is some lack of uniformity in defining "administration" and the distinction between it and "management" tends to be blurred. In general, it is accepted as referring to the processes concerned in carrying out the procedures laid down to achieve the objectives planned; as such, it refers to routines and techniques and the personal relationships involved.

3. Defining "organisation". This is generally regarded as having reference to the *structure*—that is, the determination of responsibilities, the inter-relationships of responsibility areas and the channels of information (*see* VIII).

4. A specific or an incidental function. The modern trend has been to give the practice of management the status of a specialist function, recognising it as a separate skill. This has lead to the development of techniques, an increase in theories and a vast literature. The advantages of any form of specialisation thereby accrue, but the disadvantages must also be recognised. Any extreme form of specialisation involves the risk of "isolation", in that the practitioner may become too separated from the main stream of human activity. Because a fundamental of management is its complete dependence upon co-operation by other people, any failure to give adequate recognition to that principle will be particularly dangerous.

Whilst admitting the particular skill required by people *as* managers, it is nevertheless obvious that *any* activity which is not wholly automatic must involve, even unconsciously, a degree of management. A shopping expedition, for example, requires firstly some planning—what to buy and where to buy it; the route to be followed; financial budgeting, etc. Like all forms of management, there must be a system of check—to determine what is still to be purchased and what is not available for purchase, etc. The plan and the check must contain an element of flexibility—it may be found necessary or advisable to buy something other than that planned; an adjustment to the budget may be required.

At all levels in a business, there will be "incidental management" such as this, by those who are not described as "managers" and who are not expected to have managerial expertise. The simplest clerical operation will require a certain amount of planning and control.

5. The functions of management. Broad definitions of the functions of management are as follows:

(a) *Planning.* This is largely concerned with the determination of policy; that is, the overall objectives and principles. Below that level will be the establishment of aims of the various divisions, co-ordinated and subject to the overall plan.

In support of the plan will be the setting up of the organisation structure, defining the duties and responsibilities of persons and departments and their inter-relationships. The whole must be designed to operate in fulfilment of the major policy and will therefore require a structure of delegation and a system of communication.

Relative to this pattern of human relations will be the management "tools". These include such techniques as market research, budgeting, procedures, etc.

(b) *Control.* This refers to the checking of performance against the plan and must be carried out continuously. Any divergence from the target may affect the functions to be performed at the next stage and may result in the final target not being reached. Control must therefore include a system of efficient communication so that action may be taken to allow for or to correct any discrepancies.

Control also allows for the recording of the performance to provide a guide for future similar operations.

(c) *Co-ordination.* This refers to efficient organisation of work within a team as a contribution to the total efficiency. The manager responsible may not be required to use special techniques of management but must have the quality generally known as "leadership".

(*d*) *Motivation.* All managerial activity depends upon human reactions. To be efficient, the concern must have a staff willing to make the required contribution. As part of the function of co-ordination, there must be the ability of managers, supervisors, etc., to inspire and lead their subordinates. In general, it may be said that the degree to which this is achieved will largely depend upon the motivation policy of top management. This is not only because *attitudes* of top management are usually repeated throughout lower levels, but also because *laid down* personnel policies, decided at the top, will determine the extent to which lower-level managers may improve relations with their staffs.

PLANNING

6. Planning decisions. Planning may be said to be the fundamental of management and is relative to *policy formation.* Firstly, decisions have to be made as to:

(*a*) *what to do.* This may entail a choice between two or more objectives;
(*b*) *how to do it.* This will involve technical problems and matters of estimating;
(*c*) *who will do it.* This relates to the labour and the management structure required.

7. Corporate planning. "Corporate planning is the systematic development of action programmes aimed at reaching agreed business objectives by a process of analysing, evaluating and selecting from among the opportunities which are foreseen" (*Preparing Company Plans,* Harry Jones, Gower Press, 1974).
Corporate planning is not now regarded as being a specialist function at top level, almost as an appendage to the mainstream of management. It is now established as a method for the global active management of a business, reaching from the chief executive officer down to heads of divisions and departments, operating according to a strategy by the use of prescribed procedures.

8. Forecasting. This is concerned with the estimating of future events and is thereby directly related to planning. It can include such matters as the amount of sales, the cost of materials, the cost of machine maintenance, labour requirements and their cost, the potential of a new market, etc.

Forecasting is now a sophisticated science and many techniques are in use. The accuracy will, however, always be influenced by the following considerations:

(a) *The extent of unknown factors.* In most cases, some of the factors can be predicted fairly easily because they derive from published information or are based on past performances. Often, however, there will be unknown factors and the number and importance of such factors, relevant to the known factors, will affect the degree of accuracy.

(b) *The relevance of known factors.* It cannot always be assumed that known factors will remain constant. Future sales of a product may not be the same as past sales of the same product because outside influences may change them. The degree of probability and the extent of such changes will therefore be unknown.

(c) *The range of the survey.* An estimate based on too narrow a survey will tend to be inaccurate.

(d) *The validity of the forecast.* This will largely depend upon the skill of the forecaster. The sources of the data must be validated and the forecaster must clearly understand what is required of him.

(e) *The length of the forecast.* In general, long-term forecasts are less reliable because of the longer period during which distorting features can emerge. Particular difficulty is therefore likely when the forecasting *must* be long-term, e.g. estimating costs and sales of a new car model.

(f) *External factors.* Long-term forecasts are particularly prone to changes which cannot be anticipated, e.g. Government policy or taxation changes; political events abroad; invention of new processes; changes in public taste, etc.

9. Organisation structure. The organisational framework must be planned so that the right amounts and types of personnel will be available to implement the plan. Any change in the plan may require a re-structuring of the organisation. It must be seen that responsibilities are clearly allocated, that the delegation system is efficient and that information channels are effective (*see* VIII).

POLICY

10. The nature of policy. Policy may be said to be the defining of objectives. The establishing of a policy must be based on efficient forecasting.

Planning, as a precursor of action, is the determining of the methods whereby the policy is to be carried out.

The making of a policy requires the following:

(a) *Objectives.* The objective must be clearly stated.

(b) *Information concerning external factors.* For example— an assessment of the market; the availability of finance, materials, etc.; the availability of the required types of labour and their cost; any relevant legislation or Government policy.

(c) *Information concerning internal factors.* For example— production capacity; composition of the present labour force; organisation structure; types of specialist staff.

11. Types of policy. A business will have more than one type of policy. One may relate to its "image" and will be largely concerned with ethics; another will express its attitude to staff relations. As such, the policies are not capable of definitive measurement but, nevertheless, they serve as declarations of objectives in those fields. Thus the targets can be compared with the subsequent achievements.

There will be policies capable of measurement concerning financial objectives and other targets. Such quantifications will be in the form of standards to be achieved (*see* **15**(*a*) below), and will exist in respect of almost every aspect of the business.

12. Formulation of policy. Major policies will be determined by the directors of a company, or other governing bodies in other concerns. Subsidiary policies will be established at lower levels, but within the confines of the policy made at higher levels.

(a) *Communication.* Policy must be clearly communicated to those with the responsibility of implementation and, where any latitude is allowed to subordinates, it must be explicitly stated. Adequate information is necessary not only in the interests of efficiency but as a form of motivation; good and adequate information promotes a feeling of participation and reduces a tendency to the "them and us" attitude.

(b) *Statements.* These may be broadly classified thus:

(i) General policy, giving the principles and sets of standards concerning business attitudes, such as those concerning relations with customers, the public and employees.

(ii) Sectional policy, giving guidelines and instructions to various sections of the business.

Policy statements should be written and should result from consultation with those directly concerned and who can make personal contributions.

13. Policy programme. The process relevant to policies can be summarised as follows:

(a) Assembling the information required.
(b) Deciding on the policy.
(c) Communicating the policy to those concerned.
(d) Planning implementation by the management.
(e) Implementing the policy.
(f) Controlling the implementation.
(g) Reviewing the policy and, where necessary, amending it to meet changed circumstances.

Flexibility is important but, as far as possible, any changes should not be unduly disruptive of the management structure.

14. Implementing the policy. This is in the realm of management, but it is the responsibility of the policy-makers to ensure that the management facilities are such as to make attainment of the objectives possible. There should therefore be a form of communication with management before a policy decision is made so as to ensure that all the requirements are or could be available.

Similarly, there must be a communication system for subsequent information as to the progress being made and for any policy changes to be promulgated.

CONTROL

15. Function of control. Having established a plan and put it into operation, it is necessary to have a system for comparing one stage with the other. The purpose of control is to check the performance against the target and to make any adjustments which may be indicated as being unavoidable or advisable. The process consists of the following steps:

(a) *Setting standards.* This will establish standards to be reached at various points in a sequence of events or for different areas in the total plan. The scales of measurement can be various. For example, it may be a time scale within which a certain target must be reached; a unit scale, such as output or sales; a monetary scale, showing expenditure or return on capital; or a ratio, such as sales related to selling costs.

(b) *Comparing performances with standards.*

(c) *Feedback of information.* The methods to be used to pass back information on progress and any deviation must be clearly established.

(d) *Correcting deviations.* When the feedback indicates that external factors, faulty planning, mistakes in operation, etc., have caused a deviation, adjustments will be made accordingly.

16. Methods of control. The methods of measurement used in control are many, some of them being specific to types of activity. In general, they take the form of budgets, ratios, audits, inventories, etc., in addition to special techniques. In this HANDBOOK they are dealt with in the appropriate chapter where they are specific to particular departments; others will be found in chapter IX.

17. Effectiveness of control. The degree to which control is effective will be influenced by the following considerations:

(a) *Flexibility of the plan.* The establishment of control implies that some deviations may be expected. Whilst the plan must be capable of adjustment where necessary, there must be no indication given that laxity in attempting to conform to standards will be tolerated. An example would be the failure to meet a delivery date because it is generally known that the date could be postponed. It must be understood that any deviation not caused by external factors must impose accountability on the person responsible.

(b) *Speed of feedback.* Deviations must be reported quickly so that adjustments can be made before the target becomes more remote. Even though the deviation may result in failure to reach the original standard (because the report will be made *after* the event), if it is an unavoidable one it can be built into the next similar plan, so that the target will be more realistic. Alternatively, if the deviation could have been avoided by prior knowledge, a suitable adjustment can be made to future procedures.

(c) *Control through the organisation.* The organisation structure must clearly indicate the areas of responsibility so that control will thereby be more effective. The structure will also indicate the channels through which deviations are to be reported.

(d) *Degree of deviation.* A certain amount of tolerance in respect of deviation may be acceptable. If the plan allows for that tolerance, then no adjustment will be required for permitted deviations. Those responsible must be certain they know what degree of deviation must be acted upon.

18. Management by objectives. This term relates to the setting of objectives as part of a strategy, departmental and personal targets being supplementary to and co-ordinated with the main objective. A feature is that those responsible for reaching targets, either as individuals or heads of departments, have the maximum possible amount of freedom in attempting to achieve their objectives.

This freedom entails the following considerations:

(a) *Initiative.* The person or group concerned is allowed to exercise initiative in working towards the target. An individual would thereby receive personal satisfaction; a group would be made more cohesive because of the internal co-operation required. Thus, in both instances there would be personal involvement which should provide effective motivation.

(b) *Clarity of objectives.* The target for each person or group must be clearly established, both as regards the ultimate objective and the performance standards.

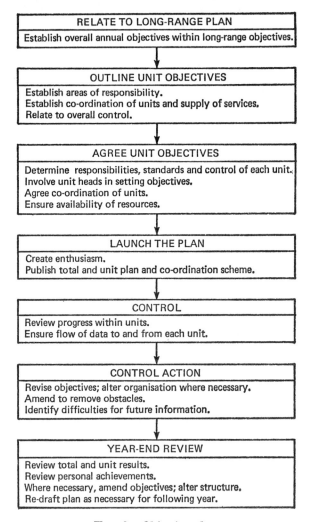

RELATE TO LONG-RANGE PLAN

Establish overall annual objectives within long-range objectives.

OUTLINE UNIT OBJECTIVES

Establish areas of responsibility.
Establish co-ordination of units and supply of services.
Relate to overall control.

AGREE UNIT OBJECTIVES

Determine responsibilities, standards and control of each unit.
Involve unit heads in setting objectives.
Agree co-ordination of units.
Ensure availability of resources.

LAUNCH THE PLAN

Create enthusiasm.
Publish total and unit plan and co-ordination scheme.

CONTROL

Review progress within units.
Ensure flow of data to and from each unit.

CONTROL ACTION

Revise objectives; alter organisation where necessary.
Amend to remove obstacles.
Identify difficulties for future information.

YEAR-END REVIEW

Review total and unit results.
Review personal achievements.
Where necessary, amend objectives; alter structure.
Re-draft plan as necessary for following year.

FIG. 2—*Objective plan.*

(c) *Feasibility of the objectives.* To ensure that achievement is not impossible or unduly difficult, consideration must be given to the following:

(*i*) The group must be provided with the necessary facilities.

(*ii*) Control information must be provided regularly and promptly.

(*iii*) Allowance must be given for any deviation caused by factors external to the group (e.g. the failure of a group at a preceding stage, or the failure to provide promised services or support).

(*iv*) The organisation structure must allow the group to operate freely in relation to other groups, with adequate flows of information and geared to a realistic timetable.

(*v*) The objective must be decided in consultation with those to be responsible for its achievement.

An objective plan on an annual basis as part of a long-range plan is illustrated in Fig. 2.

PROGRESS TEST 7

1. What are the generally accepted distinctions between "management", "administration" and "organisation"? (1–3)

2. To what extent may management be regarded as a specialist function? (4)

3. Name the generally accepted functions of management. (5)

4. What is meant by "corporate planning" ? (7)

5. What factors may influence the accuracy of forecasting? (8)

6. Define "policy" and state the requirements for establishing a policy. (10)

7. What are "policy statements"? (12)

8. Outline the stages in a policy programme. (13)

9. What are the purposes of control and what are the stages in its establishment? (15)

10. What principles apply concerning standards and deviations in control? (15–17)

11. Concerning control, explain the significance of: (a) flexibility; and (b) feedback. (17)

12. What is meant by "management by objectives" and what is its connection with motivation? (18)

13. What is required to ensure the success of a management by objectives scheme? (18)

CHAPTER VIII

THE FRAMEWORK OF MANAGEMENT

ORGANISATION STRUCTURE

1. The nature of organisation structure. In broad terms, one may say that organisation is concerned with the grouping of activities in a co-ordinated whole, to achieve the objectives of the business. In more detail, it requires inclusion of the following principles:

(*a*) *Division of activities.* The total of the functions must be divided into logical groupings which must each contain appropriately qualified staff and adequate facilities.

(*b*) *Determination of responsibilities.* The extent of the responsibility of each group must be established and each group must contain a structure which determines the functions and responsibilities of each of its members.

(*c*) *Delegation.* General principles of delegation must be understood, both as regards the whole structure and the structure of each group.

(*d*) *Co-ordination.* Groups must be arranged so as to co-operate in furthering the purpose of the whole.

(*e*) *Communication.* There must be firmly established lines and methods of communication (*see* IX).

(*f*) *Hierarchy.* There must be a vertical structure indicating the links between levels of responsibility and authority.

(*g*) *Flexibility.* As business is not conducted in static conditions, so must the organisation be capable of adaptation to meet changing circumstances.

2. The necessity for a structure. In a small business there would be no requirement to draft a structure, because the members would know what their duties were, to whom and for whom they were responsible and the flow pattern of the work. At a certain stage, however, an attempt must be made to compile some picture of the organisation as it is at that time. From then onwards, the drafting of structures would be a continuous process to meet changing conditions. The reasons for a structure are as follows:

(a) *Personal identity.* Every member of the enterprise can see his position and that of his department in the whole and can relate those positions to others in the organisation.

(b) *Determination of responsibility.* Combined with job specifications (*see* XIII, **19**), the structure indicates the responsibility of each department and each person.

(c) *Establishment of authority.* The structure will indicate to each person who are his immediate and ultimate superiors and those who are accountable to him.

(d) *Co-ordination.* The flows of activity between one area and others are established so that the routing of work, of responsibility and of communication are understood.

(e) *Increased efficiency.* A structure may indicate unduly long lines of authority, duplication of functions, dual responsibilities, etc. It can thus be used to compile a more efficient structure.

(f) *Staff distribution.* If the representation shows the number and type of staff at each work point, it can contribute to the more efficient use of staff.

(g) *Specialisation.* As the organisation shows the scope of work at each point, it is possible to allocate staff with attributes specific to the work. Also, if increased growth indicates the need to split a department to achieve a greater degree of specialisation, the structure can be amended accordingly and still retain the co-ordination required.

3. Formal and informal organisation. The formal organisation is the structure which has been officially drafted and to which personnel consciously work, but within any such structure there will always be an informal organisation. Groups of people with common interests will work together beyond the confines of the formal structure. This tendency may not be ignored by management, even when it recognises that it may, on occasion, detract from attainment of the business objectives. It would be a matter of judgment to recognise when an informal organisation should be formalised because of its contribution to the common objective.

AUTHORITY AND RESPONSIBILITY

4. The hierarchic channel. This concept recognises the necessity for *unity of command*. Also known as the *Scalar Principle*, it states that there must be an unbroken line of authority and command from the highest level to the lowest.

5. The strata of management. This refers to the levels of management which accommodate the handing down of authority and responsibility and the consequent upward accountability. The granting of authority and the imposing of responsibility on a lower stratum may be:

(*a*) *specific*. For example, the chief executive officer may impose upon the chief accountant the task of computerising the pay department; a sales manager may make a clerk responsible for checking salesmens' expense accounts;

(*b*) *comprehensive*. An officer may have authority and responsibility for a set range of tasks. Within that authority he could grant authority to his subordinates. In (*a*), the chief accountant would be responsible for all matters generally relevant to accounting, in the same way that the sales manager would be responsible for the conduct of the sales department.

6. Forms of authority.

(*a*) *Line authority*. This indicates the vertical line of direct authority, the superior/subordinate relationship being expressed throughout its whole length. An absolute line organisation is impossible except in the smallest and simplest structures because at an early stage of development specialists will be required. These functional and staff officers will have a *width* of responsibility which will partly upset the strict vertical pattern of line authority. But at any point in the organisation, each person will have immediate and ultimate superiors and subordinates.

(*b*) *Functional authority*. This recognises functional relationships; that is, between those who are specialists in their own spheres. Each expert is responsible for a specified type of activity throughout the business. For example, a personnel officer at a head office would have authority in respect of the work of personnel officers in divisions or branches. This would ensure uniformity in the business's personnel policy, but would not interfere with the branch personnel officers' direct responsibility to their branch superiors.

(c) *Staff authority.* This relates to relationships outside the vertical and lateral relationships discussed above. It concerns those with specialised knowledge who are able to assist and advise the business generally. Examples are public relations officers, legal officers, etc. Clearly defining an officer as having only staff authority is frequently impossible. For example, an organisation and methods officer is available to advise generally, but if he is given instructions to install an office system he is thereby given *authority.* He therefore assumes functional authority and also line authority in that he may command.

7. Delegation of authority and responsibility.

(a) *Authority.* This relates to transferring to another person (which could be a committee or body, *see* **14** below) authority to carry out a specified task which is within the authority of the delegating body. As such, it is therefore part of line organisation.

(b) *Responsibility.* *Ultimate* responsibility is retained. The subordinate has responsibility to his superior for carrying out the delegated task but the superior remains responsible for ensuring the work is done.

8. Effective delegation. Effective delegation requires the following to be observed:

(a) *The scope of delegation.* The delegate must firmly be made aware of the limitations to his authority. In the case of a committee, this would be stated in its terms of reference.

(b) *Delegate's ability.* It must be established that the delegate has the necessary experience and ability to carry out his task. Where necessary, he should be given instruction and guidance.

(c) *Control.* The delegator must supervise the work of the delegate, the extent of the supervision being dependent upon the delegator's knowledge of and faith in his delegate. An unduly extensive amount of supervision will become irksome and frustrating to the delegate and will indicate a lack of confidence by the superior in his ability to delegate. Little or no supervision may leave the delegate unfairly exposed and may indicate that the delegator is abdicating some of his responsibility.

(*d*) *Single subordination.* A person should have only one direct superior, otherwise confusion and clashes of interest may result.

9. Justification for delegation.

(*a*) *Fundamental.* The system of delegation is basic to management.

(*b*) *Specialisation.* Sections of work can be delegated to those with particular expertise.

(*c*) *Sharing work load.* The delegator is relieved of some duties, leaving him time to concentrate on other matters.

(*d*) *Training.* Delegation results in wider experience and increased confidence for the delegates.

10. Span of control. This term relates to the number of immediate subordinates a superior is responsible for. The optimum is often difficult to determine and depends upon a number of considerations.

(*a*) *If the span is too wide* there will be little opportunity for contact between the leader and his subordinates and supervision will be difficult.

(*b*) *If the span is too narrow* subordinates will be discouraged by the lack of opportunity to learn and gain experience.

In establishing the span, the following factors should be considered:

(*c*) *Nature of the work.* Where the work is complex, with a degree of inter-locking, the span should be narrow because actions of one delegate will affect many others. The span can be wider when each job is comparatively self-contained.

(*d*) *The ability of the superior and the delegates.* One

superior may be more able to cope with a large number of subordinates than another. The experience and reliability of the subordinates has an obvious effect on the amount of work which may safely be delegated to them.

(e) *Team work.* A group able to work cohesively would be able to relieve the superior of a greater amount of work. This attitude can be affected by the leadership qualities of the superior (*see* 25 below).

(f) *Management aids.* Increased mechanisation and the use of management services can reduce the amount of supervision necessary.

ORGANISATION CHARTS

11. Illustrative purposes. An organisation chart is a diagrammatic representation of the structure of a business. It is an attempt to show the following:

(a) *Demarcation of responsibility.* The nature and extent of responsibility of each person and section can be indicated.

(b) *Lines of authority.* Vertical lines show the downward flow of authority and the upward flow of accountability.

(c) *Channels of communication.* The main lines of communication can be regarded as being parallel to the lines of authority, but there will be others which take different routes.

(d) *Relationships.* This concerns the connection between units and the place of line, staff and functional duties.

12. Advantages and disadvantages. The *advantages* may be as follows:

(a) *Information.* A chart presents a "picture" of the organisation which can be used when reorganisation is being considered. It is also useful to show new staff members their positions and that of their departments in relation to the whole organisation.

(b) *Indicator of inadequacies.* A chart may make inefficiencies apparent by indicating areas of duplicated work, overlong lines of authority, etc.

Possible *disadvantages* are as follows:

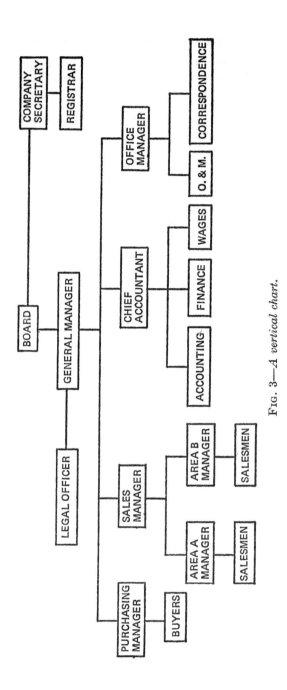

Fig. 3—*A vertical chart.*

(c) *Difficulty in designing.* An over-simplified chart contributes little and may be positively misleading. On the other hand, too detailed a chart is confusing.

(d) *Topicality.* A chart shows the position as at the time of drafting. Consequently, it will rarely be up to date.

(e) *Rigidity of outlook.* There is a tendency for people to be too conscious of the boundaries of their own areas. In practice, people go beyond the set limitations (*see* 3 above), and it is generally good for the enterprise that they do so, but charting may nevertheless develop too strong a feeling for "territorial rights".

(f) *Status problems.* The placing of people in relationships to others sometimes creates offence and jealousy.

(g) *Formality of relationships.* The human relationships which exist cannot be shown.

(h) *Expense.* The cost of compiling will not be justified if the chart does not add to efficiency.

13. Types of chart.

(a) *Vertical charts.* This is the traditional method, showing direct lines of authority. Figure 3 is a simple example.

It will be seen from Fig. 3 that four line executives are directly responsible to the general manager but that the secretary is answerable to the board. The fact that the four executives are on the same line does not imply parity in status but merely indicates their relationships with the general manager.

(b) *Horizontal charts.* This is an attempt to avoid emphasis on levels of authority. The chart is read from left to right, with the most senior members on the left.

(c) *Circular charts.* Again, the objective is to eliminate "levels" but comparative relationships are nevertheless indicated by the position of any one member's circle to that of the circle of the most senior (*see* Fig. 4(a)). Within each circle are the circles of subordinates; the drafting problems of showing smaller and smaller circles are obvious.

An alternative method is to identify the senior officer by a circle in the centre (*see* Fig. 4(b)) and to arrange the subordinates in sectors within concentric circles.

From a study of Fig. 4, the difficulty of drafting so as to show other than simple structures is apparent.

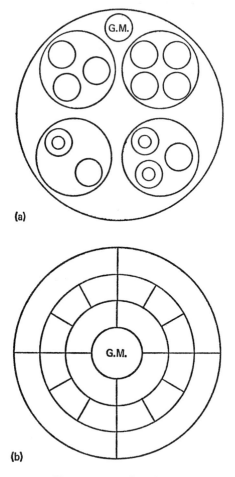

(a)

(b)

FIG. 4—*Circular charts.*

THE COMMITTEE SYSTEM

14. A form of delegation. A committee is a body of persons (occasionally, one person) with delegated functions. As such, it obtains those powers which are delegated to it and is accountable to the appointing body.

15. Terms of reference. The scope of responsibilities and duties must be clearly defined, preferably in writing. Any power exercised by a committee within its delegated authority will, in respect of its conduct with outside persons, be binding upon the appointing body. If a committee's function is advisory only, this must be clearly understood by its members. Failure to do so could have unfortunate results if, as a consequence, the committee used power it was not entitled to. A committee may therefore:

(*a*) make decisions and take action (usually described as an *executive* committee); or

(*b*) investigate and report; or

(*c*) investigate, report and recommend.

It may be:

(*d*) *a standing committee,* carrying out routine work of a continuous nature;

(*e*) *an ad hoc committee,* formed for a special purpose, on completion of which it would be dissolved.

16. Advantages.

(*a*) *Joint effort.* A committee facilitates the pooling of ideas. Thus, the decision would be a consensus, without the danger of undue bias by one person.

(*b*) *Specialist knowledge available.* A committee can be formed to bring together those with a knowledge relevant to the subject and so report to those without that expertise.

(*c*) *Sharing of work.* Work can be spread by allocating members to different committees.

(*d*) *Speed.* A small committee is likely to reach a decision quicker than a large body.

(*e*) *Democratic decision-making.* More people can play a part in decision-making.

17. Disadvantages.

(a) *Expense of time.* An ineffective chairman can allow deliberations to be protracted. The time spent going to committees and that spent on paper work may be uneconomical.

(b) *Weakened authority.* A committee with executive authority will take that amount away from the appointing body. There can also be the danger of "key" committees (such as those responsible for finance) becoming too powerful.

(c) *Politicising.* Committees can be mis-used to exert "political" power and may encourage manoeuvring to be appointed to powerful committees. A person or group may dominate a committee or be obstructionist.

(d) *Indeterminate decisions.* Decisions may be reached as a result of compromise between opposing views and will thereby lack positiveness.

(e) *Loss of personal responsibility.* A member may consider himself personally unaccountable for a group decision.

CENTRALISATION AND DECENTRALISATION

18. Extent of centralisation and decentralisation. Absolute centralisation is not practical because although major decisions are made by the controlling body, day-to-day decisions must be made at lower levels.

Similarly, decentralisation cannot be absolute because there must be a central body to decide major issues.

Decentralisation, therefore, means moving authority to lower points in the organisation and is thereby analogous to delegation. As such, it refers to *decentralisation of management.*

19. Federal decentralisation. This relates to the setting up of what in effect are separate businesses. Allocations of capital are made, the unit is responsible for its own profits and losses, and management has a large degree of autonomy. These are sometimes *product divisions.*

20. Functional decentralisation. Applicable where units have total responsibility for separate stages in the business, functional decentralisation occurs in such sections as production and supply. It has the possible disadvantage of an isolationist outlook and co-ordination may therefore be difficult.

21. Centralisation of services. This refers to centralisation within one unit, e.g. typing pools, and centralisation within a group, e.g. statistical services available to all branches.

22. Aspects of centralisation.

(a) *Recognition of local conditions.* A uniform attitude or procedure may ignore factors specific to one section, e.g. an overall marketing policy may be inappropriate in one geographical area.

(b) *Uniformity.* Economies may result from uniformity of systems, etc., but may be conducive to rigidity.

(c) *Decision delays.* Problems which have to be referred to a central authority could often be dealt with more quickly at a lower level.

(d) *Loss of initiative.* If centralisation reduces the scope of managers, initiative and personal involvement is lessened.

(e) *Bureaucracy.* Centralisation results in an increase of personnel at the controlling centre and a proliferation of procedures. This can lead to the disadvantages associated with "red tape".

(f) *Economies of specialisation.* The increase of specialists serving all areas and levels should add to efficiency and reduce costs.

(g) *Development of the business.* The stage of development which the business has reached may affect the choice between centralisation and decentralisation. Beyond a certain size and degree of complexity, it may be beneficial to decentralise. There may be other stages when it would be advantageous to combine some operations of separate units into a single unit.

DIRECTION

23. Direction and leadership. The superior/subordinate relationship and its derivative, the delegation principle, give rise to the concept of direction. All human activity must be directed by the relevant superior levels of management. Direction, therefore, means the action of a leader in ensuring that those for whom he is responsible carry out the duties allotted by him in furtherance of the objectives of the business.

24. Leadership. As the head of a group within the organisation, a leader must have recognition of the following principles:

(a) *Human relations.* The leader must have the ability to understand people and handle them so as to obtain the best results from a group.

(b) *Responsibility.* The leader accepts responsibility for the actions of his group in achieving the objectives.

(c) *Authority.* It is the responsibility of higher management to ensure a leader has the authority and support necessary for him to carry out his duties.

(d) *Influencing attitudes.* It is a truism that the personality and ability of a leader is reflected in his group. No group can be better than its leader and the attitude of the leader will permeate the group.

25. Human relations in leadership. The success of a leader in creating an efficient group is dependent to only a lesser degree on his technical ability. An efficient leader who cannot get co-operation because of his personal attitude to others will have an inefficient group. Aspects of behaviour which will influence the group performance include the following:

(a) *Availability.* A leader should always be available to his subordinates. Friendliness should not be confused with familiarity, however. A leader should be recognised as being fair in his dealings with others, but it can be dangerous to court popularity.

(b) *Authoritarianism.* The giving of orders is necessary, of course, but a leader who behaves in a brusque manner and uses threats will get little co-operation. He must *explain* what he wants, advise where necessary, give any reprimand with fairness and acknowledge good work. Where possible, subordinates should be allowed to participate in decision-making, e.g. how a certain job is to be tackled by the group.

(c) *Delegation.* A leader must delegate to the extent of allowing initiative. A leader who keeps everything to himself is unfair to his staff and himself.

(d) *Impartiality.* Unfair treatment, either in the form of

victimisation or favouritism, can create a cancer in a group.

(e) *Recognition of individuality.* People are individuals and a leader must treat each subordinate according to that person's nature. He must have the ability to discern the way each person should be treated, recognising weaknesses and strengths in the other. In the event of a "personality clash" which cannot be resolved, the subordinate should be moved from the control of the superior.

DECISION-MAKING

26. The incidence of decision-making. Decisions are made continuously and at all levels of management. In considering this, the following points are relevant:

(a) *Chain of command.* Decisions are passed downward in the organisation. Each level forwards decisions for action by lower levels which in turn make decisions within the responsibility it receives.

(b) *Decisions of amendment.* The carrying out of its responsibilities by any one level may be frustrated by unexpected difficulties or by a change in the original plan. Decisions would therefore have to be made to amend the procedure, but any changes must be within the original authority or further authority should be sought.

(c) *Basis of full understanding.* The decision-maker must clearly understand the basic objective of the part for which he is responsible; the consequences of taking a decision must be known as far as possible; there must be awareness of any external factors which may influence the decision.

(d) *Comparability of decisions.* Where alternative decisions are available, there must be the means of assessing the comparative costs and results.

(e) *Accountability for decisions.* Circumstances will dictate whether any choice of decision or any decision consequent upon a change of circumstances can be made by the leader directly responsible. The degree of autonomy must be established, although a decision made in an emergency, where there is no time to seek special authority or advice, should be supported by higher levels.

(f) *Co-ordination.* The effect of any decision on any other part of the organisation must be allowed for.

(*g*) *Degree of authority.* There may be limitations set on the extent to which a leader may make a decision. For example, there may be a restriction on the amount of cost he may incur. In general, where a wrong decision could result in undue cost, or be particularly damaging, the decision should be made by a higher level of management.

(*h*) *Use of techniques.* Many quantitative techniques are available for decision-making, but it must always be accepted that their value lies in *understanding and applying them.* "Management tools" in themselves are no substitute for management.

27. Decision trees. Where a series of decisions reaching some way into the future have to be made, it is possible to draw a "decision tree" showing the decisions to be reached. Where choices of decision have to be made at various stages, the possible outcome of each choice is shown as a "branch", thereby aiding management in making its choice.

28. Types of decisions. Various classifications of decisions have been made, such as the following:

(*a*) *Strategic decisions* are made by management in attempting to attain objectives in a condition of competition and are formulated as policies or plans.

Tactical decisions are matters of routine in carrying out a strategic plan. It may, for example, relate to the efficient use of resources.

(*b*) *Organisational decisions* are those made by staff within their authority and responsibility limitations, as prescribed by the organisation structure.

Personal decisions are those attached to personal responsibility that cannot be delegated.

(*c*) *Programmed decisions* are routine decisions made within prescribed situations and which are subject to set procedures.

Unprogrammed decisions are unique. They are those for which no procedure has been established: they may refer to "emergencies", or they may relate to fundamentals.

(*d*) *Basic decisions* are those which have a long-term effect and which will involve many consequences, e.g. to decide which factory to close or which product to promote.

Routine decisions are those which have to be made in day-to-day activities and which are not fundamental.

THE DIRECTORS

29. Responsibilities of the Board. Directors are appointed by the shareholders in that a director may be appointed or removed by the holders of a majority of the voting shares. There may therefore be said to be a voluntary delegation of authority in favour of directors.

The responsibilities of directors differ according to whom they have responsibilities.

(*a*) *To the shareholders.* Directors are required to:

(*i*) conduct the affairs of the business in the interests of the company as a whole and to not favour one or more sections of it;

(*ii*) make no secret profits or benefit personally by reason of any information privy to the directors;

(*iii*) disclose to other directors any interest they may have in contracts with the company.

(*b*) *To the company.*

(*i*) Directors are agents of the company and any agreement made by them in the name of the company, provided it is within their powers to do so, are binding on the company.

(*ii*) Directors form the highest level of management and are empowered to determine major matters of policy.

(*c*) *To the law.* Stringent legislation applies to directors concerning disclosures in the accounts and of such matters as their personal dealings in the company's securities, etc.

(*d*) *To the Stock Exchange.* If the shares of the company are listed on the Stock Exchange, further obligations are placed upon the directors—mainly to ensure fuller disclosure to investors than the law requires.

30. Constitution of the Board. Directors may be classified as:

(*a*) *full-time and part-time.* Full-time directors will be executive directors; part-time directors *may* be executives;

(*b*) *executive and non-executive.* An executive director is an officer of the company with specific administrative duties.

A non-executive director is not in an administrative position, although he may be available as a consultant or adviser.

The legal responsibilities appertaining to directors *as* directors apply to all members of the Board.

31. The managing director. The managing director is the chief executive officer of the company and answerable to the Board. His basic function is to ensure the implementation of policies decided by the directors, thereby providing the link between the Board and general management.

32. The chairman of the Board. The chairman of the Board is also chairman of the company. His duties are those devolving upon the chairman of any body but, as chairman of the company, he also acts as spokesman for the company in making public statements, etc.

The functions of a chairman are often carried out with those of the managing director but, in general, it is regarded as being unsatisfactory for both positions to be held by the same person. The functions of one differ from those of the other and the result can be a clash of interests, in that the managing director is closely involved in management, whereas the chairman should be somewhat detached.

33. Managerial duties of directors. The duties of directors as generally applicable to the management of a company may be summarised as follows:

(*a*) *Policies.* General policies and specific policies of a fundamental nature are formulated by the Board, which also has the responsibility of ensuring their implementation.

(*b*) *Financial.* The objectives should be that maximum amount of profitability, over a long period, which can be achieved without undue risk. Management must therefore be directed to include the preservation of assets, the maintenance of reserves, the ensurance that working capital is available, that expenditure is controlled, etc.

(*c*) *Senior staff.* Key positions in the organisation should be filled by appointments made by the directors or by their control. The establishing of such personnel is a vital managerial function and the responsibility for it should rest at the highest level.

(*d*) *Morale.* The directors should set standards of behaviour and attitudes. They should ensure that the efficiency of management is influenced by enlightened human relationships.

PROGRESS TEST 8

1. What principles are relevant to organisation? (**1**)

2. Why is an organisation structure necessary? (**2**)

3. Distinguish between formal and informal structures. (**3**)

4. What is "the hierarchic channel" or the "Scalar Principle"? (**4**)

5. Compare line, functional and staff authority. (**6**)

6. What is the relationship between delegation of authority and delegation of responsibility? (**7**)

7. What are the requirements for effective delegation? (**8**)

8. Define span of control. What factors determine the span? (**10**)

9. What are the objectives of organisation charts? (**11**)

10. List the advantages and disadvantages of organisation charts. (**12**)

11. Distinguish between the following types of committee: executive; standing; *ad hoc.* (**15**)

12. Consider the importance of the terms of reference of a committee. (**15**)

13. List the advantages and disadvantages of the committee system. (**16, 17**)

14. Define: federal decentralisation; functional decentralisation; centralisation of services. (**19–21**)

15. What could be the advantages and the disadvantages of centralisation? (**22**)

16. Define "direction". (**23**)

17. What are the principles of effective leadership? (**24, 25**)

18. What factors contribute to efficient decision-making? (**26**)

19. Outline the nature of directors' responsibilities to different areas. (**29**)

20. Indicate the difference between executive and non-executive directors. (**30**)

21. Compare the functions of the company chairman and the managing director. (**31, 32**)

22. What are the general managerial duties of the Board of Directors? (**33**)

CHAPTER IX

COMMUNICATION

PRINCIPLES OF COMMUNICATION

1. The scope of communication. Communication may be said to be the process by which a thought is transferred from a person or persons to another person or persons. Communication may be in the following forms:

(a) *An order*, in which case it would be part of the direction process.

(b) *A request or appeal*, such as one from the work-force to management.

(c) *An observation*, being perhaps a contribution to decision-making or merely an expression of a viewpoint.

(d) *As information*, such as the provision of data for the use of management.

(e) *As instruction*, perhaps related to training or as part of the delegation process.

(f) *In policy-making*, whereby principles and standards are promulgated.

2. Effective communication. This means that the intention contained in the communication is conveyed in such a manner as to be fully understood by the recipient; there must be a coincidence of thought by both parties. One of the major areas of failure in management is the frequent inability of communication to meet this criterion. The achievement of effective communication is therefore vital if management is to be successful. Management is concerned with working with others and unless understanding can be reached between people, the job of management is made very much more difficult.

Some of the essentials for effective communication are as follows:

(a) *Adequate briefing of the recipient.* The communicator must appreciate that facts which are known to him may not be available to the other party. Telling the recipient "all he needs to know" may sometimes require giving him more than may at first seem necessary. Circumstances may make it necessary to:

> (*i*) show how the recipients' duty is part of a larger process;
> (*ii*) outline the history leading to the communication;
> (*iii*) define the terms used.

(b) *Use of a suitable language.* In making the communication, the language used must be related to the knowledge and intellectual ability of the recipient. For example, an instruction-manual written for machine-minders by an engineer must be so worded as to be understandable by those for whom it is intended. Again, a technical report to the Board must be in a language comprehensible by non-technical directors.

(c) *Clarity.* The value of a communication is reduced if there exists verbosity, complicated phrasing, lack of objectivity, etc.

(d) *Use of appropriate media.* Different vehicles of expression are appropriate to different circumstances. There are many sub-divisions to the two broad categories—oral and written—but the choice of which to use can be very important.

3. Barriers to communication. In addition to failure to meet the requirements of effective communication as outlined above, the following can also make understanding more difficult:

(a) *Organisation inadequacies.* The danger here can be that of poorly designed channels of communication (*see* **4** below) in that:

> (*i*) information does not reach all those who should receive it;
> (*ii*) the channels are too long, thereby slowing the flow of information;
> (*iii*) too few (and, sometimes, too many) are involved in consultation before communication is made;
> (*iv*) quick access of workers to management is not available.

(b) *Physical conditions.* A noisy atmosphere, for example, (such as in a factory) can make communication difficult.

(c) *Inadequacies of the communicator.* Poorly laid-out written communications or those vaguely worded, a speaker unable to express himself clearly—all these failings can seriously detract from effectiveness.

(d) *Interpretation failure.* An excellent report can fail because of the inability of those receiving it to interpret it fully. A report from a specialist may be unacceptable to management, either because:

(i) it refuses to agree to something it does not understand and rejects the knowledgeable opinion of the expert; or

(ii) of personal prejudice—a Board largely consisting of technical people may be suspicious of recommendations by accountants, in the same way that financial experts sometimes react contrarily to technicians.

(e) *Personal animosity.* A communication may be almost deliberately misconstrued because of the pre-existing attitudes of the parties. Where bad labour relations exist, the most innocent statement by management may produce a completely unwarranted reaction; an order from a foreman to a labourer, where personal friction exists between them, is likely to be unsuccessful.

4. Channels (or lines) of communication. This refers to the *flows of communication,* some of which conform to defined patterns, whereas others do not.

(a) *Informal.* These relate to the countless communications passing every day between equals and near-equals whose work brings them into close relationships. It covers all that which follows from the procedure of work, the giving of instructions, and the discussions which have no positive objective but which contribute to the morale of the business.

(b) *Downward.* This is the passing of instructions down the line of command, each tier delegating within the authority it has been given.

(c) *Upward.* This is the system for:

(i) *procedural feedback,* whereby the results of work delegated are fed back to the authorising body;

(ii) *workers to approach management,* whereby complaints, suggestions, demands, etc., can flow upward.

Where such lines flow in reverse of the lines of delegated authority, danger exists. Dissatisfaction amongst employees will have time to fester if complaints have to go through many stages. With the growth of a business there is a tendency for lines of communication to lengthen and it is essential that "short cuts" exist so that matters of contention can be dealt with quickly. Overlong lines mean a wider separation of the two sides and are conducive to the corrosive "them and us" attitude.

(d) *Broadcast*. This concerns statements from the management to the staff generally or to certain sections of it. It can also relate to public announcements and to communications to shareholders (*see* 5 below).

(e) *Horizontal*. In the same way that absolute vertical organisation is not practical, so communication will not invariably flow upwards and downwards. Information must flow *across* between the various functional areas in the normal work pattern. There must also be provision for the mutual exchange of information between managers of different departments.

(f) *"The grape-vine"*. Unofficial flows of information, largely based on rumour, will exist in any business, and management must recognise its inevitability. Managerial skill will consist in recognising when any particular rumour has reached dangerous proportions. Stories gain in dramatic effect with re-telling and may soon be completely distorted. It is essential, therefore, that before a dangerous level is reached management issues a definitive statement. The ideal would be to *anticipate* staff concern (e.g. about possible redundancies) and make a statement at an early stage.

(g) *Committees*. These form part of the communication system and are dealt with in Chapter VIII.

5. External communications. The standard of communication between a business and those outside it is important for reasons of efficiency and good public relations.

(a) *Efficiency*. An impression of efficiency as well as its actuality is enhanced by the standard of communication in the use of letters and the telephone. Correspondence should be answered promptly. Letters should conform to a style common throughout the business, should be well laid out and be unambiguously worded. Telephone operators should be trained, so that good service is given to callers.

(b) *Public relations.* A business should aim to present an acceptable "image" to the outside world. Judicious use of the national press about its activities can be made; the trade press should be kept well informed. In these ways, relationships with customers and potential customers will be improved. The company's attitude to its shareholders and the financial world can be shown by the style of presentation and the openness of its disclosures.

VERBAL COMMUNICATIONS

6. Face-to-face contact. This relates to direct speech between two people or between small groups of people. Obviously, it is the most common form of communication and consists of orders, instructions, requests, the passing of information, etc.

(a) *Advantages.*

(i) The communicator can recognise the aptitude for understanding in the recipient and can speak in a manner suitable to that ability. Thus, the recipient's general intelligence and knowledge of the subject matter will determine the style of delivery.

(ii) It allows the recipient to ask for elucidation where necessary. Thus, the communicator can be finally satisfied that the instruction has been fully understood.

(iii) If the contact is in the form of a discussion, each can contribute to the achievement of a decision without further consultation being necessary.

(b) *Disadvantages.*

(i) The recipient may subsequently require guidance in carrying out his task, the necessity for which was not obvious at the time of communication. With no record of the communication to refer to, he will be disadvantaged. His position may be compared to that which it would have been had he been given written orders.

(ii) Another disadvantage of the lack of written record is the absence of evidence of what was agreed. There may be a subsequent dispute as to exactly what the instructions were or what authority had been given.

(iii) The relationship existing between the parties may make verbal contact unsatisfactory. This would be the case if bad feeling existed between them; if the communicator acted brusquely or even belligerently; or if the recipient was resentful.

(*iv*) The communicator may be inadequate in his vocal expression, so that the message is misinterpreted. A written communication can be the result of time being spent in making it completely understandable but this is not possible for verbal communications.

7. Interviewing. This is largely a two-way exercise, in that both parties aim to make statements and ask questions. It will apply to interviewing prospective staff members; interviews for promotion; disciplinary interviews; discussions of business and personal problems, etc. As the basic aims are to obtain and give information and for personal assessments to be made, there must be contributions from both sides. The following principles should apply:

(*a*) *The interviewer.* The interviewer should *control* the discussion but not *dominate* it.

(*b*) *Atmosphere.* As far as possible, the atmosphere should be relaxed. The aim should be not to interrogate but to allow both sides to make points. The interviewee should be "drawn out" to speak, if necessary.

(*c*) *Information.* The interviewer should have all the necessary data available, but not conspicuously so. Personal details about the interviewee would, for example, be available when a staffing interview takes place.

(*d*) *Note-taking.* A record should be compiled immediately the interview is ended while the information is still fresh in the mind (*see also* XIII, 27).

8. Joint consultation. This is a forum for discussion between employees and employers or their representatives (*see* XIII, 62).

9. Public delivery. This may relate to:

(*a*) the announcement of a policy-decision, e.g. an address by a director or the labour relations officer to the work-force in the course of an industrial dispute;

(*b*) the giving of lectures as part of an education programme;

(*c*) a speech to those with a common interest (e.g. at a conference of professional people) or to those seeking information (e.g. a press conference).

In general, good speakers have a natural aptitude, although

the art can be acquired to an extensive degree. Certain principles are, however, always essential:

(d) *Presentation of points.* All the facts to be included must first be assembled and arranged in a logical order. Almost invariably, this will entail the compiling of notes, the style being that most acceptable to the speaker.

(e) *Reserve information.* If the speaker anticipates being questioned, he should have available information he has not included in his speech.

(f) *Type of audience.* The speech must be "pitched" in a style relative to the type of audience. A "paternalistic" attitude to employees or any form of "talking down to" would be unacceptable, as would any talking "over the heads" of the listeners.

(g) *Objectivity.* A public delivery should be aimed at establishing certain points and must be constructed to lead logically to that end. Repetition must be avoided, although it may be advisable to conclude with a short and positive reiteration of the objectives as a summing up.

VISUAL AIDS

10. Purpose. In many circumstances, the inadequacy of unsupported verbal communication is obvious and it is therefore frequently necessary to communicate by visual methods in conjunction with verbal ones. Visual methods may be used to:

(a) *provide data for decision-making.* For example, reports, analytical statements, etc., can be used as illustrations to support verbal debate;

(b) *educate.* As part of training, manuals may be used and displays may be employed in lectures;

(c) *inform.* All types of visual aid can be used in helping to provide information about such matters as staff pension schemes, wage rates, safety precautions, etc.

11. Methods. The choice of visual aid must be appropriate to the subject matter and the circumstances in which it is to be used.

(a) *Literature.* Any discussion or talk is made more effective if it is supported by written material. This makes it possible for members of a meeting to relate what the speakers are saying to literature in their possession. A person delivering a talk will find it easier to speak to written material already held by his listeners. Frequently, it is advantageous to distribute the material before the meeting to give the opportunity of prior study.

(b) *Displays*. A speaker can make his delivery more effective by demonstrating various points on a blackboard, by projecting prepared material onto a screen or by using film slides.

REPORTS

12. Types of report. Reports may be classified by reference to the circumstances making them necessary.

(a) *Routine reports*. These are reports made on a periodic basis according to a prescribed procedure. As such, they provide a regular flow of information as part of the work routine. Examples are:

> (i) annual reports on staff members;
> (ii) monthly returns of sales;
> (iii) reports of overdue accounts.

(b) *Commissioned reports*. These are reports called for in respect of non-routine matters. The report may be required from one person or a committee; in either case the principle is that of requiring experts to inform the appointing body. It usually demands the making of an investigation and the reporting of findings. The reporter may or may not be required to make recommendations, but in either case any action resulting from the report will be by the appointing body. Examples are:

> (i) considering the financial viability of a project;
> (ii) investigating the circumstances and extent of losses by pilfering.

(c) *Reports occasioned by specific events*. There should be laid down those events which must automatically result in a report being made. It should be prescribed who is to make the report; to whom it must be made; and the content. Examples would be the reporting of:

(*i*) an accident to staff by the works manager;
(*ii*) a traffic incident by a driver;
(*iii*) a machine failure by the operator.

13. Report layout. Rules may prescribe a standard method of layout but the general principles applicable are as follows:

(*a*) *Address.* The report must be headed by being addressed to the person or body requiring the report and by naming the reporter. Indication should be included of those to whom copies are being sent.

(*b*) *Identification.*

(*i*) The report should have an indicative *title*. All subsequent reports on the same matter must have the same title.

(*ii*) An agreed system of *coded identification* should be used. For example, AK/T/5 would refer to the fifth report of a series generally coded AK/T.

(*c*) *Terms of reference.* The opening paragraph in the body of the report should explain the circumstances leading to the making of the report, e.g. "As instructed by the Board at its meeting on . . ., I submit my report".

(*d*) *Salutations.* The general rule is that the opening salutation and complimentary close are omitted, but practice may require the inclusion of such phrases as "Gentlemen" and "yours faithfully".

(*e*) *The subject matter.* The following rules apply in connection with the body of the report:

(*i*) Each section (which frequently will consist of a single paragraph) must deal with one point only.

(*ii*) Sections must be headed and numbered.

(*iii*) Sections must be presented in a logical sequence.

(*iv*) The opening section may consist of a preamble, showing facts already known or outlining any relevant history.

(*f*) *Recommendations.* These should be given only if asked for and then they should appear at the end of the report.

(*g*) *Appendices.* These may be included to show graphical matter, extracts from other documents, sources of the data used, etc.

(*h*) *The report must be dated.*

(*i*) *Signing.* The signing must be done by the person making the report or a representative of the reporting body.

14. Essential factors. An efficient report must meet the following requirements:

(a) *Clarity of appearance.* Layout should be neat, with judicious use of sub-margins and underlining.

(b) *Simplicity of expression.* The findings should be presented in a language comprehensible to the reader, using short sentences and avoiding convoluted phrasing.

(c) *Cross-referencing.* The paragraph numbers should be used when referring to material in other parts of the report or in previous reports.

(d) *Abbreviations.* These must be consistent and conform to an agreed system.

(e) *Quantitative material.* Where figures are included, it must be made very clear which figures are *factual* and which are *conjectural.*

15. Standardised reports. For the making of routine reports, the reporter may be required to mark a standardised form instead of submitting one in essay form. This method ensures that all the required information is given and that time is saved. It also facilitates the compiling of statistics.

Thus, a sales representative may be required to report on the amount of publicity material he can persuade each customer to display. The form may require the ticking or underlining of one of the following:

Nil. Spasmodic. Regular. Current special display.

COMMUNICATING MANAGEMENT INFORMATION

16. The necessity for information. Management needs to be fed with information to facilitate its work in:

(a) *planning.* The necessity for forecasting as a basis for planning produces a need for techniques capable of making estimates;

(b) *control.* The continuous checking of performance against objectives requires systems for providing up-to-date data.

17. Management requirements. The demands of management in respect of information communicated to it may be regarded as being as follows:

(a) *Accuracy.* Data concerning past or current events can, of course, be very accurate, but mention must be made of any exceptional factors which may make the figures not truly representative. This is particularly important when using historical figures to forecast future trends. Estimated figures must be accompanied by statements of the assumptions on which they are based. Frequently, it is necessary to include alternative estimates calculated on different assumptions.

(b) *Speed.* The feedback of control data must be produced quickly, so that deviations are identified before it is too late to take corrective action.

(c) *Form of presentation.* The style of communicating must be such as to present the information in a quickly understandable form and must be appropriate for the purpose.

(d) *Extent of information.* The *"exception principle"* should be used in control, whereby only exceptions to the standard are drawn to the attention of management.

18. Types of presentation. Information can be presented in the following broad categories of methods:

(a) *Textually.* This relates to the various types of report (*see* **12–15** above).

(b) *Statistically.* This covers a very wide range of methods, including graphs, charts, pictorial representations, etc.

19. Statistical presentations. The rules generally applicable to the presentation of information in statistical form may be summarised as follows:

(a) *Purpose.* The purpose of the presentation must be made clear and the conclusions drawn must be directly identifiable with the purpose.

(b) *Interpretation.* It must be capable of interpretation by those for whom it is intended and therefore the style will be geared to the readers' ability.

(c) *Title.* There must be a clearly indicative title.

(d) *Period.* The range of time covered must be shown distinctly.

(e) *Measurement unit.* The unit of measurement being used must be clearly indicated.

(f) *Comparables.* Figures to be compared should be immediately adjacent if possible.

(*g*) *Sources of data.* These must be shown.

(*h*) *Quantities.* If large numbers are used, they may be "rounded up" or "rounded down" or given as the nearest whole number. The method which is adopted must be indicated.

20. Graphs. There are many types of graphs and the list below gives only a summary of them and their characteristics. Graphs indicate the relationship of associated figures by means of "curves" (which can be straight lines connecting points on a scale).

(*a*) *Line graph.* This is the most well-known type. It is plotted against two axes, which thereby permit two variables. Such graphs indicate *absolute* changes—that is, the vertical scale provides equal divisions representing equal amounts.

Where the data is portrayed over a period of time it is known as a *time series graph* or *historigram.*

(*b*) *Rate-of-change graph.* Unlike the line graph, this graph is plotted against a log scale so that equal gradients indicate equal *rates* of change and not equal *amounts* of change. Thus, if the profit on Product A rose from £500 to £550 and the profit on all products rose from £6,000 to £6,600, a line graph would show increases of £50 and £600 respectively. A rate-of-change graph would give a more useful conclusion—that in each case the rise was 10 per cent.

(*c*) *Distribution graphs.* Distribution graphs indicate the frequency of the occurrence of data which is measured on the vertical axis.

21. Charts. Some of the more common types of chart are summarised as follows:

(*a*) *Bar charts.* These show the magnitude of an item by the length of a bar or upright rectangle based on a regular scale.

(*b*) *Compound bar chart.* This is an elaboration of the bar chart in that the constituent parts of each bar are indicated, thus showing variations in the constituents as well as in the whole.

(*c*) *Band curve chart.* This is a further extension whereby the constituents in a compound bar chart are joined together in curves, the changes in the constituents being then displayed as distinctive bands.

(*d*) *Gantt charts.* This is a horizontally read chart where each regular division represents a period of time. The whole width of each division relates to the *planned* figure (e.g. output) for that period. The *actual* figure is drawn underneath as a horizontal bar, its length being determined by the proportion of the actual figure to the planned figure. Thus the extent to which the planned figure was achieved (or exceeded) for each period is apparent; by the use of a cumulative bar the total achievement for any length of time can be measured against the planned figure for that period.

(e) *Pictograms.* These present simplified expressions of relative values by the use of pictorial representations. Money, for example, may be shown as piles of coins, the number of coins indicating the amount of money. They are inadequate for use within a business but can give a somewhat dramatic presentation for the benefit of those unversed in statistics.

(f) *Pie charts.* These show the comparability of components of a whole as segments in a circle. The presentation is almost entirely graphic and is inadequate for normal commercial use.

(g) *Z charts.* These are "moving charts", giving static and cumulative figures on one chart. Thus monthly sales could be shown; the total sales to date for the year; and the total sales for the twelve months just ended.

(h) *Break-even charts.* These indicate the point of balance between two related sets of figures. Thus, if total sales to date are plotted against accumulated costs, the point where profitability will commence can be determined (*see* XIV, **27**).

22. Aids to management. Many techniques have been and are being developed to provide management with information to facilitate forecasting and control, but the value of any technique does not lie within itself but in its application. A technique can be only an aid, and its usefulness will depend upon the accuracy of its design, its relevance to the problem, its interpretation and the recognition of its limitations.

Some of the techniques specific to a branch of business are mentioned in appropriate chapters of this HANDBOOK. The following is a selection and brief description of those which have general application.

23. Operational research (O.R.) This is a broad term covering various advanced techniques, but it is distinctive in that it analyses operations *as a whole*, often by constructing mathematical models within which formulae and equations are employed. The approach is inter-disciplinary in that the skills of various specialists are combined within a total concept. Being largely mathematically orientated, the system has benefited by the development of computers. It has been stated (by Richard Field in *The Principles and Practice of Management*, ed. E. F. L. Brech, Longman, 1975) that:

> "Operational research provides management with a quantitative basis for decisions or the solution of specific problems through the ascertainment and measurement of facts, the probability of their accuracy or error, and the use of mathematical techniques and analogies for predicting results."

Techniques developed included the following:

(a) *Simulation.* This involves the building of mathematical models which are representative of the problem. The alternative policies or actions are applied to the model in order to assess the probable result if such measures were used in reality.

(b) *Linear programming.* Linear programming is used to assess the most advantageous choice between a number of alternative actions or the optimum level of operation. It calculates in known terms of constancy; that is, for example, it assumes that costs will move in direct relationship with production rates. There is thus a tendency to produce unrefined assessments because factors incapable of precise measurement are not taken into account.

(c) *Queueing theory.* This is a mathematical study of queueing behaviour. Queueing can relate to streams of components to the assembly points, ships waiting to unload, etc. The purpose is to calculate the waiting time and its cost and to produce methods for reducing them.

(d) *Network analysis.* Network analysis is a general term covering *critical path analysis* (*CPA*) and *programme evaluation and review technique* (*PERT*). The methods are similar to the extent that both use planning networks to control complex large-scale operations. The basic feature is the planning of the sequence of events so that the target date is achieved. The distinctive feature is the determination of the *critical stages* due to the dependence of one stage upon others. The starting times of certain stages will be determined by the completion time of another or others; delay at some stages will affect the next consequent stage and may be cumulative as regards later stages. The completion time for each stage must therefore be planned in relation to all other related stages, the whole being built up into a complex network. Calculations are also included for adopting alternative methods where a critical stage cannot otherwise be overcome.

PERT elaborates on CPA in that the calculations include those of the component costs.

PROGRESS TEST 9

1. What is the importance of effective communication? What are the essentials necessary to achieve it? **(2)**

2. What are the barriers to communication? **(3)**

3. Distinguish between the following channels of information: (a) informal; (b) downward; (c) upward; (d) broadcast; (e) horizontal; (f) committee. What are the special features of the "grape vine"? **(4)**

4. Consider the importance of speed in respect of communications. **(4)**

5. Discuss the importance of effective external communication. **(5)**

6. What are the features specific to verbal communications? **(6)**

7. What principles apply in respect of interviewing? **(7)**

8. What are the essentials of good public delivery? **(9)**

9. What are the purposes of visual aids? **(10)**

10. Distinguish between the following types of report: (a) routine; (b) commissioned; (c) those occasioned by events. **(12)**

11. What rules prevail concerning the layout of reports? **(13)**

12. What factors contribute to an effective report? **(14)**

13. What are standardised reports and what advantages have they? **(15)**

14. What are the essentials in providing information to management? **(17)**

15. What are the requirements for statistical presentation to be efficient? **(19)**

16. What are the distinguishing features of the following types of graph: (a) line; (b) rate-of-change; (c) distribution. **(20)**

17. Define: (a) bar chart; (b) compound bar chart; (c) band curve chart; (d) Gantt chart; (e) pictogram; (f) pie chart; (g) Z chart; (h) break-even chart. **(21)**

18. What are the limitations on the usefulness of management aids? **(22)**

19. Define: (a) operational research; (b) simulation; (c) linear programming; (d) queueing theory; (e) CPA; (f) PERT. **(23)**

CHAPTER X

PRODUCTION

THE NATURE OF PRODUCTION

1. The scope of production. In the strictest sense of the word, production means the making of things by the conversion of materials and/or the assembly of components into marketable objects. This physical action is, however, only part of the wider process covered by the general meaning of "production" and will include the following aspects:

(*a*) *Consideration of the market.* Except in the case of production which has been commissioned, all production must take place in advance of sales, which, by their very nature, can only be estimated. An attempt must be made to assess the potential sales of a new product or the degree to which sales of an existing product can be expanded. Included in that survey must be an estimation of the price at which the product will find a market. This price must be related to the anticipated unit cost of production in order to establish the economic viability of the project. (This enquiry will take the form of market research, which is discussed in Chapter XII.)

(*b*) *Production to order.* Where production is in response to an order, the above considerations will not apply except, of course, that the price must be economic.

(*c*) *Design and technical problems.* The design of the product and the method of production have mutual influences on each other. Therefore, there must be co-operation between the designer and the production engineers.

(*d*) *Availability of resources.* The required amount and type of plant and equipment must be available, as well as the necessary number of workers of various skills. Plans must be made to ensure supplies of materials, components and power.

(e) *Purchasing and marketing.* Organisations must be established to purchase and store materials, and to market the product. Transport of various kinds will be required.

(f) *Assimilation into existing production.* Assuming this is *additional* production, then arrangements must be made to merge the new production into the present structure. Machine-sharing may be possible, there may be some flexibility in the use of labour, and overheads will probably be reduced. Against these may be the necessity to physically expand if present facilities are inadequate, unless the new production can be combined with some phasing out.

2. Production policy. The production policy of a business is concerned with deciding what should be produced and in what quantities and the method of production. Production policy is subject to the following constraints:

(a) *Limitation of range.* A business must establish the optimum range of products. There must be a degree of specialisation, although too narrow a range may prove uneconomic (*see* **8** below).

(b) *Availability of resources.* This will include the premises, plant, labour, etc. which are or could be available.

(c) *Level of production.* The amount to be produced will be largely determined by the demand for the product but it will also be affected by the unit cost at different levels of production. The reduction of unit cost when a high number are produced will be of no benefit if the amount of units is more than that demanded by buyers at a profitable price.

(d) *Costs and prices.* There must be a viable relationship between the two but both figures are largely conjectural. Costs may rise after production has commenced; a change in demand or in purchasing power may reduce prices.

(e) *Finance.* The cost of financing until the point of profitability is reached must be an influencing factor.

(f) *Managerial expertise.* An extension of production or the venturing into new fields must raise the question as to the ability of the present management to cope, as against the problems which may follow the introduction of new management. It must also be assured that managerial facilities (such as techniques and equipment) will be adequate.

3. Types of production. The method of production depends on the product and the quantity produced. A broad classification is as follows:

(a) *Job production.* This relates to "one off" products, that is, the production of one or a small number of identical products to the specification of the buyer. Usually this refers to the supplying of components to a larger manufacturer; the provision of one area of production to a larger one; or the making of special equipment or material.

Because such production is in "short runs", the benefits of large-scale are lost. Because the work is not in regular demand, the producer will be subject to "peaks and troughs" of activity, resulting in inefficient use of labour and equipment. These two factors make scientific assessment of costs difficult.

Jobbing production is not, however, confined to small firms. For example, civil engineers, marine engineers, building contractors, etc., are mainly occupied in carrying out specialised work to the specification of others as forms of sub-contracting.

(b) *Batch production* refers to *repetitive* production (unlike job production) which, however, is *not continuous*. It refers to the production of goods the quantity of which is known in advance. It may be to meet a specific order or it may be for stock-piling. It frequently occurs where the trade is seasonal, either as regards supply (e.g. fruit canning) or demand (e.g. ice-cream). The benefits of repetitive production are available to a degree, provided the batch is of a sufficient quantity. A series of batches of different products may, with careful planning, constitute what is, effectively, continuous production (e.g. canning a range of fruit and vegetables).

(c) *Flow production.* This is otherwise known as *line* or *continuous* production. It refers to production on a large scale to provide a continuous supply. The characteristic feature is the "flow" of units from one operation point to another throughout the whole process. For each process there would be one type of machine which will carry out one operation (*single-purpose machines*), but as some processes take longer than others there will be points where there will be more machines than at others. The objective is to have a regular, continuous moving flow and planning must therefore be a complex operation. It is typified by the *assembly line* or *conveyor-belt system.*

4. Production engineering. This relates to the organisation of the production process as a whole. Thus the total period from the design and layout of production facilities to final inspection of the product comes within its orbit and represents the implementation of the production policy. It is concerned with every stage and every aspect within the production span and includes the establishing of standards, the design of tools and equipment, the measurement of performance and the working within cost limits.

5. Simplification and standardisation.

(a) *Simplification* is the practice of reducing the variety of components and/or final products. Reducing the range of components entails producing more of any one type and thereby gaining the advantages of large-scale production.

(b) *Standardisation*, in many respects, is closely related to simplification. In production, it can refer to the interchangeability of standard components and between different end-products (e.g. all models of cars using the same door handles; three car models can be basically the same but can be marketed as different models by varying some of the components).

6. Advantages of simplification and standardisation.

(a) Reduction of unit costs.
(b) Easier inspection.
(c) Reduced costs at the design stage.
(d) Reduced variety of skill required, resulting in reduced training costs.
(e) Lower tooling costs.
(f) A more efficient customer service for spares and repairs.
(g) Simpler organisation.
(h) Less complex purchasing and storage.

7. Disadvantages of simplification and standardisation.

(a) A mistake in the choice of product or design (i.e. it is unpopular with buyers), will be more costly to correct because of the commitment to a narrow range.

(*b*) The buyers' desire for something different may present opportunities for competitors.

(*c*) Introduction may mean losses on existing stock, materials and plant.

8. Specialisation.

(*a*) *Specialisation of product* relates to concentration on a fairly narrow range of products. There are obvious advantages for a manufacturer to remain in those areas where he is most experienced, because he will have well-established production processes, the labour and technical skill required and a sound knowledge of the market. The dangers would include that of being dependent upon one market, of being overtaken by a new technology which replaces his own, and of inflexibility generally.

(*b*) *Specialisation of labour* means reducing the range of skill required of each worker so that efficiency is improved by concentration of effort.

9. Diversification.

This is the reverse of product specialisation and means the venturing into new areas of production. The reasons for diversification can include the following:

(*a*) To reduce the risk of being dependent upon the success of one product.

(*b*) To utilise spare capacity, either because:

(*i*) there has been a reduction or termination of production in the previous area because of unprofitability; or

(*ii*) because of seasonal fluctuations in the market.

(*c*) To offer a wider range within the same market.

(*d*) To put by-products to profitable use.

(*e*) As a result of integration (*see* V, 11).

FACTORY LOCATION AND LAYOUT

10. Site location. Influencing factors in the choice of a factory site will include the following:

(*a*) *Effective cost.* Building or rent costs are lower in some areas than others. Certain areas may be attractive because of the availability of Government grants. The level of local rates must be considered. Costs may be lower where the local authority encourages new factories, e.g. "new towns", trading estates.

(*b*) *Labour availability of the required types.* Difficulty will be experienced if the producer uses a type of labour already in short supply in the area. The predominant requirement may be, for example, for part-time women workers, for unskilled workers, for technicians of a particular kind.

(*c*) *Labour costs.* Related to (*b*) above will be the effect of shortage or abundance of particular skills on local wage rates.

(*d*) *Transport facilities.* Access to a motorway would be an obvious advantage, proximity to ports would benefit exporters.

(*e*) *Local bye-laws.* Some local bye-laws concerning building restrictions, etc., may have a bearing.

(*f*) *Housing and social facilities.* A shortage of these will affect the labour supply.

(*g*) *Possibility of expansion.* Expanding the site may be a consideration.

(*h*) *Proximity of commercial services.*

11. Type of building.

(*a*) *A custom-built factory* would be specific to the production requirements. It would also probably have better lighting, heating and ventilation than one which had to be converted.

(*b*) *Single-storey buildings* are more convenient for accommodating heavy machinery and for the movement of materials. Modern buildings of this sort can be of simple construction and therefore cheaper to build, but the relative cost of land would be higher. A single-storey building is more capable of alteration and extension than a multistorey building.

(*c*) *Multi-storey buildings* should be cheaper to heat because of less heat-loss through the roof but more artificial lighting would probably be required. Traffic would be largely confined to separate floors except where gravity chutes and lifts were used.

12. Factory lay-out.
Planning the layout of a factory can be an almost continuous process because of the need to cope with changing circumstances. There is thus an advantage in having

as few permanent structures as possible, such as roof supports and interior walls. Wide-span roofs and movable partitions make this possible as well as reducing "unprofitable space" to a minimum.

13. The objects of planned layout. Layout is planned to:

(a) *economise on space*;

(b) *minimise cost of heating, lighting and ventilation* by having as many open areas as possible;

(c) *produce smooth work-flows* so that materials travel the shortest possible distance;

(d) *provide transport entry and exit points* as near as possible to raw materials and finished-goods departments, and to provide parking and turning areas nearby;

(e) *provide traffic flows for materials* by planning adequate gangways and temporary storage bays, augmented where possible by facilities for overhead movement;

(f) *facilitate supervision and inspection*;

(g) *segregate noisy machinery* as far as is possible;

(h) *reduce human traffic* to a minimum by efficient work flows;

(i) *relate the positioning of departments logically* (*see* **17** below);

(j) *provide access to machine servicing points and safety devices*;

(k) *provide acceptable working conditions*.

14. Product layout. This refers to the system of arranging machines to coincide with the sequence of processes. Thus there would be minimum movement between the raw materials stage and the finished product. This would be the normal layout for flow production.

15. Process layout. Process layout applies where machines are grouped according to their functions, regardless of the product. Thus there would be, for example, a welding bay for welding work relevant to all products. Such a system is more suitable for job and batch production.

16. The installation of services. Services such as electricity, gas, water, air, etc., can present problems. The methods available are those providing access by:

(*a*) *overhead* pipes and cables with "drops" to the usage points;

(*b*) *underfloor* supplies with plug-in and tap-off points;

(*c*) *islands* whereby pipes and cables run along low gangways from which power can be taken.

17. Positioning of departments. The largest open space should be used for the major processing stage, such as the machine shop, and other departments should be positioned in a logical proximity to it and to each other. The following principles apply:

(*a*) *The first processing section* must be near the store for raw materials or components.

(*b*) *The final inspection department* should be near the production terminal; *intermediate inspection* should be built into the production line near the work stage to be inspected.

(*c*) *The finished-product store* should have direct access to the final inspection department but be separate from it and conveniently placed in relation to the *despatch department*.

PLANT AND EQUIPMENT

18. The choice of plant and equipment. In the selection of plant and equipment the following must be considered:

(*a*) *Special-purpose machines.* These will be designed to meet the processing requirements. There must therefore be consultation between the prospective user and the manufacturer at a stage well in advance of when it will be required.

(*b*) *General-purpose machines.* Included here are machines not designed for a function specific to the buyer, such as welding and cutting equipment, etc. They are likely to be standardised and available "from stock".

(*c*) *Effective cost.* This must take account not only of the initial cost but also the cost of maintenance and depreciation, and of running costs.

(*d*) *Size.* The floor area must be planned to accommodate the machines and therefore overall sizes will have to be known before the layout is finalised. Size must include allowances for any "swinging parts" (e.g. the arm of a crane), for the operator's working position, for access, and for passing traffic.

(e) *Maintenance and repairs.* Servicing may be included in the contract of sale. The design must allow for easy access for maintenance and repairs.

(f) *Obsolescence.* The estimated life of the machine should be known. The manufacturer may offer "trade in" terms for when a larger or more efficient machine becomes necessary.

(g) *Power.* The requisite power must be available and the cost taken into account.

(h) *Labour cost.* A very simple machine may require a low-paid operator. The cost of labour replaced must be considered.

(i) *Output.* A costing exercise will be required to calculate the earning capacity of each machine.

19. Maintenance. Maintenance must be a continuous process and should be the responsibility of a specialist staff. Its responsibilities would include:

(a) *regular inspection and servicing;*
(b) *repairs,* carried out on an emergency basis;
(c) *supervising proper use* by operatives;
(d) *compiling records* of breakdowns, performance, etc.;
(e) *advising management* about replacements, etc.

20. Maintenance policy. This should be concerned with:

(a) the cost of production lost through breakdowns;
(b) the cost and effectiveness of inspection and maintenance;
(c) principles concerning obsolescence and replacement;
(d) buying policy as affected by maintenance cost.

21. Materials handling. This relates to the moving of raw materials, components, finished parts and completed goods within the production stage. This requires planning, taking account of the following principles:

(a) *Economy of movement.* The transporting distance must be as short as possible and, ideally, should coincide with the flow of production. There should be no "back-tracking".

(b) *Economy of floor space.* Where possible, movement should be off the floor. This is possible by using overhead conveyor belts, gantries, etc.

(*c*) *Traffic ways.* These must be established so that floor movements do not interfere with other work.

(*d*) *Combining movement with processing.* For example, paint spraying a unit whilst it is on a production conveyor may be possible.

22. Handling equipment.

(*a*) *Bulk materials* can be moved by specialist methods, e.g. suction pipes, vacuum tubes.

(*b*) *Conveyors* can be mechanically motivated; light packages can be slipped manually along roller belts; heavy goods can be moved overhead by conveyors which also lift and lower.

(*c*) *Trucks* take many specialised forms, such as:

(*i*) dumper trucks for holding and discharging bulk or collections of items;

(*ii*) fork-lift trucks which pick up and carry a load and then stack it;

(*iii*) pallet trucks which pick up and transport standard "pallets" on a platform, made up into "unit loads".

(*d*) *Gravity chutes, hoists, lifts, etc.,* are used for vertical movement.

PRODUCTION PLANNING AND CONTROL

23. Planning and control.

(*a*) *Planning* the method of production will follow the *pre-planning stage.* That is, after the type of product has been decided upon and designed, output agreed in conjunction with a sales organisation, and all matters of cost, price and delivery times have been settled.

(*b*) *Control* implies the setting of standards and objectives, the co-ordination of the various stages and the variation of plans as circumstances dictate.

The two functions are closely related and are usually the responsibility of one department.

24. The objects of planning and control. Planning and control aim to:

(*a*) co-ordinate labour and machines in the most effective and economic ways;

(*b*) establish targets, check them against performance and take any consequent action;

(*c*) achieve smooth continuous production with the elimination of "bottle necks" and under-employed resources.

25. The responsibilities of the planning and control department. These are:

(*a*) to liaise with the marketing and purchasing departments, and as a result to adjust the production rate or "product mix" where necessary;

(*b*) to decide the method of production and determine any priorities;

(*c*) to determine the allocation of labour and machines;

(*d*) to establish time schedules for various stages;

(*e*) to establish continuous inspection;

(*f*) to operate a system of cost control.

26. The planning programme. This will usually conform to the following plan:

(*a*) *Decide the process* to be adopted.

(*b*) *Schedule the sequence of operations.*

(*c*) *Establish time-schedules* for the completion of each operation and the final completion.

(*d*) *Determine machine-loadings*, that is, allocate work to machines and work groups.

(*e*) *Ensure materials availability*, so that the right types and adequate amounts are ready when required.

27. Progress control. Progress control is the method of ensuring that production performances accord with the time schedules. The system of checking and taking any necessary action is known as *expediting* or *progress-chasing*.

(*a*) *Its necessity* can arise from incidents such as the following:

(*i*) Failure of materials to be delivered.

(*ii*) Machine or power breakdown.

(*iii*) Industrial action.

(*iv*) Delays at an earlier point on the production line or in an outside group (such as a sub-contractor).

(*v*) Staff absenteeism.

(*vi*) Errors of design, planning or human activity.

(*b*) *Its duties* are as follows:

    (*i*) To check progress continuously.
    (*ii*) To determine the cause of any deviation.
    (*iii*) To resolve the difficulty.
    (*iv*) To adjust materials delivery and to advise the sales department of any change in completion date due to deviations.

28. Aids to control. Standard methods to assist control include the following:

(*a*) *Flow charts* show the planned sequence of operations.
(*b*) *Production schedules*, such as Gantt charts (*see* IX, 21), compare targets with performances.
(*c*) *Automatic control* gives a continuous feedback of information by computer with the ability to automatically adjust. (This is an aspect of *cybernetics*.)
(*d*) *Machine loading charts* state the different operations completed by each machine.
(*e*) *Inspection schedules* establish a programme for inspection and the criteria to be applied.
(*f*) *Materials lists* specify the type and quantities of materials and components for each product.

29. Inspection. This is a method to ensure that finished products reach a required standard, but it also entails inspection at all stages in order to reduce the amount of "scrap" and wasted labour.

Its *purposes* are to:

(*a*) *establish standards*;
(*b*) *ensure conformity* with standards;
(*c*) *identify contributory factors to deviations*, such as faulty design, machine malfunction, bad workmanship, faulty materials;
(*d*) *determine permitted deviations*, if any. (This is also known as *tolerance*);
(*e*) *schedule inspections*, to ensure that periodic checks are continuous, the frequency depending upon the proclivity to deviation;
(*f*) *provide management data* about costs of deviations, the effect on deliveries, etc.

Its *forms* can be:

(g) *inspection of raw materials* to ensure they conform to stipulated standards;

(h) *inspection of work in progress*, a series of tests carried out at various stages of production;

(i) *process control*, applicable to some industries to ensure that production conditions conform to standards, e.g. temperature, humidity, etc., in chemical industries;

(j) *running tests* (practical operational tests). For example, an engine may be run on a test bed, electrical circuits can be meter-tested;

(k) *quality control*, the inspection of the final product to ensure it complies with standards acceptable to buyers. This is therefore the culmination of all the stages of inspection (inspection generally may be regarded as being quality control);

(l) *statistical quality control*. It would be impossible, other than for small-scale production, to inspect every item at every stage. This must be accepted because the cost of so doing would more than outweigh the financial benefits of having a 100 per cent perfect output. Accordingly, samples are taken and tested at the various stages. The selections and the deviations are then charted to portray the areas and degree of deviation. This will indicate levels of deviation above the accepted tolerance and call for action; it may also result in an adjustment of tolerances. The statistical theory of probability applies and, provided the selection is wide enough to be representative, trends will be apparent.

30. Methods of inspection.

(a) *Centralised inspection*. This method requires work to be sent to an inspection department or bay before it proceeds to the next operational stage.

(i) Delays result from the time spent in transporting to and from the inspection point.

(ii) It allows for easier supervision.

(iii) Inspection records are centralised.

(iv) The shop floor is kept clear for operatives.

(b) *Floor inspection* requires inspectors to examine at the work point.

(i) Less time is lost in handling and transporting.

(ii) Space must be found for the inspectors at the work point.

(*iii*) Fault-finding is immediate and may be remedied without delay.

PRODUCTION MANAGEMENT TECHNIQUES

31. Work study. This is a general term relevant to the detailed study and analysis of every operation with a view to increasing efficiency. The two major techniques of work study, whilst each has its distinctive area, are interdependent. They are:

(*a*) *method study*, which studies the ways in which work is done and considers alternative ways;

(*b*) *work measurement*, which is concerned with the time and effort to perform a task.

32. Method study. This relates to a scientific analysis of every operation and of the way in which all operations are co-ordinated, including the contribution of machines and labour. Its broad purpose is to criticise the current system where justified, and to devise better methods.

33. The objectives of method study. These are to:

(*a*) improve individual processes;

(*b*) improve the inter-relationships of processes;

(*c*) improve the layout;

(*d*) make more efficient the use of manpower, machines and materials;

(*e*) improve working conditions;

(*f*) economise in human effort and reduce fatigue.

34. Method study procedure. The usual steps in conducting a method study are as follows:

(*a*) *Determine the work to be studied* and define objectives.

(*b*) *Record the facts* which are established. Some of the many recording devices are:

(*i*) process charts and flow diagrams, which show the progress of materials and components through the production process;

(*ii*) multiple-activity charts, which show the movements of man and machine in co-operation on a task;

(*iii*) motion charts show the movements of an operative. It allows for analysis and, where possible, the elimination of unnecessary movement or the design of more economic movement;

(*iv*) simo-charts record the simultaneous movements of an operative's hands or other body parts;

(*v*) layout models and templates;

(*vi*) string diagrams. Work-positions are marked with pins and connecting lengths of string indicate the paths an operative takes during the course of his work and the total distance travelled during a period. It allows for a more economic movement plan to be made;

(*vii*) films and still cameras may be useful for recording some operations.

(*c*) *Analyse the record* and quantify where appropriate. Attempts to improve may take the form of:

(*i*) eliminating an operation or part of it;

(*ii*) combining one or more operations;

(*iii*) devising different physical movements;

(*iv*) altering machines or tools;

(*v*) altering the sequence of operations.

(*d*) *Design a new method.*

(*e*) *Record the new method* and produce mathematical comparisons with the old method.

(*f*) *Install the new method* and provide instruction for its use.

(*g*) *Record the new method in operation* and adjust where appropriate.

35. The objectives of work measurement. Work measurement aims to use *time study* to:

(*a*) establish standard times for completion of specific tasks;

(*b*) check performances with standards;

(*c*) measure machine output;

(*d*) facilitate costing;

(*e*) provide a fair basis for incentive schemes.

36. Work measurement procedure. The procedure is broadly the same as for method study except that the emphasis is on quantification.

(a) *The unit* is usually time, but it can be "work units" related to time.

(b) *Calculation* is usually by stop-watch.

(c) *Allowances* are made for fatigue, variations between operations, unavoidable delays, etc.

(d) *The standard time* is based on the day-long average time it is calculated a task should take a competent operative, maintaining a set standard of quality performance.

37. Work measurement techniques. These include the following:

(a) *Direct time study* is applied usually to repetitive tasks. It entails recording the time taken to perform a specific part of a task, the measurements being made at different times.

(b) *Predetermined motion time system* establishes set times for completion of certain tasks, taken from observations of a number of operatives on varying occasions.

(c) *Analytical estimating* is applicable to non-repetitive jobs, such as maintenance. As the jobs vary in size and complexity, a standard is set for the time taken for an average job. It can be applied to a non-repetitive element in a repetitive operation.

(d) *Activity sampling* entails making observations and recording what is happening on an agreed number of visits in a period, but at a frequency picked at random. "Idle time" of a machine could be calculated by noting, at the random samplings, if the machine is working.

38. Attitudes to work study. The problems connected with work study are largely human ones and are often deep-seated. They can be summarised as follows:

(a) *Resentment of being watched.* A study engineer holding a stop-watch can cause ill-feeling.

(b) *Effect on incentives.* Where remuneration is linked to output, the introduction of a new time study may arouse suspicion that "speeding up" by improved methods may not benefit workers proportionately. If the standard is set too high, earnings may even fall.

(c) *Reliability of the standards.* Workers being watched

may deliberately go slower in order to get a lower standard set. Worker representatives may aim to have added allowances which may not be justified.

(d) *Fear of redundancies*. Improved methods may result in a reduction of labour content in an operation.

39. Value analysis. This is a technique, the application of which is known as *"value engineering"*. It is concerned with cost-reduction by first making a detailed study of the function of each element in a process with a view to economy. This may take the form of redesigning a component, introducing a substitute, altering the process, etc. The analysis *goes back* to the design stage instead of starting from it.

The function of the part is considered and *then* related to its cost. The *importance* of each part is evaluated so that the costing is made more realistic. For example, increased mechanisation may reduce the labour content so that the important cost factor becomes that for power instead of for labour.

40. Ergonomics. This is otherwise known as *"human engineering"*. It is the study of man in relation to his working environment, mainly as regards physical posture. It aims to reduce fatigue and increase efficiency by the scientific design of seating and, for example, the improved positioning of hand and foot controls on machines.

41. Plant records.

(a) *Plant budget*. This entails budgeting for the cost of plant replacement. It must therefore estimate the cost of replacing worn-out machines and those which have become expensive to run because of obsolescence and repair costs. Accordingly, it must be closely related to maintenance records.

Consideration must be given to comparison of the cost of a new machine with the true cost of an existing machine (that is, allowing for repairs, lost production because of breakdowns, and the output).

(b) *Plant registers*. These contain the history of each machine as regards maintenance costs, repair costs and "idle time" due to breakdown or under-employment.

RESEARCH, DEVELOPMENT AND DESIGN

42. Research. Basically, industrial research is concerned with the acquisition of technical knowledge, particularly new products, processes, techniques, materials and sources of energy. Such research can be divided into two categories:

(a) *Fundamental (or pure) research.* This is research with the general objective of extending knowledge, with no apparent practical application. It is therefore not undertaken by industry generally but it can have an important place in the work of large, scientific businesses such as those engaged in pharmaceuticals, aircraft, etc. Much of such research must, by its very nature, be financially unproductive but there always exists the possibility of a discovery which could be commercially exploited. Occasionally, a discovery is made which is peripheral to the main research objective (known as "spin off") which is financially rewarding.

Such research is therefore long-term and uncertain in outcome.

(b) *Applied research.* This is far more common and relates to direct investigations with a view to financial benefit.

43. Research policy.

(a) *Responsibility.* This must be determined by establishing a research department, specifying its scope and to whom it is answerable.

(b) *Areas of research.* These must be decided by top management. Management and scientists often differ widely as to what should be investigated. Even more difficult is the stage when management wishes to end a research project which the scientists are anxious to continue.

(c) *Cost/benefit.* Much of the expense of research may be unproductive and it is not always easy to measure the profitability of research which is successful, particularly as it may be impossible to determine the cost areas where several types of research are taking place simultaneously.

(d) *Production feasibility.* It may appear that a projected line of research will probably be scientifically successful, but the decision as to whether such a discovery would be capable of conversion to profitable use may be taken by someone other than the researcher. For example, solar energy is scientifically possible but at present it is not commercially viable.

44. Development. Development relates to the practical application of the results of research and is often the responsibility of the research team, operating as a *research and development department.*

The discovery must be tested in working conditions, it must be capable of being manufactured at an economic cost and it must have a potential market.

Often, development is not strictly linked to research by the same firm in that it includes study of ways in which a discovery can be *adapted* for use in a particular firm or industry.

Development may sometimes be fairly long-term because it is often necessary to test the new product to see how it stands up to normal usage, which design faults appear with time, and what the breakdown rate is. This is often done by *"user-testing"*, whereby trial products are used by potential buyers to discover latent faults.

45. Design. This requires a detailed specification for the product. The designer's problem is the reconciliation of the ideal functional version and the version which will appeal to buyers. He is also very concerned with cost: to produce something which will meet both ideals may make the cost prohibitive.

The following distinctions may therefore be made:

(*a*) *Functional (or technical) design* relates to the structure and working of the product. Where consumer preference for appearance is not relevant (such as machine tools for industry), functional design is the only consideration.

(*b*) *Formal (or aesthetic) design* is concerned with the appearance of the product and is of vital importance for, say, domestic consumer goods. In fashion trades it is often of overwhelming importance.

46. Design errors.

(*a*) *Commitment to a design.* Once a design has been finally decided it becomes incapable of alteration in the short-term. Any errors in function or any misjudgment of consumer preference will mean that time must be spent on modification. The manufacturing process may require alteration; new materials may be required; all this will result in delays in production as well as losses on the goods already manufactured. There may also be some loss of goodwill because of dissatisfaction by the first buyers.

Design must, therefore, be the result of considerable testing before scale production commences. Obviously, the simpler the design the more capable it will be of modification.

(b) *Evidence of errors.* These can arise from:

    (i) consumer complaints of malfunction and maintenance costs;

    (ii) decline of sales (unattractive or too expensive);

    (iii) undue amount of scrap in production (bad design resulting in wasteful methods).

ESTIMATING

47. Estimating. Estimating means the determination of the selling price (either as a quotation for a commissioned order or as a market price), by calculating the cost of production. Accuracy is essential because:

(a) *under-estimating* will result in a loss;

(b) *over-estimating* may result in too high a price, leading to lost sales.

The following steps are necessary in estimating:

(c) Compiling the technical data relevant to design, e.g. sizes, voltage, clearance spaces, etc.

(d) Costing materials, labour, tooling, etc.

(e) Calculating the overheads and profit margin.

(f) Deciding the method of production and ensuring the necessary capacity is available, e.g. work areas, equipment, supplies, etc.

(g) Establishing the delivery date, allowing for other commitments of resources.

PROGRESS TEST 10

1. What is meant by "production policy"? Under what constraints does it operate? (2)

2. Consider the problem of relating cost of production to demand at an acceptable price. (1(a), 2(c), (d))

3. Under what circumstances would the following be most appropriate: (a) job production; (b) batch production; (c) flow production? (3)

4. Define "production engineering". (4)

5. Define "simplification and standardisation". What are the possible advantages and disadvantages of such practices? (5–7)

6. What are the features of production specialisation? (8)

7. What could be the justifications for diversification? (9)

8. What factors will influence the choice of factory site? (10)

9. Compare the attractions of single-storey buildings with multi-storey buildings. (11)

10. What are the objectives in planning factory layout? (13)

11. Define: (a) production layout; (b) process layout. (14, 15)

12. What rules apply for the planning of departments in relationship to each other? (17)

13. What factors influence the choice of plant and equipment? (18)

14. List the responsibilities of maintenance staff. (19)

15. What are the contents of a maintenance policy? (20)

16. What factors must be considered when planning the handling of materials? (21)

17. List the various classifications of handling equipment. (22)

18. What are the objectives of planning and control, and the consequent responsibilities? (24, 25)

19. What are the purposes and functions of "progress control" (or "expediting" or "progress chasing")? (27)

20. What management aids are available in respect of control? (28)

21. What are the objectives of an inspection system? (29(a–f))

22. Define: (a) process control; (b) running tests; (c) quality control; (d) statistical quality control. (29(g–l))

23. Compare centralised inspection and floor inspection. (30)

24. Define: (a) work study; (b) method study; (c) work measurement. (31)

25. What are the objectives of method study? (33)

26. Outline the stages in a method study programme. (34)

27. Name some of the devices available for the practice of work study. (34)

28. What is "time study"? (35)

29. Name the more common techniques of work measurement. (37).

30. What suspicions may exist concerning the use of work study? (38)

31. What is meant by "value analysis" and "value engineering"? (39)

32. What are the purposes of: (a) plant budgets; (b) plant registers? (41)

33. Contrast pure research and applied research. (42)

34. What are the usual areas covered by a research policy? (43)

35. What is the connection of "development" with "research"? (44)

36. What conflicting attitudes may have to be reconciled at the design stage? Contrast functional design and formal design. (45)

37. Consider the consequences of design errors. (46)

38. What are the problems of estimating selling price? What factors must be allowed for? (47)

CHAPTER XI

PURCHASING AND STOCK CONTROL

PURCHASING

1. Purchasing in the organisation structure. The importance of the purchasing department will vary between one type of business and another. In service industries, purchasing would play only a minor role; for example, it may be restricted to the buying of office supplies, furniture, etc. In other businesses, it would occupy a key position. Its position in the structure will also differ in those businesses where purchasing *is* an important function.

(*a*) *In a manufacturing business* a purchasing department would be responsible for obtaining materials and/or components. The amount and type of purchases would be dictated by the requirements of the production sector and the purchasing officer would be responsible to the production department. In this instance, buying orders would be given for *known needs.*

(*b*) *In a selling concern* the extent and types of purchases would be determined by the sales department, which would thereby be the controlling department. As the purchases would be those required to meet expected sales, the buying orders would be for *anticipated needs.*

2. The functions of a purchasing department. These may be regarded as being within the following areas:

(*a*) *Knowledge of the suppliers.* It is essential to have up-to-date information about the ability of potential suppliers as regards delivery times, the relative merits of their goods, and their prices. This will entail keeping records and having available comprehensive price-lists, specifications, etc.

(*b*) *Experience of the market.* The department must be knowledgeable about the type of purchases required and, in the case of raw materials, have accurate information about the condition of commodity markets.

(c) *Seek quotations.* Comparisons will be made of prices quoted but account must also be taken of delivery times and each supplier's record for quality.

(d) *Orders on requisition by a department requiring goods.* The specification will be made by the requisitioning department, but it must be guided by the purchasing department about the length of delivery time so that it will requisition sufficiently in advance.

(e) *Ensure delivery.* Records must be kept of promised delivery dates and "follow ups" must be instituted where necessary.

(f) *Administration.* This will include:

    (i) checking goods to delivery notes;
    (ii) certifying invoices for payment;
    (iii) issuing purchases to requisitioning departments;
    (iv) maintaining records of orders made, orders outstanding and stocks held.

(g) *Legal.* The purchasing officer must be well versed in the law of contract and experienced in the framing of contracts to buy, futures agreements, etc.

3. Purchasing policy. The main objectives should be to:

(a) *buy at the lowest price* without sacrificing quality or endangering delivery targets;

(b) *buy at the right time* to take advantage of any price movement;

(c) *use the method most appropriate* (*see* **4** below);

(d) *buy the most appropriate amounts.* Goods could be purchased in those minimum quantities which would ensure meeting demand. By this method, goods are stored for a very short period with a consequent saving of storage costs. However, the price to be paid must be that prevailing at the time, which may be a disadvantage. Also, even a short delay in delivery may hold up production. The alternative is to *buy a stock* of goods when the price is low, offsetting the gain by the cost of storage.

4. The buying methods. Buying methods will not be the same for all purchases, and may include the following:

(a) *Contract.* This is an agreement to purchase an agreed quantity over a period (e.g. a year), at a fixed price. Deliveries could be as demanded or could be at a regular rate (e.g. fuel oil), but in either case the purchaser has an assured supply. Also, the price will be known in advance and could not be changed (which could be a disadvantage if market prices subsequently fell). This price may be lower than if other methods were used because the supplier would have the advantage of an assured market.

(b) *"Spot" purchases.* These relate to orders given "on the spot", e.g. to a visiting representative, or at a showroom.

(c) *Quotation.* Quoting applies when standard forms are sent to suppliers giving specifications, amount required, delivery dates, etc. Suppliers quote prices accordingly and the buyer accepts the most suitable. Supplies of this sort to public authorities, etc., are usually referred to as being *by tender.*

(d) *"Futures".* This refers to established practices within certain commodity markets. Cocoa, for example, is purchased by agreeing a price well in advance of the harvest. This method, obviously, is speculative for both buyer and supplier.

5. Purchasing department organisation.

(a) *Centralisation.* The extent of centralisation will differ between businesses. A degree of centralisation exists in most concerns because it provides the *advantages* of:

(i) bulk buying and reduced costs;

(ii) specialisation by buyers with particular expertise;

(iii) a higher degree of standardisation of goods and uniformity of procedures.

The possible *disadvantages* are:

(iv) local management (at branches, etc.), are better aware of local demand;

(v) purchases (particularly edibles) may be obtained more economically from local suppliers;

(vi) delays and increased paper work.

(b) *Specialisation.* This may be practical within a large department in that buying staff may be divided:

(i) according to the materials ordered. Thus there would be experts for each type of purchase; or (*ii*) in relation to specific areas of the business, e.g. components, fuel, furniture and office supplies.

6. Purchasing routine. The usual procedures may be summarised as follows:

(*a*) *Requisitions* would be received from departments requiring supplies to be ordered. These would be on standard forms and signed by a responsible official (the holders of authority and the extent of their authority must be notified to the purchasing department). On receipt, the requisitions would be numbered for reference purposes.

(*b*) *Orders,* assuming supplies are assured and prices agreed, would be sent on standard order forms to the suppliers. A *goods ordered* record would be kept by the purchasing department and (if a separate function) by the stores department.

(*c*) *Goods received* would be checked by stores to the supplier's delivery note and to the goods ordered record, and then confirmed to the purchasing department which would note its records accordingly.

(*d*) *Invoices,* when received, would be checked with the order to ensure the correct price is charged and any discounts allowed. The quantity invoiced would be checked with the record of goods received. The invoice would then be vouched and passed to the accounts department for payment.

(*e*) *Follow-up* is necessary to ensure goods are received on time. A procedure must be laid down as to when action must be taken. Records should be kept to identify suppliers with unsatisfactory records for deliveries.

STORES AND STOCK CONTROL

7. Materials control department. This relates to manufacturing and is the department responsible for ensuring the right amount and quality of materials are available as required. It embraces purchasing and the storage of goods, and operates in relation to financial control.

8. Objectives of stores control.

(*a*) *To ensure availability* of goods when required.

(*b*) *To reduce storage costs* as much as possible.

(c) *To preserve goods*, i.e. to avoid deterioration, wastage, theft, etc.

(d) *To maintain accurate records* and provide management data.

9. Classification and identification of stores.

(a) *Classification*. Storerooms may be specialised according to the classification of their contents, e.g. raw materials, components, consumable stores (such as cleaning and lubrication materials), tools and jigs, finished parts and finished goods.

(b) *Identification*. Types of stock should be identified by a system of coding. The code should be used on all records, on bin cards and bays, and in a *stock manual* listing and describing all items of stock.

10. Stock levels. One of the most important duties of a stores officer is to maintain the optimum level appropriate to different sorts of stock.

Too high a level will result in an undue amount of capital being tied up in stock; increased storage costs of rent, lighting, insurance, etc.; greater risk of deterioration, damage, etc.

Too low a level will endanger supplies needed immediately for production, and may involve having to purchase immediately, irrespective of price.

(a) *Minimum, maximum and reorder levels*. This is the fixing of the level of stock below which it would be dangerous to go; fixing the maximum above which it would be uneconomic to store; and deciding the level at which goods must be reordered.

(b) *"Lead time"*. This is the allowance to be made for delivery. Thus, re-ordering must take place before the minimum level is reached because of the time taken for delivery.

(c) *Deterioration risks*. Where these are high, stock should be kept as low as it is safe and economic so to do.

(d) *Storage costs*.

(e) *Risk of obsolescence*. For example, tools may become outdated if kept too long.

(f) *Price movements*. It may be economic to stockpile if prices are expected to rise.

(*g*) *Economic amounts.* Storage costs may be partly offset by the economies of buying large quantities.

11. Stores layout. The following general principles apply:

(*a*) *Appropriate storage.* Small items should be in bins, related articles being adjacent. Large items should be in special stores, e.g. timber, fluids, heavy metals.

(*b*) *Economy of movement.* Small items should be near the issuing points; large items should be close to appropriate transport; finished goods should be near the despatch department.

(*c*) *Transport* should be near and relevant to types of goods, e.g. low loaders for timber, fork-lift trucks for packages.

(*d*) *Access.* Goods in bins should be at a suitable height for withdrawal and filling; space must be available for unpacking and inspection; gangways must allow for free movement.

12. Stores procedure.

(*a*) *Stores inward.* Co-operation with the purchasing department is discussed in **6** above. On accepting goods for stock, entries must be made in:

(*i*) the stock records. These contain separate sections for each item, which would have a description and a code reference. The record would give a "running total", showing the balance held at any one time, incoming stock being added to the existing total;

(*ii*) bin cards. These are attached to bins holding the stock relevant to the cards or, in other cases, on or near the stock itself. They contain similar information to that in the stock records. The cards are altered to show the new balances as stock is physically placed in the store.

(*b*) *Stores outward.* The document demanding stores may be a signed requisition, works order or some other standard document. Rules must be prescribed as to who may make withdrawal requisitions.

The requisitions should be numbered upon receipt. As stock is withdrawn the reference number of the requisition is placed on the stores records and the bin cards to facilitate any subsequent checking which may be necessary. The runnings totals are adjusted by the amounts withdrawn.

13. The necessity for stock-taking. Account must be taken of stock-in-hand for the following reasons:

(a) *To value for the purposes of the accounts.* The figure must, of course, appear in the published year-end accounts, but many firms also produce monthly accounts for internal use.

(b) *To determine insurance cover.* Where cover is based on a fluctuating asset such as stock it may be necessary to make monthly valuations.

(c) *To calculate the cost of carrying stock.* This involves relating cost to the value of stock held.

(d) *To detect pilferage and deterioration.*

14. Methods of stock-taking.

(a) *Annual.* This entails the counting of every item to enable a valuation to appear in the annual accounts. This valuation will be certified by the firm's external auditor who usually states he has accepted a written statement of the valuation by the directors, who, in turn, will rely on a certificate by the internal auditors conducting the stock-taking.

The system has the disadvantage of using much labour over a period of concentrated activity. The reception and issue of stores must continue meanwhile and this complicates the calculating.

(b) *Perpetual inventory.* This means a continuous process of checking and counting. This is done to a programme in order that a permanent staff of unchanging size may check every section of the store so that the whole is checked over a period. Preferably, this would be more than once a year.

The physical count is reconciled with the records, the latter being adjusted where any discrepancy is found. Differences due to a reasonable amount of deterioration must be accepted but any apparently due to pilfering must be investigated.

At the year-end, the figures in the stock records are accepted for the purpose of the balance sheet.

The *advantages* of perpetual inventories are that:

(i) disruption of the stores is minimised;

(ii) no extra staff is required for short periods, a regular constant staff being used;

(iii) the stock-takers have time to check thoroughly;

(*iv*) discrepancies are identified early;

(*v*) slow-moving stocks can be identified.

15. Pricing of stock. For the purpose of costing, materials issued from stores to production must be valued. Materials in constant use may be purchased at different prices according to that prevailing at the time of purchase. It may therefore be difficult to decide the cost of any item as part of production costs because the market price when the purchase was made may differ from that prevailing when the item was used in production.

According to circumstances, there is a choice of the following methods of costing:

(*a*) *Cost price.* Cost price is not usually used, except where the purchase is specific to a particular job and can be directly related to it.

(*b*) *Average price.* This method means adding the total of the variety of prices and dividing by the number of prices.

EXAMPLE

> 100 units purchased at 50p
> 500 units purchased at 60p
> 400 units purchased at 70p

The average price would be the total of the different prices in the range (180p) divided by the number of price variations (3). The average would thus be 60p.

(*c*) *Weighted average price.* This gives a more realistic figure by allowing for the quantities purchased at different prices. Thus the price of a purchase of a larger than normal amount would have a marked effect on the average price. The formula is to add to the total cost of the stock already held the cost of the new purchase, and to divide by the total units (including the latest purchase) in stock.

EXAMPLE

If one assumes that the first two purchases in the above example are still in stock and that there is no earlier stock, the weighted average after the final purchase would be calculated as follows:

> 100 units at 50p = 5,000p
> 500 units at 60p = 30,000p
> 400 units at 70p = 28,000p

Total stock: 1,000 units   *Total cost:* 63,000p

Weighted average: 63p

(d) *First in, first out price (FIFO).* This method assumes that the materials received first are issued first and issues are charged out on that basis. Although issues would normally conform to this pattern, it is obvious that the issue price may not, in fact, be the same as the purchase price because the frequency of purchases may not coincide with the rate of usage.

(e) *Last in, first out price (LIFO).* In this method, the price paid for the last purchase is taken as the issue price. When the amounts of issue at that price are equal to the amount purchased at the last price (that is, when the last purchase has been exhausted), the issue price is changed to that paid for the next previous purchase.

PROGRESS TEST 11

1. Why may purchasing departments be of different degrees of importance between one business and another? (1)

2. Compare the purchasing functions in a servicing industry, a manufacturing business and a selling business. (1)

3. What are the broad functions of a purchasing department? (2)

4. What should be the objectives of a purchasing policy? (3)

5. Define purchasing by: (a) contract; (b) "spot"; (c) tender; (d) quotation; (e) futures. (4)

6. What could be the advantages and disadvantages of purchasing being a centralised function? (5(a))

7. What is meant by specialisation in the purchasing department? (5(b))

8. What records should be kept following a request to order goods? (6)

9. State the objectives of stores control. (8)

10. Discuss the importance of setting the optimum levels of stock. (10)

11. Consider, in relation to storage, the importance of: (a) lead time; (b) costs; (c) price movements. (10)

12. State the principles of efficient layout of stores. (11)

13. Define: (a) stock manual; (b) goods ordered record; (c) bin cards; (d) withdrawal requisition. (6, 9, 12)

14. Why is stock-taking necessary? (13)

15. Compare annual stock-taking and perpetual inventory. (14)

16. Compare the following methods of valuing stock: (a) cost; (b) average; (c) weighted average; (d) FIFO; (e) LIFO. (15)

CHAPTER XII

MARKETING

THE SCOPE OF MARKETING

1. The marketing function. In essence, the function of marketing is to provide and distribute those goods and services required by customers and to do so in the most efficient manner. The function is, however, more comprehensive than that and includes recognition of the following aspects:

(*a*) *Assessing consumer demand*. This will entail a study of the potential market and will result in decisions as to:

(*i*) what to produce. This will be based on the anticipated preferences of the customers;
(*ii*) how many to produce. This will be the result of assessing the strength of the demand;
(*iii*) the sale price. This will be decided partly by what consumers would be prepared to pay and would be influenced by the strength of the demand and the extent of competition.

(*b*) *Ability to provide products*. If the marketing is to be of goods which have been purchased, the supply of the goods must be assured. If the seller is to manufacture the goods, then he must be sure that:

(*i*) he has the productive capacity and ability, e.g. space, equipment, expertise, labour, etc.;
(*ii*) production costs and selling price will have a profitable ratio to each other;
(*iii*) production materials will be available.

(*c*) *Adequacy of finance*. Buying or production must take place ahead of income being received from sales. The amount of these costs, and the length of time they must be met out of capital, has to be added to the costs of marketing.

(*d*) *Organisation*. There must be an efficient system of:

(*i*) *co-operation between the various sections*. For example, production rate must equal anticipated sales; finance must be

132

available at the right times; changes in demand must be reflected in adjustments within the business;

(ii) *information between sections.* This will *flow back* from marketing so that all sections will be aware of targets and any changes in targets or strategies.

(e) *Advertising.* The method of advertising and its cost must be decided.

(f) *Distribution.* It may be necessary to make a choice between methods of distribution. The matters of cost, convenience and customer-preference must be considered.

2. The marketing concept. In the past, manufacturers were primarily concerned with the techniques of production and the reduction of costs. The philosophy was to produce goods with the right mixture of quality and cost, but with comparatively little concern with what the potential buyers wanted. Their attitude can be described as being *product-orientated.*

This concept of efficient and economical production must still prevail, of course, but of itself it can be destructive. The increased sophistication of buyers, the extension of demand to what were once regarded as "luxuries", the effects of increased competition and the force of advertising have combined to put the decision of what shall be produced into the hands of the *consumers.* The extent and direction of demand is now recognised as being the dominating factor. Consequently, the efforts of the marketing division to assess what the consumers want, and for production to be geared to meet those preferences, are of paramount importance. This has resulted in the *"marketing concept",* whereby the business as a whole is *"customer-orientated".*

3. Marketing policy. This involves appraisal of all the factors relevant to marketing in conjunction with the most efficient deployment of the firm's resources, and will include the following:

(a) *Choice of market.* The marketing may be aimed at one section of a market, e.g. the "top end" or the low-price, mass market. This will determine quality and price.

(b) *New or existing markets.* It may be decided to remain in the same market, possibly taking an increased share of it; to move to a new market; to add a new market to the existing one. A new type of product may be necessary if a new market is to be breached, e.g. to mass-produce for a wider and "lower" market, cheaper versions of what was previously an "exclusive" product.

(c) *The extent of competition.* To combat competition it may be necessary to:

(i) produce a cheaper product;
(ii) produce at lower costs;
(iii) make the product more attractive;
(iv) persuade consumers by advertising.

(d) *Distribution channels.* Cheaper and/or more efficient methods may be considered, e.g. direct sales to consumers by eliminating retailers.

(e) *Sales force.* The adequacy and ability of the sales force and the supporting administration must be considered.

4. Marketing strategy. This is concerned with planning market activity and usually involves consideration of various alternatives, such as the choice of production models, promotion methods, prices, etc. These choices are known as the *"marketing mix"*.

The plan must be flexible to allow for change because of:

(d) *internal factors,* such as production problems, finance, changes in costs, etc.;

(b) *changes in consumer demand,* due to altered social attitudes, the introduction of substitutes, etc.;

(c) *external factors,* such as Government action (e.g. increasing a tax), competition, economic depression, etc.

Implementation of a marketing plan will result in strategies such as the following:

(d) *Penetration strategy.* This relates to a high output with the aim of a high volume of sales with low profit margins per unit. Obviously, the market must be wide and the goods capable of mass production. Planning must be long-term and detailed because of the considerable losses following any miscalculation.

(e) *Segmentation strategy.* This relates to variations of a standard product to appeal to different markets. For example, various models of the same domestic appliance, such as a vacuum cleaner, may be marketed. A degree of similarity in the models, whereby there are standard parts and interchangeable parts, will obviously make production simpler and marketing more flexible.

5. The marketing division. The marketing division would be headed by a marketing manager. The structure will differ between firms but will normally be similar to that shown in Fig. 5.

6. The responsibilities of the marketing division. These are to:

(*a*) *determine marketing policy* within the broad policy of the directors and subject to financial constraints;

(*b*) *advise the Board on marketing policy*;

(*c*) *conduct market research*;

(*d*) *liaise with production* to ensure co-ordination of effort;

(*e*) *promote sales* by advertising and promotion schemes;

(*f*) *control distribution*;

(*g*) *forecast* sales, price movements, costs, etc., advise management of trends and prepare sales budgets;

(*h*) *maintain statistics* of sales, and report;

(*i*) *control staff*. This would include the selection, training and supervision of sales staff, stores and distribution staff, and administration personnel.

7. Pricing policy. Because of improved technology, the cost of production, in real terms, has tended to fall in recent years. There has, however, been a marked increase in marketing costs, due to increased spending on advertising, packaging, after-sale service, etc.

Determining the optimum selling price is a complex operation and must take account of the following:

(*a*) *Production costs.* There will be a rate of production at which costs per unit are lowest, but this production figure may not coincide with the extent of the demand. Production costs will therefore be those appertaining to the rate of production which matches demand.

(*b*) *Quality.* The degree to which customers will pay for superior quality may mean that achieving the optimum sale revenue will depend upon reducing the quality. Alternatively, the product and the demand may be such that optimum returns would result from charging higher prices to a limited market. The restriction on sales may, in itself, constitute an asset because of the "exclusiveness" of the product.

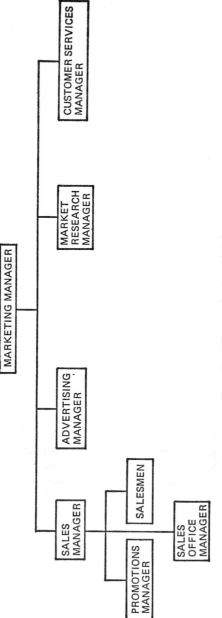

Fig. 5—*The marketing division.*

(c) *New products.* New products which appeal to the public may command a high price, which should compensate for the comparatively high cost of production at an early stage. Later sales, because of "familiarity" with the product or because of the emergence of competitors, may result in lower prices being necessary. The total income arising from both price levels must relate favourably to the production cost at the total level.

(d) *Demand elasticity.* The market may be sensitive to price changes. The effects of substitutes or market saturation must be considered.

(e) *Advertising.* Effective advertising will increase demand and so improve profitability, but advertising which is insufficiently productive will have the reverse effect. If advertising is an unrewarding expense, the price may have to be increased with a consequent loss of competitiveness.

MARKET RESEARCH

8. Application. Market research is a set of techniques for obtaining and analysing information about a market with a view to planning sales in that market. It may be:

(a) *initial research* to establish the potential of a prospective market;

(b) *continuous research,* applied to a market which the researcher is already serving, in order to forecast changes within that market or to change the selling strategy.

9. The objectives. Objectives are to determine:

(a) *the degree of acceptability.* This establishes to what degree a product is acceptable to consumers and, within that survey, the consumers' preference for any variation of the product. For example, it may be learned that there is a bias in favour of a particular colour;

(b) *the amount of sales which could be anticipated;*

(c) *the price which would be acceptable;*

(d) *the most appropriate method of appeal.* This would include those aspects it would be most beneficial to stress in advertising.

10. The necessity for research. As production must take

place in advance of selling, the importance of accurate assessment of the market arises from the following factors:

(a) *Deference to consumer preferences.* The producer should market not what it is the most convenient for him to make, or what he considers to be the most efficient or attractive. He must concentrate on what his customers *want* (*see* 2 above).

(b) *The extent of the demand.* If the product is one sold to individuals occasionally (e.g. washing machines) or continuously (e.g. detergents), the producer must, in either case, be able to determine the amount he can sell over a period. This amount would then be related to the unit-cost of producing that total. Thus the benefits of large-scale production will not accrue if the demand is insufficient to warrant extensive production.

(c) *Effective use of advertising.* Assessing consumer reaction to the product allows advertising to be directed to exploiting those attitudes.

(d) *Financial commitment.* Once a decision has been made as to what to produce and in what quantities, the producer is committed to financial outlay. This may be lost if a miscalculation has been made.

(e) *Changing conditions.* In an established market, the seller must remain in contact so that his strategy can be changed to meet new conditions. For example, the "composition" of the population in an area may alter, a fashion change may re-direct demand, a substitute may be discovered, or social habits or attitudes may alter.

(f) *Competition.* The extent of competition in selling the same type of product must be assessed and account taken of the methods used to provide that competition. Regard must also be paid to competition in the form of *different* products being introduced as substitutes for present products.

11. Research methods.

(a) *Desk research* is a preliminary stage of research and involves the collection and analysis of published data. This is available from Government publications, agency surveys, trade journals, etc.

(b) *Internal research* entails an analysis of the producer's own records to indicate, for example, the comparative popularity of the variety of his products, trends between geographical areas, seasonal fluctuations, and the effects of price movements.

(c) *Consumer research* is a form of "field survey" in that checks are made on the buying habits, preferences, etc., of the public.

(d) *Motivation research* is a refinement of consumer research (which is entirely mathematical). Motivation research aims to establish *why* people have preferences. The system requires the use of psychological methods so that, for example, the answers are more truthful (consider the validity of answers to: "How many cigarettes do you smoke?"). The reason for a preference may not always be consciously known to the interviewee and motivation research aims to establish the true reasons. Such knowledge also enables a producer to base his advertising on appeals to aspects of human nature which may be subliminal (for example, two identical perfumes in different bottles could be rated differently by prospective buyers).

(e) *Product research* is designed to assess the acceptability of a product and the degrees of preference relevant to variations of the product.

12. Research techniques. There are various techniques used in carrying out the methods outlined above, some of which are as follows:

(a) *Quantitative surveys* are usually carried out by agencies and relate to fast-selling consumables, e.g. foods, tobacco, etc. It is a continuous process, showing volume of sales and indicating trends in various components of a market.

(b) *Attitude surveys* are used in motivation research, particularly in "emotive" products such as pharmaceuticals, cosmetics, baby foods, etc. It entails the use of subtle methods to discover true attitudes by "depth interviews", group discussions, etc.

(c) *Test marketing* entails using a small area as a test market. The product is promoted and sold locally, and a detailed examination made of the buying pattern.

(d) *User tests* can be employed, by asking consumers to use a product and report back on it. If different versions of the product are given to different users, comparisons can be made. The method is also employed in industrial markets where a product (e.g. a floor-cleaning machine) is lent to an industrial user for him to give his opinion of its performance.

(e) *Retail audits* are regular surveys carried out at selected shops to calculate demand for competing products.

(f) *Random sampling* requires members of the public, selected at random, to give answers to a questionnaire. The answers are coded and by a system of totalling and analysing all the answers to each question, a global set of answers is compiled. This is then regarded as representative of the attitudes of the buying public as a whole.

The failings of this system are:

(i) the difficulty of compiling a scientific questionnaire;
(ii) reliance upon the honesty of the answers;
(iii) the degree of skill of the interviewers;
(iv) the fact that a random selection may not, in fact, be truly representative, e.g. fewer old people will be interviewed on a wet day.

(g) *Consumer panels* consist of a team of volunteers regularly reporting their purchases, preferences, etc. Examples are the systems of assessing the size of television audiences. This has the disadvantage that the cross-section is unchanging and consists of those who are already committed to some degree, e.g., it would not include those who do not watch television, as a random sample would.

13. Conducting a consumer survey. The stages may be summarised as follows:

(a) Determine the objectives of the survey.
(b) Decide on:

(i) the number to be interviewed;
(ii) the geographical areas to be covered (the class of district may be important);
(iii) the length of the survey.

(c) Assemble the questionnaire, including a scheme of "marking".
(d) Build a team of interviewers and train them. Appoint supervisors and co-ordinators.
(e) Arrange for the submission of completed questionnaires.
(f) Devise a scheme for counting and analysing the results.
(g) Report on the findings.

SALES MANAGEMENT

14. Sales forecasting. This is a specialised aspect of marketing and is concerned with estimating the future trends in sales. This can be partly achieved by continuous market research and the analysis of past performances of sales. The degree of possible accuracy is largely dependent upon the nature of the product, those which are subject to the whims of fashion being the most unpredictable.

Information which can also be taken into account includes the experience of the sales force ("grass-roots experience"), the views of retailers, the opinions of economists and that available from the expert use of statistics.

15. Product life cycle. In most cases, the rate of sales will not remain static or even move at a regular rate of change. New products must be constantly planned because increased sophistication of buyers, the development of new techniques, the pressure of competition and the influence of advertising mean that the sales of most products must eventually go into a decline. The problem is the assessing of the time and extent of the decline.

The initial stage may show a sharp rise in sales if the product is unique and attractive to the public. More probably, however, the rise will be slow until the product becomes established and thereafter sales would rise more steeply. There would then follow a period of "maturity" with sales fairly steady. At this point, its success may attract competitors, the "novelty" may begin to pale, or the market may become saturated. This would lead to a decline in sales.

The skill required is in determining when the decline is to take effect so that planning ahead will ensure that a replacement product is marketable before sales of the first product have declined.

In Fig. 6 the periods shown across the top of the chart and the continuous line relate to the first product. The periods on the bottom and the charted broken line relate to the replacement product. This indicates that planning the introduction of the new product facilitated a beneficial overlap of the sales of the two products.

16. Functions of the sales department. The department must

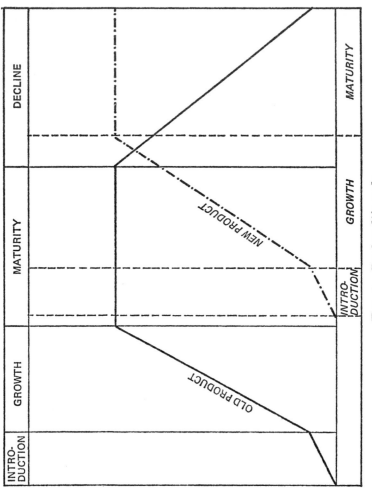

Fig. 6—*Product life cycle.*

operate as a member of the marketing team. As a department, its functions are mainly concerned with actual selling, although as part of the team it will be involved in all aspects of marketing. Its contribution to the team effort is vital because it is the only member of the team which is *directly* involved in selling. It thus has intimate knowledge of conditions in the field; it is not "desk bound" as are the other departments. Information flowing back from salesmen in close contact with customers must therefore be interpreted and passed to the marketing team.

17. The duties. Duties specific to the sales department may be said to be as follows:

(*a*) *Co-operation with other departments* in reaching decisions.

(*b*) *Implementing the marketing policy.*

(*c*) *Interpreting information from the field* by seeking reports from salesmen on customer reactions, market conditions, activities of competitors, possible new outlets, etc.

(*d*) *Establishing sales targets* for the department and for any sub-divisions of it, e.g. sales areas and individual salesmen.

(*e*) *Provision of statistics* for higher management.

(*f*) *Organisation of the sales department.*

(*g*) *Responsibility for staffing*, including the selection, training and supervision of the sales force.

(*h*) *Corresponding with customers* concerning complaints, suggestions, etc. (this may be the responsibility of a special customer relations department).

18. Organisation of the sales force.

(*a*) *Territories.* The size and number of territories will largely depend upon the nature of the product. The geographical range of a representative visiting grocers, for example, would be comparatively small because of the concentration of customers. A firm selling specialised equipment to industrial concerns would have larger territories because the customers would be less concentrated and the number of sales within a period would be far fewer.

Where selling is in concentrated areas, the comparatively high number of salesmen would lead to the establishing of *areas*, with area managers in charge. Thus there would be delegation from the central sales department.

(b) *The "call-rate"*. Each salesman would have a programme of calls to make on customers and potential customers. The frequency of calls would be graded according to their importance to the firm; thus, in some cases it may be sufficient to visit only occasionally to "keep in touch", whereas others would be called on often.

The "call-rate" is the frequency of calls on each customer. This is related to the *"call-costs"* which equates the total cost of the sales force to the value of the sales. This comparison will indicate which customers it is rewarding to call on frequently and, at the extreme, those which can be removed from the call list.

(c) *Quota-selling*. This refers to the establishing of targets for each salesman and, where appropriate, each area. It can also include the setting of targets for each of several products. The quotas must be realistic by being based on past performances and allowing for external factors, seasonal demand, etc.

(d) *Salesmen's reports*. These should be made on standard forms whereby each salesman must provide all the answers required.

    (i) *General reports*. These reports will show the number of calls made and the orders taken. The latter would, where required, be analysed into type of customer and the class of product. This information would be recorded and analysed by the sales department to provide data indicating trends, etc., as a basis for future strategy.

    (ii) *Call reports*. There would be one of these for every call made. It would give an outline of what was discussed, what complaints or suggestions were received, how the product was displayed (if a retail outlet), etc.

    (iii) *Sales record*. This would consist of order forms in respect of sales made. They would be processed in the sales department and the goods despatched.

19. Sales department records. These will include:

(a) *salesmen's personal records*. They would summarise each salesman's history—positions held, territories, staff reports, etc. They may also record his sales and expenses, although these may be recorded elsewhere;

(b) *sales records*. These would record sales, usually on a monthly basis, analysed into products, areas, etc. The figures should be cumulative over the year and be capable of comparison with the monthly and cumulative figures for the same time in previous years;

(c) *customer records.* Index cards should be maintained, showing the characteristics of each customer, such as the names of their buyers, any preferences concerning purchases, any special terms agreed, the record for prompt payment, normal size of orders, etc. Prospective customers may also be recorded, with information which may be useful in attempting to obtain their custom;

(d) *statistics.* These should show the firm's share of the market, costs of salesmens' cars, analyses of distribution costs, etc.

20. Selection and training of the sales force.

(a) *Personal attributes.* A salesman must be self-reliant, able to work in comparative isolation and have confidence in himself and the product.

(b) *Technical ability.* A salesman must be thoroughly trained to be knowledgeable about the product and so be able to talk authoritatively.

(c) *Office training.* Office training should come first so that the new salesman can see what happens in the office and learn the staff structure.

(d) *Field training.* A new salesman should first accompany one who is experienced. Later he would be given his own territory but should be helped and supervised in the early stages.

(e) *Refresher periods.* From time to time, salesmen should be brought into the office for short periods. This is partly to enable them to keep in touch with other staff members, including the "desk officers" who support them. Another reason would be to bring them up to date concerning developments, to attend conferences and, possibly, undertake courses.

EXPORT MARKETING

21. Features of overseas selling. Each country has specific characteristics which must result in marketing approaches being different for each country. "Business etiquette" varies between countries, some types of advertising are unacceptable in certain countries, packaging may have to be specific in some areas because of attitudes to colours, etc. In general, regard must be paid to different social attitudes, religious sensitivity, nationalistic feelings, etc.

(*a*) *Language* may constitute a difficulty in creating understanding.

(*b*) *Specifications*, measurements, etc., may differ.

(*c*) *Market research* is more difficult because fewer facilities may be available for obtaining field data.

(*d*) *Remoteness of the market* may mean lack of close contact with customers, potential customers and with the market generally.

(*e*) *Transport* will add to costs and make efficient packing essential and, perhaps, more costly.

(*f*) *Documentation* will be more complicated and will require the employment of specialist staff or the services of an agency.

(*g*) *Credit control.* There may be a higher risk of bad debts because information services and collection facilities may be less reliable.

(*h*) *Political and economic factors.* Suddenly-altered conditions in overseas markets could include nationalisation following a change of government, imposition of import and export controls and restrictions on the transfer of currency out of the country, etc.

(*i*) *Rates of exchange* may move adversely so that the true price when paid would be less than the agreed price.

22. The Export Credits Guarantee Department (E.C.G.D.). This department provides insurance against risks which, because they are specific to exporting, are not normally covered by commercial insurance concerns. Because the Department of Trade has intelligence reports from embassies, etc., it is better able to judge the risks (national as well as those pertaining to individual buyers), and can provide such information to exporters. It is also thereby in a better position to determine the extent of risks and so can offer insurance in acceptable instances.

In general, risks covered are as follows:

(*a*) The insolvency of the buyer.

(*b*) The failure of the buyer to pay for goods he has accepted.

(*c*) Default by the buyer before acceptance of the goods but after they have been shipped.

(*d*) Failure to receive payment because of exchange restrictions imposed by the foreign government.

(*e*) The imposition of import restrictions.

(*f*) Civil disturbance in the importing country.

(*g*) Outbreak of hostilities between the U.K. and the importing country.

The maximum amount of cover is 95 per cent of the risk.

Because of the security provided by an E.C.G.D. policy, banks are willing to provide assistance in financing such exports.

23. Export channels. A company exporting on a sufficiently large scale can afford to have its own exporting department, with specialist staff. Others have access to the services of the following:

(*a*) *Buying agencies* (*or confirming houses*) act on behalf of overseas buyers in placing orders with exporters. As the agencies attend to shipping, documentation, etc., they provide a convenient method for exporters.

(*b*) *Export merchants* in this country buy from manufacturers and sell the purchases to overseas buyers. To the producer this, in effect, is identical to selling on the home market.

(*c*) *Export agents* may act on behalf of a number of home-based producers of non-competing goods. They are knowledgeable about specific overseas markets and sell in those markets on behalf of the producers.

(*d*) *Importing houses* are based abroad. They buy from home producers and sell in the overseas market. Thus marketing is facilitated but the producer retains responsibility for the shipping formalities. Frequently, the house has an exclusive contract in respect of the products.

(*e*) *Overseas branches* can be set up by the exporter (and which may be a locally-registered subsidiary company) in the overseas country. Thus the benefits of local knowledge and closer control of sales, after-sales services, credit, etc., are available.

ADVERTISING AND SALES PROMOTION

24. Objectives of advertising. The broad purpose of advertising is to induce sales. A distinction can be made between the various methods used, however, by linking them to the particular objective *within* the global objective.

(*a*) *To inform.* In its simplest form, this is an announcement that a particular product or service is *available*. For example, a department store may announce a forthcoming sale. In other cases, more detailed information is given, often of a technical nature, e.g. the specifications of a refrigerator, or the refinements incorporated in a camera.

(*b*) *To persuade.* The objective is to induce the market to exercise a preference for the advertised product as against competing products. This is done by:

(*i*) *being factual.* Thus the low petrol-consumption of a car or the economic price of a piece of furniture may be emphasised;

(*ii*) *emotional appeal.* This is usually non-factual. For example, subliminal sex appeal can appear in advertisements for toothpastes, packaged holidays, chocolates, etc., which has no scientific justification;

(*iii*) *exploiting fears.* There are obviously desirable limits to such approaches but many medicaments are advertised by hinting at the dangers their use would prevent. Attitudes of social inferiority and other human weaknesses can also be exploited.

(*c*) *To remind.* These are forms of advertising which do not inform or directly persuade, but merely serve to keep the name of a product in the eye of the public. In its simplest form it can be a sign (such as on a bus) giving the name of, say, a cigarette. Other advertisements could be more expansive, such as a humorous television commercial, which *say* little but serve to keep a name fresh.

(*d*) *To create market attitudes.* These are attempts to change social attitudes in order to sell products never (or less frequently) sold before, by making their use socially acceptable or desirable. An obvious example is provided by the charges which have been laid against the tobacco industry. More recent examples include the marked increase in sales of men's toiletries.

25. Effective advertising. Spending on advertising will not, of itself, produce or increase sales. Successful advertising must exist within conditions which are conducive to selling and be in a form which is relevant. The following considerations apply:

(a) *Choice of media.* The media must have users who are potential buyers of the product. The limited selling range of a specialist journal is obvious, because its readers will have specific interests, but even in unspecialised journals, such as daily newspapers, distinctions can be made. There is some relationship between newspapers and the social classes of those who read them. A product which would not appeal to all classes would not be advertised in all papers and a product with a universal appeal may be advertised in different styles in one newspaper and another. Advertising appeal must be made to receptive markets, and those markets differ between the different forms of media.

(b) *Extent of demand.* If a demand does not exist, it is pointless to attempt to create the demand if it is impossible to do so or, if successful, the cost could not be justified. A product which has been overtaken by improved technology, one uncompetitive in price and/or quality, or one which the public no longer wants because of changed social attitudes— none of these would warrant the expense of advertising.

(c) *Presentation.* Ill-advised presentation can turn buyers *against* a product. This can happen when an "emotional" appeal is made and the anticipated response is misjudged.

(d) *Inadequate coverage.* There must be a minimum amount below which it would be unproductive to spend. Impact is rarely instant and it is usually necessary to seek a cumulative effect.

(e) *Economic climate.* Demand cannot be created when economic conditions are overwhelmingly against it. In a period of depression there will be a much-reduced demand for luxuries and other degrees of reduced demand for other goods. Certain conditions will have a more adverse effect on some sales than others. For example, the imposition or increase of a selective tax will reduce demand for those products affected by the tax; substitutes not affected by the tax may even *benefit*.

(f) *Market research.* If this has not been efficient, the advertising strategy may well fail.

26. The cost-benefit of advertising. When an advertisement includes a coupon to be completed and sent to the advertiser, it is possible to measure the *response* to the advertisement. (Coding the coupon would enable the "pulling power" of the various media used to be compared.) If returning the coupon is a form of buying (that is, the reader *orders* when he despatches the coupon), the amount of sales can be directly related to each advertisement. When, however, the coupon indicates an *enquiry* (e.g. a request for a brochure), the extent to which subsequent sales can be related to the number of enquiries will depend upon the circumstances. For example, information provided by a brochure may lead the enquirer to purchase at a local shop and therefore the sale could not be linked to the enquiry.

In general, it is not possible to relate sales directly to the cost of advertising, except to the extent outlined above. Review may indicate a rise in sales following an advertising campaign, but it would not be possible to determine which part of that rise could be attributed directly to the advertising. Also, most advertising is on a *continuous* basis, striving to keep the product before the public. Sales would be expected to fall if there was no advertising or if it was reduced but, again, the influence of one on the other could not be quantified.

Advertising, in its attempts to increase sales, will aim to prevent the erosion of its sales by competitors and to that extent advertising may be regarded as being "defensive". The concept could therefore be said to include not only the increasing of sales but also the reduction or prevention of lost sales. Any attempts at measurement must, therefore, include the cost of "standing still" as well as of expansion.

27. Economic justification of advertising. The often enormous expense of advertising is frequently said to be justified on the grounds that it increases sales, which thereby results in increased production. This in turn reduces unit costs which are passed on to consumers in the form of reduced prices. Thus the contention is that the consumer benefits because of the cost of advertising.

This is true to the extent that some goods could not be sold at an economic price unless production was on a large scale, but the following reservations may be made:

    (*a*) *Diminishing returns.* There is a limit to which production can be increased with an accompanying reduction in costs.

    (*b*) *Duplicated advertising.* Much advertising is aimed at increasing the sales of products which are not in competition.

Large sums are spent on publicising soap powders, for example, which appear to be in competition but which, in fact, come from the same manufacturers.

(c) *Defensive advertising.* Money may be spent on fighting competitors, when the free force of demand should result in the product being withdrawn because it is no longer truly competitive.

(d) *Artificial demand.* Advertising can create a demand for something which would not otherwise be desired. Thus social attitudes can be changed by exploiting fears and by pandering to human failings.

(e) *Efficiency and complacency.* An assured market, as a result of advertising, can reduce the spur given by competition. The resulting complacency could lessen the advertiser's urge to reduce costs and, in turn, prices.

28. Sales promotion. This term can embrace all methods for increasing sales, including advertising. It is often used, however, for shorter-term policies and may be referred to as "buying incentives". It can be used as:

(a) a form of intensive activity in promoting a product; or
(b) a method of maintaining the impetus of sales as a continuous process.

Sales promotion is almost entirely restricted to the domestic consumer market and the methods used include the following:

(c) *"Special offers"*, e.g. reduced prices available for limited periods; two complementary articles in a "bargain pack".
(d) *Competitions.*
(e) *Special displays*, arranged in conjunction with retailers.
(f) *Premium offers*, e.g. customers submit packet tops or coupons with cash in exchange for an article below the market price.

29. Public relations. The sphere of public relations may be said to be that of "projecting the image" of a business. Whilst it has no direct effect on sales, it can be regarded as part of marketing in that the reputation of a business can influence the amount of its sales.

The broad policy is to obtain publicity, outside the bounds

of formal advertising, which is advantageous to the firm. The public relations officer (P.R.O.) is usually someone with journalistic experience and he carries out his functions by the use of methods such as the following:

(a) *Press releases.* These consist of items of news which are circulated to the press.

(b) *Press conferences.* If a business is "in the news" it may be decided to meet the press so that statements can be issued and questions answered. The skill of the P.R.O. is very necessary here when the aim is to combat publicity which has been adverse.

(c) *Exhibitions.* These can take the form of either an exhibition by the business or participation in trade fairs, etc.

(d) *Literature.* Various sorts of literature may be used, e.g. expertly designed annual statements to shareholders, the City press, etc., and staff handbooks and house journals.

(e) *Sponsoring public events.* Such events could include tennis tournaments, sailing races, etc.

(f) *Providing information.* Information can be provided to the press and the public in response to questions. Within this definition could be included a "customer relations department" dealing with enquiries and complaints from customers.

30. Packaging. Packaging may be regarded as an aspect of marketing because, particularly in the domestic consumer market, it has a considerable influence on sales. The technique of packaging is comparatively new but it now plays a pre-eminent part in the marketing of many products.

The choice of packaging, obviously, must satisfy technical criteria concerning durability, cost, etc., but the *psychological appeal* of packaging can be equally important. For such products as cosmetics, the style of packaging may well be a greater influence on sales than the contents.

The following factors are relevant in designing packages:

(a) *Psychological appeal.* This takes account of the shape, colour and, in some cases, even the feel of the package.

(b) *Protection.* The extent to which the packaging must protect will depend upon:

(i) the nature of the product (e.g. plastic is generally preferable to glass as a container of fluids);

(*ii*) the "shelf life" (i.e. the time the article normally remains on a shop shelf);

(*iii*) the use of the product (e.g. cardboard may be unsuitable if the product has a long usage life, particularly if the contents are susceptible to damp);

(*iv*) the amount of handling in transport.

(*c*) *Special requirements for the contents.* Containers for special requirements include vacuums, "squeeze bottles" and anti-corrosives.

(*d*) *Size.* Products should not be in over-large packets because of possible wastage before they are fully used and because customers would be deterred by the bulk and weight. Many products must be packed according to *standard measurements*.

(*e*) *Legal requirements.* Legislation lays down standards of safety and prescribes rules about describing the contents fairly, warnings of possible dangers, etc.

31. After-sales service. Some products, because of their nature, almost automatically carry an after-sales service, the most obvious example being home-appliances. The *efficiency* of that service will not be established until after a sale has been made. Accordingly, the promise of service may not be a selling point, because a customer would expect all producers to offer it, but *subsequent* sales will be affected by the supplier's reputation for service.

The service may be provided directly by the supplier which, because of the cost and time spent in returning the appliance, may inconvenience the customer. In other cases, the service would be provided by the retailer or by an agency.

The following considerations are specific to after-sales service:

(*a*) *Spare parts.* There must be co-ordination with the production department to ensure an adequate supply of spare parts—including those for outdated models.

(*b*) *Servicing agents.* There must be control of agents and retailers who provide the after-sales service to ensure the maintenance of acceptable standards.

(*c*) *Statistics.* If a record of malfunctions is kept and analysed, technical weaknesses can be identified. This would assist in the designing of new products.

CREDIT CONTROL

32. The importance of credit control. A business relies upon income from its customers to provide working capital. Where difficulty is experienced in obtaining payment for sales, the resulting deficiency may have to be borrowed, involving the creditor in the payment of interest. Where payment is not received *at all*, the result is a complete loss.

33. Establishing credit periods. The limitations on the period of credit granted depend upon two broad considerations:

(a) *The general limit.* The limit granted to customers generally will be influenced by the period which is customary in the industry—what may be regarded as the "traditional" period. A seller who gives a shorter allowance for payment will be disadvantaged in that buyers will be attracted to those giving longer credit. (A buyer requires credit to be as long as possible because funds retained pending payment can be used in production. In effect, the buyer has the use of the creditor's money for the period of the credit without paying for it.) A seller giving a shorter period of credit may tempt potential buyers by reducing his prices, as the gain from receiving early payment may compensate for the lower profit-margin.

(b) *Specific limits.* These are limits applied to each customer and are determined by individual credit-ratings.

34. Establishing credit-ratings. The *period* and the *amount* of credit to be granted to each customer is influenced by several factors:

(a) *New customers.* Before an account is opened for a new customer, enquiries are made into his financial standing by means of bank references, through trade enquiry agencies, etc. An agreement will be reached with the customer as to the value of goods he may have on credit and the length of time granted for payment.

(b) *Established customers.* The credit ratings of customers will be reviewed *generally* as a continuous process and *specifically* when the customer requires an extension of credit. The determining factor will be the customer's record for payment, in addition, possibly, to further enquiries as to his financial standing.

(c) *Importance as a customer.* A customer providing extensive and continuous business will be more favourably considered as regards credit than the average customer.

35. Reducing credit risks. The losses due to non-payment or the expense of unduly slow payment may be reduced by the following methods:

(a) *Offering inducements.* This can be in the form of generous discounts for immediate or early payment.

(b) *Credit control department.* A staff delegated to control strictly the granting of credit and the collection of debts can reduce losses, provided the administration expenses are not uneconomic when compared with the savings.

(c) *Factoring and invoice discounting.* These systems consist of a finance house paying the creditor at least the major part of the debt on the due date, thus ensuring his cash flow. The house collects payment from the debtor and the final settlement is made with the creditor, less a deduction for the fees of the factor or discounting house.

(d) *Credit insurance.* This relates only to bad debts.

(e) *Efficient accounting.* A system whereby accounts are kept fully up to date will contribute to debt reduction. A business which is slow in sending out invoices and statements, and which does not react quickly to "danger signals" in the accounts, is liable to unnecessary losses.

PROGRESS TEST 12

1. What principles prevail concerning the relationship of the marketing division with other sections of the organisation? (**1**(*d*))

2. What is meant by the "marketing concept" and what is its importance? (**2**)

3. What, in general, is included in the marketing policy? (**3**)

4. What is meant by the "marketing mix"? (**4**)

5. Why must marketing strategy be flexible? (**4**)

6. Define penetration strategy and segmentation strategy. (**4**)

7. Outline the responsibilities of a marketing division. (**6**)

8. What factors go to determine the selling price? (**7**)

9. What are the objectives of market research? (**9**)

10. What considerations make market research necessary? (**10**)

11. Define the following methods of market research: (a) desk;
(b) internal; (b) consumer; (c) motivation; (d) product. **(11)**

12. Define the following research techniques: (a) quantitative;
(b) attitude; (c) test marketing; (d) user tests; (e) retail audits;
(g) consumer panels. **(12)**

13. What are the stages in conducting a consumer survey? **(13)**

14. What sources of information are available for sales forecasting? **(14)**

15. What is the "product life cycle"? **(15)**

16. What are the usual duties relevant to a sales department?
(17)

17. What factors may determine the size of a sales territory?
(18(a))

18. What is the "call rate" and what is its relationship with the
"call cost"? **(18(b))**

19. What is quota selling? **(18(c))**

20. What should a salesman's training include? **(20)**

21. What problems are specific to export marketing? **(21)**

22. What services are provided by the Export Credits Guarantee
Department? **(22)**

23. List the various organisations which facilitate export
marketing. **(23)**

24. What are the main objectives of advertising? **(24)**

25. What are the requirements to ensure effective advertising?
(25)

26. To what extent is it possible to relate the cost of advertising
to its earning ability? **(26)**

27. What arguments are put forward to justify the cost of
advertising? **(27)**

28. Give examples of sales promotion methods. **(28)**

29. What is the purpose of "public relations"? **(29)**

30. What are the principles involved in the designing of packaging? **(30)**

31. Discuss the importance and characteristics of after-sales
servicing. **(31)**

32. Define credit control and state its importance. **(32, 33(a))**

33. What factors determine the length of credit offered a customer? **(33)**

34. Why and how is a customer's credit-rating established? **(34)**

35. What can be done to reduce credit risks? **(35)**

CHAPTER XIII

PERSONNEL

HUMAN RELATIONS

1. The human aspect of management. All aspects of management not only *include* management of people in the normal process of direction and delegation, but also all management *depends* upon the successful management of people. No matter how extensive mechanisation is or how sophisticated management techniques are, any business must ultimately depend upon the efforts of human beings. In turn, this must mean *relationships* between people. Failure to take account of human behaviour and attitudes must result in poor personnel management and could make management, no matter how otherwise efficient, ineffective.

2. Responsibilities for effective relationships. The establishment of relationships conducive to management efficiency requires certain attitudes from those responsible for personal relationships. The categories of those with that responsibility are as follows:

(*a*) *Top management.* It is a truism that the morale of a staff will be largely determined by those responsible for the policy and overall management of a concern. The attitude of those at the top will affect most directly those immediately below them. In turn, they will act in a similar manner to *their* subordinates and this will be extended downwards throughout the organisation. Managers who are subjected to dictatorial attitudes by their superiors, who are given unrealistic targets, and who experience no compassion, will adopt the same policies towards their subordinates—even if only out of a sense of self-preservation. At the other extreme, "slack" control at the top will reproduce the same pattern at all levels.

(*b*) *Managers and supervisors.* These have a closer

relationship with the work-force. Accordingly, they should have a more intimate understanding of those people and should therefore adopt attitudes suited to the characteristics of each person or group of persons.

(c) *Personnel officers.* These may be regarded as specialists in human relations, whereas others must practice it as an addition to their other duties. A chief accountant, for instance, must be able to manage people but his prime responsibility is elsewhere. Personnel officers, however, do not have continuous day-to-day contact with employees as do other executives. They are responsible for implementing personnel policy and therefore relate to the work-force *generally.* They are, however, responsible for *specific* and personal matters when their expertise is required. Thus, a personnel officer would meet a staff member in a face-to-face situation only when he is required to do so, e.g. to help with a problem which has a psychological cause, to offer assistance when an employee has a personal problem, and to join in settling a dispute, etc.

3. Establishing efficient human relationships. Those responsible for establishing a favourable climate for human relationships must pay regard to the following:

(a) *Human understanding.* No two persons are identical and the personality features of subordinates must be considered within that precept. To produce the best efforts from one person may require the use of different approaches than those employed for others. To give a "firm talking to" to one person may be effective, but to do so to another may be disastrous.

(b) *Recognition of motives.* People do not all have the same attitudes to their work. Some welcome responsibility, others fear it; some wish to lead, others have no such desire; some prefer routine work, others are responsive to challenge. Therefore, it is pointless to impose responsibility, leadership and initiative on those with no wish for it. People are more capable when doing the type of work they prefer to do; a clerk doing routine work effectively is more valuable than one unsuccessfully trying to cope with non-routine work.

(c) *Approach attitudes.* A manager should not make a human relationship approach with a preconceived inflexible attitude. He must be prepared to listen and to try to understand the other's attitude. For example, the work of a clerk may suffer because he is a "worrier". The manager may be incapable of understanding such a state of mind because it is completely foreign to his nature, but he must recognise that it *does* exist for the clerk. Impatience on his part would only worsen the situation.

(*d*) *Recognition of talents.* A manager should be able to identify talents in his staff in order to exploit them for the benefit of the organisation and the worker himself. Such personal attributes may show themselves as part of the worker's present duties. Thus, it may be noted that an accounting clerk is particularly proficient when his work involves analysing rather than in carrying out routine work. On the other hand, a worker may be doing a job which does not allow him to use his special talents. A sales clerk may be obviously unhappy doing desk work, but if he was allowed the freedom and individuality connected with work "in the field" he may prove to be an excellent salesman.

4. Individuality differences. The attributes of one person differing from those of another may be classified as follows:

(*a*) *Mental abilities.*
(*b*) *Emotional demands.*
(*c*) *Personality characteristics.*
(*d*) *Physical and sensory capacities.*

5. The causes of changing attitudes concerning personnel. The greatest change in management thought in recent years has been in respect of personnel attitudes in the work situation. The change has been so fundamental as to warrant the description of "social revolution". The causes of such changes may be summarised as follows:

(*a*) *Demands for higher living standards.* Improved education, lower unemployment (giving workers greater bargaining power), increased sophistication in that workers have wider horizons, demands created by advertising—all these have lead to an insistence on higher standards of living. In turn, this results in the need for higher incomes.

(*b*) *Demands for better working conditions.* These stem from the same sources. A person who has improved his home and social conditions will require a similar improvement in his work conditions.

(c) *"The dignity of labour"*. The subservient attitude of workers to "masters" has been abolished and there is a greater tendency to treat work-people as human beings instead of as ciphers.

(d) *Education.* There are now greater opportunities to rise from one class level to another because of improved education facilities. Consequently, more people from "working-class" levels can enter industry at higher levels (or rise to them within an organisation), bringing with them a better understanding of those who will work under them.

(e) *Trade unions.* Collective action by trade unions provides the strength to make possible improved conditions and attitudes.

(f) *Employer attitudes.* There is an increasing tendency for employers to recognise the inevitability and justice of changing demands by employees.

6. The results of changing attitudes. In addition to the consequences mentioned above, there are others such as the following:

(a) *Emphasis on youth.*

(i) There is a demand for *increased earning power* to be achieved at an earlier age. Thus, there has been a considerable reduction in long apprenticeships, articles and probation periods at a low wage. Such practices were often regarded as being forms of cheap labour and youth now demands fair rewards at a much earlier age.

(ii) There is also a generally accepted policy of *giving responsibility* at an earlier age. Executives, for example, do not now always reach their peak of responsibility by staying with an employer long enough to be "carried up". The tendency is to recognise that the thrust and sheer hard work of being an executive can best be provided by comparatively young people.

(b) *Employer/employee loyalty.* In the past, rewards to employees were usually given for long service, so that an employee was promoted largely because of the years he had given his employer. The tendency today is for employers to prefer to give responsibility to those most capable of accepting it—either to those who have proved themselves within the business or to persons from outside it. In the same way, ambitious employees now openly seek opportunities beyond their present employers. Both sides recognise that the practice of staff movements *between* employers is not a form of disloyalty by either party.

(c) *Demands for consultation.* There is now an established pattern of consultation between employers and employees (or their representatives) on matters affecting employees. This has been extended to a limited degree to consultation on matters concerning the *business.* This practice will become more widespread and will eventually result in "worker directors".

7. Employee motivation. Personnel management requires an understanding of man's needs and this entails a knowledge of industrial psychology, but short of such a scientific enquiry it is possible to establish the different reasons why people work. They include the following:

(a) *Basic economic needs.* This indicates the lowest level of remuneration which is required to satisfy the basic economic needs for living.

(b) *Financial differentials.* A worker requires recognition of his worth in comparison with others and this will take the form of gradings of remuneration, possibly with the addition of non-financial benefits (*see* **8** below).

(c) *Security.* This can stem from the fear of unemployment. Other things being equal, an occupation carrying a less-than-average risk of unemployment will be that much more attractive.

(d) *Status.* This can be an important factor in some instances. The prestige attached to some positions is attractive, even though the related increase in remuneration may not be fully commensurate.

(e) *Self-expression.* A post may be attractive to some people if it carries the opportunity of projecting the occupant's personality or allows them to express themselves in their work.

(f) *Development.* This includes the acquisition of new skills within the employment, and personal advancement by promotion.

(g) *Satisfying a social need.* This relates to the opportunity of a social life which would otherwise be absent. A married woman, for example, may take a job mainly in order to meet people, the "pin-money" remuneration being a lesser consideration.

8. Job satisfaction. Linked to the motives for working is a consideration of the extent to which a job satisfies a person's desires. Because motivations differ, jobs can be allocated to meet the requirements of each person. The differences may be summarised as follows:

(a) *Routine or initiative-demanding.* A person requiring the opportunity to express himself would be unhappy in a routine job. On the other hand, some *prefer* routine work. When considering the "evils" of mindless production-belt work, for example, it must be recognised that some *prefer* the type of work which calls for little or no thought.

(b) *Work-groups.* Human nature demands the congregating of people in cohesive groups. Most, therefore, welcome the circumstances whereby they work in groups, such as in a department, an assembly group, a gang, etc. It has been suggested that the low morale of those working on assembly lines is partly due to the lack of social contact. A minority of people are true individualists and may find most satisfaction in "loner" jobs, such as outside representatives.

(c) *Sense of achievement.* Many people prefer to see an end-product to their work. They like to know why they are doing a job and wish to know what they have attained. Others are content to work the stipulated hours and to give no more thought to the matter.

(d) *Authority.* Some welcome authority, whereas others would prefer to reject it. This may be linked to the desire for prestige, but not necessarily so.

9. Management contributions to motivation. Recognition of the motivation of employees and of changing social attitudes (partly imposed by pressure from trade unions and legislation), requires reciprocal policies by management.

(a) *Fair remuneration.* This includes not only basic remuneration but also adequate rewards for responsibility, efficiency, expertise and, in the case of production workers, output.

(b) *Other financial rewards.* These include such things as pension schemes, profit-sharing schemes, etc.

(c) *Security.* The extent to which this can be promised will depend upon the nature of the business and economic conditions, but a reputation for fair dealing would be an advantage.

(*d*) *Participation* can include discussion and, possibly, decision-making by employees with superiors at all levels, e.g. mechanics/foremen, middle managers/top managers, shopfloor representatives/top management.

(*e*) *Recognition.* A policy of recognising contributions by employees should permeate the organisation. This reward may be directly financial or take the form of promotion or there may be no tangible reward. The important factor is an atmosphere of relationships which affords appreciation.

(*f*) *Working conditions and facilities.* Obviously, these must meet the requirements of legislation, but legal requirements should be regarded as the minimum.

(*g*) *Communications.* A group will work better if there is adequate communication between the different levels. A two-way flow of information and viewpoints makes for better understanding and less suspicion. Relationships will be improved when management, by means of communication, displays an attitude of "openness".

THE PERSONNEL DEPARTMENT

10. The scope. The scope of a personnel department varies considerably between organisations. The vital factor is that the department must be intimately involved with *every* aspect of management. The planning of production, of sales, etc., is impossible without taking account of the fact that it must involve *people*. Therefore, plans have to be made concerning the number, type, cost and environment of workers. Attitudes to workers and the mechanics of relationships are also of concern to general management.

The department could be involved with management generally in the following areas:

(*a*) *Corporate planning.* The department's function would be to participate in establishing policies and objectives to the extent that they would involve personnel.

(*b*) *Organisation.* Constant review of the organisation structure will raise problems concerning promotions, transfers, job contents, reorganisation of procedures, etc.

(*c*) *Staff development.* This will include training schemes, promotion policies, staff appraisals, etc., and will thus affect every aspect of the organisation.

(*d*) *Manpower planning.* Manpower planning is largely

concerned with forecasting and budgeting for labour requirements. It will include recruitment, training, redundancies,
promotions, transfers, etc.

(e) *Remuneration.* This will be considered in costing and
planning exercises. It will include the establishment of wage
and salary structures, job evaluation and grading, merit
rating, productivity schemes, etc.

(f) *Employee relationships.* Concerned with trade-union
negotiations, staff consultations, legal requirements, working
conditions, etc., employee relationships therefore relate to all
aspects of management.

11. The personnel officer. As has already been stated, good
personnel policies and attitudes must be exercised at all levels
of management and to that extent every manager is concerned
with personnel work. The appointment of a personnel officer
to head a personnel department does not, however, reduce the
scope of other managers. His importance derives from the
following factors:

(a) *Specialisation.* The personnel officer is a specialist.
Unlike other managers, he is *solely* concerned with personnel
work and should therefore be more efficient. He does not,
however, detract from the *personal* relationship between
each manager and his subordinates.

(b) *Co-ordinated policies.* The personnel officer has the
ability to operate a policy which is common throughout the
organisation. For example, there would be a standard
policy concerning conditions of service.

(c) *Unity of control.* The personnel officer can speak on
behalf of management generally when negotiating with trade
unions, when propounding personnel policies, etc.

(d) *Impartiality.* The services of the department would be
available to any worker, so that any friction between an
employee and a superior would not prevent an attempt to
solve a personal problem.

(e) *Staff services.* Such staff services as education opportunities, welfare, etc., would be centralised and available
generally.

(f) *Expertise.* The personnel officer would have the
services of such experts as psychologists, state welfare
bodies, legal advisers, etc.

(g) *Access to top management.* Being separate from, but

related to, all the other departments, the personnel officer is recognised as being a specialist, but who is nevertheless concerned with every aspect of the business. He therefore has direct contact with top management.

(h) *Records and statistics.* The department should maintain extensive records of staff and be able to provide management with statistics relevant not only to the business but also those published by Government departments, trade associations, etc. Thus centralisation would facilitate the provision of essential data.

12. The authority of the personnel officer. This will depend upon the size of the organisation. It will also depend on the scope given him and the degree of recognition afforded him by top management. Management is sometimes suspicious of personnel officers, and line managers frequently feel that the personnel officer is "interfering" with their staff relationships.

As he is part of management, he provides the link with staff. There may be occasions when he finds himself speaking *for* staff. (A personnel officer who sympathises with a strike is in an obviously difficult personal position!) Against this, there will often be suspicions by the work-force that he is a "bosses' man".

PERSONNEL POLICY

13. Policy formation. The personnel policy should be laid down by top management but should be the result of consulting with, or taking account of, the following:

(a) *The personnel officer should play a prominent part,* and recognition of his specialism should be given.

(b) *Trade-union attitudes* may derive from the known attitudes of the unions or may be put directly to management by union officials or shop stewards.

(c) *Consultative bodies of staff,* such as works councils, staff associations, etc, should be taken into account.

(d) *Trade associations' guide lines* and any national agreements made with trade unions should be considered.

(e) *Government directives* and known attitudes must be acknowledged.

14. The objectives of personnel policies. These may generally be regarded as being related to the following:

(a) *Wage and salary structures.* These must be related to local market rates, include provision for the calculation of differentials and bonus pay, and provide for regular reviews, including the establishment of the necessary negotiating machinery.

(b) *Disputes procedure.* A system must be established for investigating disputes at the earliest possible stage, the parties to be involved, and the action procedure.

(c) *Recruitment.* General principles will be agreed, but specific principles will be determined as part of manpower planning as circumstances dictate.

(d) *Education and training.* This will include schemes for in-firm training and for any facilities offered for education outside the organisation.

(e) *Channels of communication.* Communication upward and downward must be established to provide a quick and effective flow of information and observation.

(f) *Promotions and transfers.* The system for making decisions must allow for consultations and appeals.

(g) *Staff appraisals.* This would establish the method of staff assessment and its connection with promotion and remuneration.

(h) *Redundancies.* A policy would normally be established only if and when redundancies became necessary, but there must be prior agreement as to the extent of consultation with employee representatives.

(i) *Implementation of the policy.* Implementation would be the overall responsibility of the personnel officer but with all levels of management conforming.

(j) *Welfare.* This would include "fringe benefits" of various sorts and commonly available services. The extent, form and cost of these must be agreed.

(k) *Health and safety.* Responsibility will be placed on specified persons to ensure that at least the legal requirements are met.

(l) *Participation.* The extent and form of staff participation must be decided. This would involve building a structure of committees with rules about membership, voting, powers, etc.

(m) *Legal requirements.* Decisions must be made concerning the consequences of legislation relevant to sex- and race-discrimination, the employment of disabled persons, etc.

(*n*) *Reviews.* Agreement must be reached concerning the procedure for reviewing personnel policy as a continuous process. Changing circumstances and forward planning make it necessary for the policy to be subject to possible revision. The parties to be consulted should be agreed at the outset.

MANPOWER PLANNING

15. Objectives. The broad purpose of manpower planning is to forecast the number of employees which will be required, classifying the amount into *types* and *levels* of labour.

As with all forms of forecasting, accuracy is very difficult because of the numerous unpredictable factors which can upset calculations. Any forecast must take account of the following.

(*a*) *Analysis of current manpower (see* **16** below).

(*b*) *Total labour force required in the future,* with reference to:

(*i*) the extent and type of anticipated production;
(*ii*) any changes in methods affecting labour content.

(*c*) *Future withdrawals of labour,* such as resignations, retirements, etc.

(*d*) *Changes in the composition of the labour force,* because of promotions, etc., and changes in the organisation structure.

(*e*) *Labour availability.* This requires study of trends concerning population, migration, education, etc. It must take into account particularly the area of operation, e.g. there may be a shortage locally of the particular type of labour required, such as unskilled female workers. There will be different influencing factors between managerial, technical, clerical and unskilled labour.

16. Analysis of current manpower. The first stage is to analyse the present labour force to show where there is likely to be a shortfall or a surplus of labour of various types. This can then be related to the future demands for those types. Major methods which can be adopted will show:

(*a*) *age groups.* Thus it can be seen how many are approaching retirement and the number nearing adult status;

(*b*) *skills groups.* This will indicate a shortage or surplus according to occupations and degrees of skill within occupations;

(c) *levels groups.* This classifies each skill into levels of workers. It may show, for example, an excessive or insufficient number of foremen. This classification method must take account of *training and future promotions.*

17. Analysis of manpower utilisation. In addition to providing information as in **16** above, analysis should indicate other relationships which could be used for planning and as a contribution to increased efficiency. It could, for example:

(a) relate direct labour to indirect labour;

(b) establish ratios between production labour, supervisory labour and administrative labour;

(c) analyse the cost of overtime between departments, functions, products, etc.;

(d) determine the labour costs of maintenance and repairs;

(e) assess the effect of production peaks and troughs on the requirement for labour;

(f) determine the effect on production of piece rates, bonus schemes, etc.

18. Cost/effectiveness of labour. A fairly accurate relationship can be established between the cost of direct labour and output. Ancillary production labour, such as maintenance staff, whilst not being in direct proportion to output, can nevertheless be related to it.

Such constraints are not so rigid, however, in assessing the cost of non-production labour to earning capacity. Unless control is imposed, administration staff can grow beyond a justifiable size. This state of affairs can arise from increased specialisation by functional managers, whereby expansion results in the splitting of functional areas. The consequent increase of functional staffs, if unchecked, can justify what is generally known as *"Parkinson's Law"*, which states that "work tends to expand to fill the time available for its completion".

19. Job analysis. This is a study and statement of the facts relevant to a job. The objectives are as follows:

(a) *To make recruitment more efficient.* In seeking new staff, the first essential is to decide what the recruit would be required to do and what personal attributes he would need to have. Analysing the job will make possible the selection of persons *to suit the job,* and not vice versa.

(*b*) *To relate it to job evaluation* for the purpose of fixing remuneration and determining promotion.

(*c*) *To plan training* to meet the requirements of particular jobs.

There is some lack of uniformity in the use of terms; relevant titles used include the following:

(*d*) *Job description.* This should be a broad statement of the purpose, duties and responsibilities of a job.

(*e*) *Job specification.* This should be a detailed statement of the physical and mental activities in a job.

20. Factors in a job analysis. These include:

(*a*) *identification*—name or title of the job, location (department, branch, etc.);

(*b*) *summary*—basic duties, operations and procedures;

(*c*) *responsibility*—level and extent, subordinates and superiors, relationship with other jobs or areas;

(*d*) *physical aspects*—physical demands, dexterity required, repetitive or varied, indoors or outside;

(*e*) *training required;*

(*f*) *employment conditions*—the hours of work, remuneration, employee services available.

SELECTION

21. Sources of recruitment. These vary according to the type of labour required and will include the following:

(*a*) *Government agencies,* including specialist agencies for scientific, technical and managerial staffs.

(*b*) *Staff agencies,* mainly for clerical workers.

(*c*) *Staff selection bureaux* for "top jobs" (often known as "head hunters").

(*d*) *Professional bodies* for staff with professional qualifications.

(*e*) *Schools, colleges and universities* at which large employers mount exhibitions and arrange interview centres (commonly known as "the milk round").

(*f*) *Advertisements* in the local, national and trade press.

(*g*) *Introductions* by present staff members.

22. Recruitment v. promotion. When a vacancy occurs, a choice may have to be made between promoting a present staff member and recruiting from outside the organisation. Factors influencing such a choice may include the following:

(*a*) *Staff morale.* This will suffer if company policy appears to favour unduly the introduction of new people instead of promoting existing personnel.

(*b*) *Availability of the specialism.* If the new position is one which no present member has the ability to fill, the choice is obvious. For example, the introduction of a computer centre will inevitably entail recruiting computer staff.

(*c*) *Leadership qualities.* An existing member may have the operational ability required for the position but may have shown inability to lead. It would therefore be unwise to promote him to a position he could not adequately fill.

(*d*) *"The new broom".* A recruit to a managerial position may bring in new ideas and methods which would benefit the company. A promoted member may have too narrow an experience because it has been confined to the same business. Thus old ideas may be perpetuated and rigidity may ensue as a result of "in-breeding". Against this may be set the possible dangers of too dynamic a newcomer who upsets traditions which are, in fact, beneficial to the company.

(*e*) *The employee as a "known factor".* A present employee is known to management because of his record and character. A recruit is something of an unknown factor and may display traits which were not apparent when he was interviewed.

23. Inviting applications. The advertisement or whatever other method is used, should give sufficient information to indicate the nature of the job. If loosely worded, it can result in few applying because of its vagueness; or (more probably) a lot of people applying who are obviously unsuitable. The latter would waste the time of both applicants and employer.

Some indication of salary should normally be given. An employer who waits to see what applicants ask for is obviously seeking cheap and, possibly, inferior labour.

24. The application. This may be by:

(*a*) *letter.* This method has the advantage that the applicant can express himself in his own words and be thus more indicative than the answering of questions;

(*b*) *application form.* This has the advantages of:

(*i*) compelling the applicant to answer questions. Thus he cannot avoid disclosing what may be detrimental information;

(*ii*) clarity and uniformity. The layout clearly indicates the data required. Comparisons of specific data between different forms is facilitated;

(*iii*) some latitude for self-expression (*see* (*a*) above) can be given by including an area in which the applicant is required to give his own views on, for example, why he considers he is suitable for the position.

25. Application form layout.

(*a*) *Information required* usually includes:

(*i*) personal details—name, address, age, sex, marital status, etc.;

(*ii*) history of education and positions held;

(*iii*) qualifications and experience.

(*b*) *Clarity and practicality.* The form must:

(*i*) be neatly laid out;

(*ii*) be clearly indicative of the information required (guidelines may appear on another document or on the form);

(*iii*) provide adequate space for answers with the invitation to use a continuation sheet if required;

(*iv*) include provision for writing a reference or quoting a referee.

(*v*) indicate to whom it is to be returned and by what date.

(*c*) *Different forms.* Different forms should be required for different types of labour (unskilled, technical, clerical, managerial, etc.), because each will call for different sorts of information.

26. Selection for interview. Applications are first sorted by rejecting those obviously unsuitable. The remainder will be studied by the departmental manager concerned and probably by the personnel officer, and these will be reduced as a result of discussion. Unsuccessful applicants should be advised accordingly.

27. Interviewing. This is the vital and most difficult stage. Interviewing is an art and comparatively few people are fully proficient at it. An interview must necessarily be an "artificial occasion" and the opinions gained from it are not always proved correct. A poor candidate who "interviews well" may be preferred against a better candidate who does not do himself justice. The objective of the interviewer is to make a fair judgment in an unreal situation.

The following factors are necessary for a successful interview:

(a) *The panel*. This should include the person who will be the successful applicant's superior. He knows what the job demands and he will have to work closely with the recruit. The meeting may be chaired by the personnel officer or he may be present to support another chairman. The composition of the board will depend upon the nature of the job. In some cases there may be a sole interviewer but, in general, this is inadvisable.

(b) *Preparation*. The interviewer must be very clear as to the demands of the job, which should be set out in the job analysis (*see* **19**(a) above). He must *previously* have studied the application and not ask questions which have already been given in the form or letter.

(c) *Organisation*. Arrangements must be made to receive the applicants and to accommodate them comfortably. The interviews should be timetabled so that unnecessary waiting is avoided and, if possible, so that applicants do not meet each other.

(d) *Conducting the interview*. The main objective should be to avoid an impression of "interrogation". The applicant should be "drawn out" so that he can express himself (and thereby display his character more fully), rather than be required to give short answers to a series of questions.

Informality should be achieved as far as possible. Sitting an applicant in an isolated chair facing a line of interviewers would be daunting and would achieve no true results.

Interviewers should not make notes in an obvious manner; the sight of someone compiling a "score sheet" can be very disturbing.

The interviewee should be encouraged to ask questions. It must be remembered that *he* wishes to be assured about the future as do the interviewers.

(e) *Evaluation and result*. Interviewers should make notes immediately the interview is over while their impressions are still fresh in their minds. A discussion amongst themselves should result in a consensus of opinion. If there is more than one candidate, the timetabling should allow for this period.

Unsuccessful candidates should be informed immediately and privately—probably by the personnel officer.

The chosen candidate will be interviewed again, by the whole panel or perhaps one of them, and details about the commencing date, etc., will then be settled.

28. Selection tests. These may be used in conjunction with interviewing and include the following:

(a) *Intelligence tests.* There is controversy as to the value of intelligence tests. Because of their nature, they are compiled by various specialist institutions, but it is vital that the sort of test used is one *relevant to the job.* A test which gives a general I.Q. rating will probably be irrelevant to the particular requirements of the job.

(b) *Ability tests.* These are practical tests directly relevant to the job, e.g. a piece of typing for a prospective typist.

(c) *Aptitude tests.* These test aptitudes specifically required for the job, e.g. alphabetical sorting for filing clerks, mathematical tests of a particular kind for trainee computer programmers, dexterity tests for some technical work.

29. References. These can be obtained from previous employers and schools (references from friends and acquaintances are generally useless and rarely asked for).

They should be treated with reservation, because they are subject to the inadequacies of human judgment. Personal bias, for or against, may detract from accuracy. They are frequently not entirely truthful—either because the referee wishes to "be kind" or he is vindictive, or because of faulty memory (also, an employer may give an unenthusiastic reference in order to retain a good employee—and the reverse can apply!).

There is no legal requirement to give references. References are "privileged communications" as regards charges of defamation. (The giving of "testimonials" to those leaving a job is an outdated practice.)

30. Engagement agreements. A successful interview should be followed by a formal letter of confirmation setting out the details of the employment as agreed at the interview.

Senior officials may enter into a *service contract* which will include information such as the following:

(*a*) Identification of the parties (both must sign).

(*b*) Nature of the duties.

(*c*) Period of the engagement (if for a determined period).

(*d*) Commencing salary, salary scale or increments, commission, bonuses, etc.

(*e*) Place of employment (and, possibly, an agreement to work elsewhere if required).

(*f*) Payments in respect of illness, holidays, etc.

(*g*) Pension rights (if any).

(*h*) Staff facilities.

(*i*) Amount of notice to be given by either side.

(*j*) Circumstances leading to dismissal.

(*k*) Any special clauses concerning disclosure of company information, inventions made in the employer's time, freelance work, etc.

31. Contracts of Employment Act: 1972. This Act relates to *evidence* of employment conditions, which is not a contract in itself. The requirements of the Act do not have to be met if all the information required by the Act is contained in a service contract.

It does not apply to persons normally working less than twenty-one hours a week.

(*a*) Within thirteen weeks of commencing an employment, an employer must give the employee written particulars stating the parties, date of commencement, remuneration and intervals of payment, the terms and conditions relating to the hours of work, holidays and holiday pay, sick pay, the length of notice the employee must give and is entitled to receive to terminate his employment.

(*b*) The Act applies to all employees, whether their contract is in writing, oral or implied.

(*c*) The minimum period of notice to be given by an employer is:

(*i*) not less than one week, if the period of continuous employment is twenty-six weeks or more;

(*ii*) not less than two week's notice if the period of continuous employment is two years or more;

(*iii*) not less than four week's notice if the period of continuous employment is five years or more.

TRAINING AND PROMOTION

32. Objectives. The major objectives of a training and promotion policy are to:

(*a*) provide the skills, knowledge and aptitudes necessary to undertake required jobs efficiently;

(*b*) develop the worker so that if he has the potential he may progress;

(*c*) facilitate the introduction of new methods;

(*d*) provide for succession so that replacement workers will be available;

(*e*) increase efficiency by reducing spoilt work, misuse of machines, etc. and by lessening physical risks;

(*f*) improve morale;

(*g*) attract recruits;

(*h*) develop supervisors and managers.

33. Induction training. This is not training in the usual sense of the word but is a method of "introducing" new workers. In a large concern, it would be programmed to include talks giving a brief history of the business, its operations and its organisation structure. The regulations concerning safety, etc., would be explained as well as the staff rules concerning discipline, sickness payments, holidays, methods of pay, etc. The staff facilities about pensions, recreation, etc., would be explained. The new member would be introduced to his department and perhaps given a tour to include other areas of the organisation.

The objective is to welcome the newcomer, to project the company's image as an employer and to reach a mutual understanding about staff/management relationships.

34. Job training. Job training aims to teach the technical content of a job. It consists of the job being demonstrated and then undertaken by the trainee (often in stages) under supervision. This may be supplemented by:

(*a*) *training manuals.* These are expertly written documents, clearly showing the stages in a work process. They are used by the learner *and* the instructor. Because of the expertise employed in compiling it, a manual gives a far more efficient method of training than merely "sitting next to Nellie";

(b) *programmed learning.* This is a method whereby an operator learns by stages in following written instructions. It is done by ending every stage of teaching with a question. Giving the correct answer allows the trainee to move to the next stage; a wrong answer will divert him to a re-learning stage. This is a method of self-instruction and allows the learner to progress at his own speed. It is particularly useful where the job consists of stages and where there are alternative routes. For example, repairing electrical apparatus will require a series of operations to discover where the fault is; subsequent stages would depend on the nature of the fault identified.

35. Supervisory training. A person chosen for training as a supervisor must not only have the technical skill for the job (which he would already have demonstrated) but also the *personal attitudes* necessary. The chosen person must show he has the ability to:

(a) lead (and not drive);

(b) maintain firm, but friendly, relationships with subordinates;

(c) communicate with upper levels of management.

Internal courses will be used to explain the procedures with which the supervisor will be concerned; to involve him in various levels of participation. A large employer may be able to provide training in management techniques (e.g. in a staff training centre).

External courses in management techniques at supervisory level are provided by colleges and private institutions.

A scheme of supervisor-training is essential to ensure continuity of management and to satisfy the ambitions of personnel.

36. Management and executive training. This can be provided by colleges, etc., with senior staff members participating in the teaching. Courses are designed specifically for the employers concerned, may involve an assignment within the business as a training exercise and may include a personal assessment by the college.

Staff colleges can provide training which is specific to the employer's management philosophy and methods.

37. Education schemes. An employer may provide assistance to staff wishing to pursue education outside the organisation. Student-members of professional bodies, for example, may be encouraged to attend day-release classes, financial assistance may be given towards correspondence courses, etc.

38. Office training. This is usually concerned with improving skills which already exist. It may take the form of raising the rating of the worker (e.g. training copy-typists to become audio-typists) or teaching the company procedures (e.g. standardisation of letter layout).

39. Staff appraisals. The most common form of staff appraisal is the submission of periodic reports on staff. The aims may be said to be to:

(*a*) assess potential for promotion;
(*b*) indicate if training is necessary;
(*c*) show if a change of duties is advisable;
(*d*) link with salary reviews.

40. Disadvantages of staff appraisals. Where such schemes are used, they can have the following disadvantages:

(*a*) It is extremely difficult to compile an appraisal form which will assess truly a staff member.

(*b*) Grading of the answers must be lacking in exactness, e.g. "Answer very good/good/average/poor to the question: 'What is his attitude to the company?'"

(*c*) Assessment by a superior must be subjective. One may be more generous than another; there may be personality differences between the assessor and the assessed; bias or prejudice may be present.

(*d*) Criticisms are mainly based on personality faults, but there can be no common agreement as to the best kind of personality. For example, can an employee be faulted if he is a "worrier", if that means he is also very conscientious?

41. Promotion. Staffing policy requires a system of *planned promotion*. Employees should be aware of the various promotion routes and the facilities available in the form of training, etc.

Promotion to supervisory and managerial posts requires candidates to have administrative ability, the aptitudes of leadership, company loyalty and the ability to withstand stress.

However, promotion should not merely be a reward for loyalty. Where such a policy does exist, it is said that a person ceases to be promoted when it appears he cannot adequately cope with his present job: "In a hierarchy, every employee tends to rise to his level of incompetence" *The Peter Principle*, Lawrence J. Peter, Souvenir Press, 1969 (*see* also **22** above).

REMUNERATION

42. Wages and salaries structures. The quantifying of reward for work must take account of the following factors:

(*a*) *National agreements.* National agreements covering an industry, between trade unions and employer representatives, will establish the basic minimum.

(*b*) *Labour market conditions.* The extent to which the required classifications of labour are available, and any necessity to compete for labour, will influence the rates above any national agreements.

(*c*) *Evaluations within the business.* This refers to a system, specific to a firm, which places a value upon each job.

43. Job evaluation. This is an exercise, often carried out with participation by employees' representatives, to relate the value of jobs to other jobs. The following points are specific to the procedure:

(*a*) *The job analysis provides the basic information* (*see* **19** above). Accordingly, the characteristics which are specific to a job and those which are common to all jobs can be determined. Thus, relativities are measured against common factors.

(*b*) *Evaluation does not refer to the person performing the job.* The evaluation is of the *content* of the job, but reward based on assessment of performance may be superimposed on the standard rate for the job. If reward is to vary according to performance, a system of *merit award* must be added (*see* **47** below).

44. Methods of job evaluation. These may be classified as follows:

(*a*) *Ranking systems.* These position jobs in relation to each other according to the levels of responsibilities, duties, etc., demanded, or according to the importance of jobs. It has the advantage of simplicity but can be applied only where there is an extensive similarity between jobs, i.e. those in a similar class (e.g. fitters and fitters' mates) or in a department (e.g. senior and junior accounting clerks).

(b) *Classification systems.* Firstly, grades are defined for factors which are common to various types of jobs. Comparisons are then made and the jobs placed in appropriate grades according to the differences. Thus there will be certain duties common to clerical workers at a particular level—filing, copying, etc.

(c) *Points systems.* These involve analysis and quantification. The job analyses will indicate the requirements specific to each job; the points system entails measurement of the relative value of those demands. The maximum value of each factor is determined in advance. Each job is then analysed to determine its valuation within the context of the job. Factors to be measured may be the skill required, the responsibility and the job conditions, etc.

(d) *Factor comparison.* This is based on the points system. Key jobs are selected as points of reference for grading the others. The pay rates for the key jobs are examined and analysed to show the pay award for each factor within the key jobs. The extent to which each of these factors is present in each of the other jobs is determined and a financial award made according to its relationship with the reward given for the same factor in the key jobs.

45. Advantages of job evaluation.

(a) It is directly related to job analysis and therefore reward is based on job content.

(b) It is systematic and provides a method of measurement.

(c) It can result from agreement between employees and employers.

46. Disadvantages of job evaluation.

(a) Each worker in a category receives the same reward unless merit awards are used.

(b) The relative worth of different factors is impossible to determine with complete accuracy.

(c) It ignores the fact that remuneration is largely determined by conditions in the labour market.

(*d*) It may be too complicated and subjective to be understood by employees and may arouse suspicions about the employer's motives.

47. Merit awards. An employer may offer rates higher than those generally available (or the possibility of future higher rates) in order to:

(*a*) recruit a higher standard of worker;
(*b*) boost production by linking pay to output;
(*c*) reward outstanding performances by individuals;
(*d*) attract labour away from competitors for labour.

This may be done by *merit rating*, involving extra payment for exceptional qualities in an individual, based on personal assessment. Being based on a system of staff appraisal, it has all the disadvantages of that system (*see* **40** above). Such a system is more commonly used in promotion schemes.

Bonus schemes may also be used, related to individual or collective output (*see* **48** below).

48. Remuneration systems.

(*a*) *Time rates.* This entails payment of a stated amount for a stipulated period of working time. Work beyond a standard working day may be paid at "overtime" rates. It is mainly applicable where output cannot be directly related to wage-cost, or where the emphasis is on quality rather than quantity.

(*b*) *Straight piece-work.* Payment is made according to the output, measured in units of an acceptable quality.

(*c*) *Bonus schemes.* There are many such schemes in operation but, basically, they provide greater rewards for output above a certain agreed level. They may be based on individual output or on the output of a group.

(*d*) *Collective bonus schemes.* These provide workers generally with bonuses based on a number of factors, e.g. increased output, reduced labour costs, etc. They have the disadvantage of remoteness, i.e. a worker feels that he personally can have little influence on the determining factors.

(*e*) *Indirect incentives.* Workers not directly engaged in production and who therefore cannot derive financial rewards based on output, may receive bonuses based on company profits. They are not strictly incentives because:

(*i*) bonuses are usually shared according to staff status and length of service, which may not equate with the contribution made by each member;

(*ii*) profits are largely affected by external factors over which staff have no control, e.g. economic conditions, competition, etc.

(*f*) *Fringe benefits.* These are available to staff and may be regarded as additions to wages and salaries.

(*i*) Direct benefits may include profit-sharing, sick pay, pension schemes, etc.

(*ii*) Indirect benefits may include welfare amenities, social and recreational facilities, etc.

(*g*) *Commission and target bonuses.* These mainly refer to sales and are based on the total or the amount above a certain figure. They may be personal to the salesman concerned or may be general to a group, e.g. a bonus for a sales division exceeding a target figure.

49. Advantages and disadvantages of incentive bonus schemes related to output.

(*a*) *Advantages.*

(*i*) The increased labour cost should be less than the production cost per unit as reduced by increased output.

(*ii*) It provides incentives for workers.

(*iii*) It rewards the most efficient workers.

(*iv*) It ensures co-operation of workers in group bonus schemes.

(*v*) Less supervision should be required.

(*b*) *Disadvantages.*

(*i*) Workers are penalised when production flow is irregular or subject to breakdowns.

(*ii*) Rate-fixing is usually a subject of contention.

(*iii*) A remunerative production rate may make unreasonable demands on workers.

(*iv*) Quality may suffer. More inspectors may be required. An over-strict quality control may lead to disputes.

(*v*) Suspicion will be aroused in workers if the scheme is too complicated.

(*vi*) There may be arguments as to what constitutes the basic output on which bonus rates are mounted.

(*vii*) The effective wage-benefit may be disproportionately reduced by taxation.

LABOUR WITHDRAWALS (OR SEPARATIONS)

50. Definition. Withdrawals (or separations) refer to all forms of subtraction from the labour force in the form of resignations, dismissals, deaths and retirements.

51. Labour turnover (LTO). This refers to relating the number of employees leaving during a period of time to the average number of employees during that period. Account may be taken of "unavoidable separations" in the form of those retiring or dying. The resulting figure is expressed as a percentage:

$$\frac{\text{Number leaving during the period (excluding unavoidable separations)}}{\text{Average number employed during the period}} \times 100$$

52. Analysis of LTO. Maintenance of records for compiling labour turnover is important for the following reasons:

(a) *Indicator of morale.* The figure indicates the state of staff morale. An unduly high rate must be largely due to common factors, such as poor wage rates, unsatisfactory working conditions, poor relationships with management, etc.

(b) *Acceptable rates.* A certain amount of "natural wastage" is inevitable and assessment of the figure must allow for it. A firm employing a large number of women workers, for example, must expect a comparatively high rate of withdrawals.

(c) *Analysis into labour areas.* This may indicate regions where the problem is particularly acute.

(d) *Trends are more important than isolated figures.* A monthly index, for example, which moves around the acceptable figure would give no cause for concern, but a rising figure would demand investigation.

(e) *The cost of a high LTO can be considerable.* Training periods are usually uneconomic for employers and there can therefore be large sums spent on employees who do not stay long enough to produce compensating output. Other costs may include spoilt work and all the expenses (including administration) of recruitment and selection.

(f) *Disturbance of the labour pattern.*

(*i*) Work groups would be broken by persons leaving.

(*ii*) There may be staff gaps until replacements are received.

(*iii*) Supervision and training is made more difficult.

(*iv*) Staff morale may be affected.

53. Reducing labour turnover. An LTO exercise is pointless unless it is used to analyse the reasons why staff leave. Methods to determine the factors could include the following:

(*a*) *Interviewing leavers to ask why they are leaving.* Those departing for unavoidable reasons would probably give a true answer but others may not. A person who has quarrelled with a superior may or may not say so; one generally dissatisfied may either give vent to an outburst which would be quite uninformative or he may simply refuse to discuss it.

(*b*) *Works councils.* The validity of complaints made in works councils may be proved by examples of those leaving.

(*c*) *Supervisors and managers.* These people may advise management of the feelings of the staff on certain common matters.

(*d*) *Attitude surveys.* These may be carried out periodically amongst existing staff. Lists of questions about various aspects of company policy are answered by staff, the answers sometimes being given on a points system. The responses must be secret so that staff may answer unreservedly. The method has the considerable advantage of indicating areas of dissatisfaction *before* staff leave.

54. Redundancies. This unhappy necessity arises when staff have to be discharged as being superfluous because of a decline in trading or as part of a rationalisation scheme. The following factors must be considered:

(*a*) *Selection of areas.* Some areas will be affected more than others. It is essential that no area be reduced below a level where it will be inadequate in the new circumstances.

(*b*) *Selecting categories of workers.* Some scheme must be worked out to determine the deciding factors in choosing between those in an area to be reduced. It may be decided, for example, to favour the longer-serving members but to also retire some early.

(*c*) *Ensuring continuity.* The plan must allow for a policy of future promotions in the new reduced work-force.

(*d*) *Anticipation of redundancies.* This will allow for amended programmes concerning recruitment and training.

(*e*) *Early notification to workers.* Early warning will reduce anxiety and misunderstanding.

(*f*) *Participation in redundancy planning is essential.* Staff must be allowed to put their views and join in compiling a scheme.

(*g*) *"Natural wastage".* Those due for retirement and the proportion which it is known would normally leave must be allowed for.

(*h*) *Voluntary redundancies.* These should be encouraged.

55. Redundancy Payments Act 1965. This Act ensures financial compensation for those made redundant. It relates to men between the ages of 20 and 65 and women up to 60 years of age who have been in the relevant employment for two years. The rates are summarised as follows:

Up to 21 *years of age,* one-half week's pay for each year of service.

22–40 *years of age,* one week's pay for each year of service.

Over 40 *years of age,* one-and-a-half week's pay for each year of service.

NOTE: Service over 20 years and earnings above £40 weekly are not taken into account.

Part of the cost is recoverable by employers from a fund built up by their national insurance contributions.

EMPLOYEE RELATIONS

56. Discipline. Rules for ensuring adherence to a code of conduct must be *fair* and be *shown to be fair*. Effective discipline must, therefore, entail recognition of the following factors:

(*a*) *Communication.*

(*i*) The rules must be *made known*, preferably in the induction period although reminders may be issued from time to time, e.g. when time-keeping generally is becoming slack.

(*ii*) The rules must be *understandable*.

(*b*) *Co-operation.* A degree of co-operation by consultation can contribute to good morale. Any overbearing attitude in imposing penalties would be counter-productive.

(c) *Fairness and immediacy.* Discipline should be imposed without favouritism, be reasonable and applied without undue delay.

(d) *Authority.* It must be established who has authority to discipline and the extent of that authority.

(e) *Procedure.* There must be a procedure for referring specified stages of disciplinary action to higher levels and for making of appeals. Provisions must also be made for representation of the worker if he requires it.

(f) *Effective leadership.* This will reduce the necessity for an undue amount of disciplining.

(g) *Management should not itself break rules.*

57. Offences and penalties. It is not possible to generalise about the relationship between stated offences and specific penalties. It will differ between types of organisation, personnel policies and the particular circumstances of the offence.

(a) *Reprimands* (with or without noting the employee's personal record) may be suitable for such offences as occasional bad time-keeping, time wasting, undue spoilage, disobeying safety regulations, etc.

(b) *Suspension* would be for more serious offences, such as pilfering, wilful disobedience, malicious damage, foolish actions endangering life or property, misappropriation of funds, etc.

(c) *Dismissal* is a final resort and should preferably be preceded by suspension. To do so would allow time for appeals and further consideration. It may also avoid industrial action which may follow precipitate dismissal.

58. Trade Unions. These play a major part in employee relationships in most organisations and now extend beyond purely industrial areas. The broad aims of the movement are to:

(a) improve rates of remuneration;
(b) improve working conditions;
(c) raise the status of workers;
(d) protect members against unfair practices;
(e) strive for security of employment;
(f) take concerted action when necessary;
(g) be involved in consultation on matters affecting labour;
(h) improve fringe benefits;

(*i*) obtain facilities to meet members on the employers' premises;

(*j*) sponsor legislation relevant to labour.

59. Disputes procedures. Formal procedures for settling disputes exist in most organisations, influenced partly at least by agreements with trade unions.

The usual rule is for the employee concerned to take up the matter with his immediate superior. The subsequent stages will depend upon the procedure, but in the case of union members a shop steward would be personally involved at an early stage.

The personnel officer or labour relations officer would frequently not be involved at the early stages (if involved at all) but in some circumstances (such as the possibility of a major dispute developing) they would be involved almost at the beginning.

60. Shop stewards. Shop stewards are union representatives of workers and appointed by them. They are employees and not paid officials of the unions. They have close contact with workers and, generally, immediate access to management. Understanding reached between management and shop stewards is therefore essential for the promotion of good industrial relations. They constitute the first link in the chain of negotiation.

61. Collective bargaining. This is a comprehensive phrase meaning the method of settling the terms of employment between union representatives and employers. It first establishes recognition of the union and its right to negotiate. Thus the range of matters which can be negotiated (pay rates, working conditions, discipline, etc.) are determined and, also, a structure for negotiation is established. (Relative legislation is in the *Trade Union and Labour Relations Act* 1974.)

62. Joint consultation. Joint consultation between representatives of employees and of employers features to a larger extent than ever before, and does so at an increasing pace. It follows the recognition of the right of workers to be consulted and, indeed, to partake in decisions which affect them in their employment. It can range from discussing minor problems on the shop floor to employee representatives attending directors' meetings.

It is not intended to be merely a form of grievance procedure but a genuine working together to solve problems of mutual importance. The essential is the true acknowledgment by management of workers' rights to be consulted and to recognise the value of their contributions. Workers, on the other hand, must recognise the expertise which management has and which they have not; they must be willing to learn; they must appreciate the possible *ultimate* consequences of any action beyond the *immediate* consequences it may have for them.

Participation is part of a developing social philosophy and much "class prejudice" must disappear before it is successful. However, there is a growing understanding of the problems and attitudes of the "other side" and recognition that co-operation is essential.

WELFARE, HEALTH AND SAFETY

63. Welfare. Sundry legislation lays down minimum requirements concerning staff conditions and amenities, but most employers offer services beyond those levels. The reason for doing so are the:

(a) *demands for higher living standards.* People require an ever-increasing standard of comfort, hygiene, etc., and this must be reflected in working conditions;

(b) *competition for labour.* The offered level of staff facilities often afford sufficient inducement for workers to prefer one prospective employer to others;

(c) *contribution to efficiency.* Studies have indicated that a pleasant environment results in increased efficiency and contributes to good staff morale;

(d) *effect on staff health.* If conditions are such as to reduce the incidence of ill-health, absenteeism is reduced;

(e) *employers' recognition of their social responsibility.*

64. Employee facilities. These may be broadly classified as:

(a) *the provision of favourable working conditions;*

(b) *welfare services,* such as crèches for working mothers, health services, social counsellors, transport, etc.;

(c) *fringe benefits,* such as assistance with housing and

education, discounts on company products, holiday homes, subsidised canteens, pensions, etc.

65. The welfare department. The scope of duties and the number of officers will depend upon the size and the policy of the organisation but the department would be a sub-division of the personnel department. Its officers may include:

(a) *counsellors.* These should be trained social workers and would deal with the personal problems of employees. They would be particularly valuable where there is a large number of women workers. They would have access to the services (usually from outside the business) of psychologists, solicitors, etc.;

(b) *medical officers.* Nurses would always be available and doctors' clinics may be held at specified times;

(c) *sports and recreation officers;*

(d) *house officers.* These would be responsible for amenities within the building, such as a library, social rooms, etc.

66. Safety and health. General standards relevant to safety and health have long been prescribed in legislation relevant to factories and offices. *The Health and Safety at Work, etc. Act* 1974 extends those provisions in respect of employers' responsibilities to their employees and to the avoidance of risk to the public.

Legislation concerning health covers such matters as cleanliness, overcrowding, ventilation and heating, and sanitation. Safety regulations relate to the fencing of machinery, protection from dust and fumes, fire precautions, instruction of machine operators, provision of first aid facilities, working hours for women and young people, etc.

Procedures are laid down for reporting and investigating accidents.

67. Works safety officer. His duties will include:

(a) training employees in accident prevention;

(b) routine inspection of plant, buildings, etc.;

(c) prescribing and ensuring the use of protective clothing;

(d) creating an awareness of safety precautions by means of lectures, displays, etc.;

(e) advising on safety aspects in site layouts, ordering machinery, working conditions, etc.;

(*f*) reporting and investigating accidents, advising management about improvements, compiling accident statistics.

RECORDS AND STATISTICS

68. Personal records. A file would be kept for each employee on the permanent staff. It would commence with the original application form and be followed by a history card showing the positions held, the departments and, possibly, pay rates. Reports such as personal assessments, medical checks, attendance records, etc., would be filed as well as any relevant correspondence and interview summaries.

Separate and specially designed records should be kept for those involved in *management training*, including progress reports, personal assessments, training programmes, etc.

Confidentiality is essential. Records must be locked in an office which is not available to those outside the personnel department.

69. Management records. The department must be able to provide information for management generally and for its own purposes. These would include those relevant to:

(*a*) *staff distribution.* It should be able to provide analyses, departmentally as well as wholly, of categories according to levels of seniority, types of occupations, sex, age and length of service, etc.;

(*b*) *legal requirements.* Details are required relevant to the number of disabled persons, of those under 18 years of age, overtime worked by women and juniors;

(*c*) *labour turnover* (*see* **51** above);

(*d*) *absenteeism.* Like LTO, the aim is to identify areas of failure. The usual formula is:

$$\frac{\text{man-hours lost}}{\text{total possible hours}} \times 100$$

(*e*) *labour costs.* The method of analysis would be determined by appropriate management levels. It may be necessary to calculate these costs as a continuous process or to investigate certain areas for specific purposes, e.g. to determine the cost-effectiveness of overtime, or to relate administration costs to other costs (*see* **18** above);

(*f*) *training records.* These should include:

(*i*) details of training facilities available and those used, the extent and effectiveness of usage and relative costs;

(*ii*) costing exercises as to the effective cost of in-firm training, allowing for expenses of the trainer, trainee production time forgone, cost of materials, light and heat, etc. This effective cost can be set against the measureable benefits, particularly if more than one training method is used;

(*g*) *accident-frequency rates.* These would indicate areas which are particularly prone to accidents and should result in corrective action.

PROGRESS TEST 13

1. Consider the responsibility for personal relationships devolving upon: (*a*) top management; (*b*) managers; (*c*) the personnel officer. (**2**)

2. What attitudes are necessary by those responsible for establishing relationships? (**3**)

3. Summarise the changes which have taken place concerning attitudes to personnel. (**5, 6**)

4. Why do people work? (**7**)

5. Indicate how different motivations affect job satisfaction. (**8**)

6. Define and give examples of management motivation. (**9**)

7. In what areas would the personnel department be involved with management generally? (**10**)

8. How do the functions of the personnel officer differ from that of other executives? (**11, 12**)

9. What factors may influence the personnel policy? (**13**)

10. Define the general objectives of a personnel policy. (**14**)

11. What is the purpose of manpower planning? (**15**)

12. How may manpower be analysed? (**16, 17**)

13. Relate the cost-effectiveness of labour to "Parkinson's Law" (**18**)

14. Define and state the objectives of job analysis. (**19**)

15. Relate the sources of recruitment to types of labour. (**21**)

16. Outline the arguments for and against recruitment in preference to promotion. (**22**)

17. What principles should apply relevant to the use and design of employment application forms? (**24, 25**)

18. What are the essentials for an interview to be productive? (**27**)

19. List and state the characteristics of selection tests. (**28**)

20. To what extent are references useful? (**29**)

21. What are the usual contents of a service agreement? (**30**)

22. Outline the provisions of the *Contracts of Employment Act* 1972. (**31**)

23. What should be the objectives of a training and promotion policy? **(32)**

24. What is induction training? **(33)**

25. Contrast the forms and objectives of: (a) job training; (b) supervisory training; (c) management training; and (d) office training. **(34–36, 38)**

26. What are staff appraisals? To what extent are they unsatisfactory? **(39, 40)**

27. What principles should apply concerning promotion? What is the "Peter Principle"? **(41)**

28. What factors broadly determine wage rates? **(42)**

29. What is job evaluation and what methods are used? **(43–44)**

30. Give the advantages and disadvantages of job evaluation. **(45–46)**

31. What are merit awards and how do they relate to job evaluation? **(47)**

32. Distinguish forms of remuneration related to personal performance from those which are not. **(48)**

33. What are the advantages and disadvantages of incentive bonus schemes? **(49)**

34. Define and give the formula for labour turnover. **(51)**

35. How may LTO be analysed and for what reasons? **(52)**

36. What can be done to reduce LTO? **(53)**

37. What principles should apply relevant to redundancy schemes? **(54)**

38. What are the legal provisions concerning redundancies? **(55)**

39. What factors must be considered relevant to the imposition of discipline? **(56, 57)**

40. What are the major objectives of trade unions? **(58)**

41. What is the usual pattern of disputes procedures? **(59)**

42. Consider the importance of shop stewards. **(60)**

43. What is "collective bargaining"? **(61)**

44. Consider the changing attitudes to joint consultation. **(62)**

45. Why are welfare facilities provided? **(63)**

46. What, in general, are the functions of a welfare department? **(65)**

47. What are the general legal provisions concerning safety and health? **(66)**

48. Outline the duties of a safety officer. **(67)**

49. What records are kept in a personnel department? **(68)**

50. What statistics can be provided by a personnel department and for what purposes? **(69)**

CHAPTER XIV

ACCOUNTING

AN ASPECT OF MANAGEMENT

1. A contributor to management. Within the scope of this HANDBOOK our concern with accounting is the contribution it makes to management and not with the techniques of accounting. Its contribution may broadly be said to be the provision of:

(*a*) *current data.* In its routine work of recording financial transactions, the accounting department should provide a flow of information giving current figures such as those relating to the availability of cash, the amount of debtors and creditors, and the value of investments held, etc.;

(*b*) *estimating data.* Management decisions concern future activity and information is required on which estimates can be made. The accounting function would include the provision of past information to facilitate forecasting, and defining the probable financial results of taking specified courses of action. Accounting thereby contributes to decision-making;

(*c*) *evaluation aids.* Accounting serves as a form of control in feeding back the financial results of decisions which have been acted upon and permits management to react to any deviation indicated as a consequence of the control;

(*d*) *static data.* This includes periodic statements in final accounts form (i.e. Trading and Profit and Loss Accounts and balance sheets), which can be used in the calculation of financial ratios (*see* **5** below).

2. Divisions of accounting.

(*a*) *Financial accounting*

    (*i*) relates to transactions extending outside the business;
    (*ii*) records revenue and expenditure;
    (*iii*) analyses according to *types* of transaction.

(b) *Cost accounting*

    (*i*) relates to the internal affairs of the business;
    (*ii*) is a form of forecasting and measuring achievements;
    (*iii*) analyses functions or activities;
    (*iv*) includes a control element.

FINANCIAL ACCOUNTING

3. Functions.

(*a*) *To record transactions* and thereby:

    (*i*) establish the identity and extent of debtors and creditors;
    (*ii*) value assets;
    (*iii*) relate income to expenditure.

(*b*) *To provide summary statements* in the form of accounts:

    (*i*) to comply with legislation requiring companies to publish accounts in a prescribed manner and to disclose specified information;
    (*ii*) to meet the requirements of the Inland Revenue for the purpose of assessing tax;
    (*iii*) to provide information for the owners;
    (*iv*) to facilitate analysis by potential investors and lenders;
    (*v*) to provide information for management, e.g. monthly "final accounts".

4. Inadequacies of financial accounting.
The following limitations to the effectiveness of financial accounting must be recognised:

(*a*) *Static information.* The published figures are directly relevant only to the time at which they were compiled. Additional to the fact that final accounts are published in arrear of the accounting date (which is rarely more than twice a year), it must be realised that values are constantly changing.

(*b*) *Balance sheet valuation and market values.*

    (*i*) The figures for assets will be based on the purchase prices less accumulated depreciation, but such a mathematical assessment cannot be entirely accurate.
    (*ii*) A machine purchased for £10,000 may be worth that amount to the owner because of its contribution to profits, but if the machine is specific to the business it would realise only its scrap value if sold.

(*iii*) The market value of an asset cannot be determined accurately except upon its sale.

(*c*) *Necessity for assumptions.* Many figures must be based on arbitrary assumptions. For example, the amount allowed for doubtful debts or the sum reserved for a contingent liability may or may not approximate to the ultimate actual figure.

(*d*) *Conservative valuations.* As an accounting principle, assets tend to be under-valued, partly to avoid the risk of over-valuing and the consequent danger of a charge of producing a false balance sheet. Under-valuation may also be deliberate in order to create "hidden reserves".

5. Financial ratios. Certain calculations can be made from a study of a balance sheet, although allowance must be made for the inadequacies outlined above. A ratio relates one figure to another and the objective of the calculation will, therefore, determine the choice of the factors.

To be meaningful, a figure cannot be considered in isolation but must be compared with another figure. To say that profits have increased by £20,000 is pointless unless it is related to another figure, such as, for example, last year's profit or the total sales. The system allows for a true comparison with ratios for other periods even if the two factors fluctuate. Thus, if the ratio is of sales to expenditure, both sales and expenditure will differ from year to year, but each year a *relationship* between the two can be established and compared with the ratio for previous years.

(*a*) *Return on capital employed* (*ROCE*). This compares the net profit with the "capital employed", which is generally interpreted as being the fixed assets plus working capital. It measures the efficiency in the use of capital. It is often referred to as the "*primary ratio*".

(*b*) *Liquidity ratio.* This is concerned with the availability of cash to meet immediate and imminent liabilities. The ratio derives from dividing liquid assets by current liabilities. Liquid assets comprise cash and usually include assets which can be realised quickly, in which case it may be referred to as the "*quick ratio*".

(*c*) *Sales ratios.*

(*i*) Asset turnover relates capital employed to sales.

(*ii*) Sales/fixed assets ratio indicates efficiency in the use of fixed assets.

(*iii*) Sales/working capital ratio expresses efficiency in the use of working capital.

(*iv*) Sales/debtors ratio indicates the rate at which cash is received following sales.

(*d*) *Current ratio.* This indicates the availability of working capital and is obtained by dividing current assets by current liabilities.

(*e*) *Trade debtors/creditors.* This ratio indicates the balance between commitments to trade creditors and from trade debtors. It is particularly important when an adverse balance would be expensive because of the high cost of financing the difference.

(*f*) *Stock ratios.* Stock ratios provide guides in the control of stock in such forms as:

(*i*) raw materials/sales;
(*ii*) work in progress/sales;
(*iii*) raw materials/purchases.

BUDGETARY CONTROL

6. Budgets. A budget is defined in the *I.C.M.A. Terminology* as: "A financial and/or quantitative statement, prepared and approved prior to a defined period of time, of the policy to be pursued during that period for the purpose of attaining a given objective".

7. Control by budget. The figures in the statement as mentioned above are known as standards, objectives or targets. Set against such figures are those of actual performances, thus enabling the determination of deviations.

8. Definition of budgetary control. Budgetary control is the establishment of "budgets relating the responsibilities of executives to the requirements of a policy, and the continuous comparison of actual with budgeted results, either to secure by individual action the objective of that policy or to provide a basis for its revision" (*I.C.M.A. Terminology*).

9. Mounting a control budget.

(*a*) *Structuring.* Budget areas are determined, together with the fixing of responsibilities. The relationships between the areas are established. The link with the master budget and the information flows are agreed.

(*b*) *Subsidiary budgets* for budget areas are prepared within the quantitative ranges of the master budget.

(*c*) *The master budget* is the result of co-ordinating the subsidiary budgets. In respect of overall finance, for example, it would take the form of a projected profit and loss account, supplemented by a budgeted balance sheet and a budgeted statement of the sources and application of funds. Other master budgets would be specific to their sectional purposes.

(*d*) *The budget committee* is a body responsible for preparing the budget and will consist of representatives of the various functions involved. It is concerned with the setting of standards, and the establishment of co-ordination and effective control.

10. The budget officer. The budget officer is responsible for the administration of the budget. He is usually a senior accountant or he may be the chief accountant (often known as the "budget accountant"). His duties include:

(*a*) assembling estimates from each budget centre;

(*b*) providing historical information to facilitate the preparation of budgets;

(*c*) submitting estimates to the budget committee and leading discussions for preparing the master budget;

(*d*) collecting, recording and analysing performance data from budget centres;

(*e*) preparing frequent variance analyses reports;

(*f*) agreeing variations of standards where necessary;

(*g*) co-ordinating all budget activities.

11. Classifications of budgets.

(*a*) *Appropriation budgets* are forms of expenditure control. Such a budget would establish the upper limit of expenditure for a stated area of activity.

(*b*) *Fixed budgets* provide targets which cannot be changed because of the level of actual attainment. They *can* be altered; the principle is that no adjustment may be made merely because of a change in volume or activity. The establishing of a fixed budget is done in order to facilitate planning and co-ordination.

(*c*) *Flexible budgets* show a range of volumes of output or activity. This allows comparisons to be made of the actual figures with the budgeted figures for the actual volume of activity achieved. As defined in the *I.C.M.A Terminology*, a flexible budget is one which, "by recognising the difference between fixed, semi-fixed and variable costs, is designed to change in relation to the level of activity attained".

12. Profit targets. In preparing the master budget as an indicator of profit targets, the following must be taken into account:

(*a*) *Minimum rate of profit*. This is that rate of profit which is just worthwhile. It represents the rate below which the business would be more profitable if reserves were invested in safe securities (such as gilt edged).

(*b*) *Normal rate of profit*. This is the minimum rate plus a percentage to cover a reward for the risks involved. This addition will vary according to the degree of risk relevant to the industry or the product.

(*c*) *Target profit*. Target profit is the one appearing in the master budget. It will include provision for:

(*i*) shareholder dividends adequate to cover the risk involved and showing a return comparable with those relative to similar concerns;

(*ii*) loan interest;

(*iii*) reserves for preserving the real capital;

(*iv*) reserves for contingencies, as a safety margin, and for expansion.

13. Advantages of budgetary control.

(*a*) *Management by exception*. The comparing of performances and targets indicates areas of deviation. Control is exercised by identification of variances beyond a certain degree of tolerance so that corrective action can be taken. The *principle of exception* is that only deviations are reported.

(*b*) *Co-ordination*. Because of the links between subsidiary budgets and their total relationship with the master budget, co-ordination of effort to a common end is facilitated.

(*c*) *Responsibility*. Each functional area has its own target, and the group and personal responsibility is thereby established. Such an area subject to a budget is known as a *budget centre*.

(*d*) *Expenditure is controlled*. Each centre is set a limit.

(*e*) *Improved costing system*. The compiling of performance data in a budget operation provides historical information of value in drafting a costing system because the actual figures can be used as the basis of new estimates.

(*f*) *Policy guidelines.* The degree of success shown on completion of a budget period provides management with information useful in deciding future policy.

14. Information flows. An essential feature of budgetary control is the constant flow of information required. The following rules apply:

(*a*) Information must be provided *speedily*.

(*b*) The *type of information* required must be clearly understood.

(*c*) The *routing of information* must be agreed.

(*d*) *Reports should be standardised* to facilitate analysis.

(*e*) *Parties affected* by information must be notified as well as the controlling body.

(*f*) Where appropriate, *reports must be comparative*, i.e. target and performance.

(*g*) Distinctions must be made between *controllable costs* and *uncontrollable costs*.

The classes of reports are broadly as follows:

(*h*) *Routine reports.* These are those submitted in accordance with an agreed schedule, e.g. periodic reports within budget centres and by budget centres to the budget officer.

(*i*) *Special reports.* These deal with unusual events, such as delays due to machine breakdowns, industrial disputes, etc.; where decisions have to be made (e.g. to buy or make a component); where plans have to be changed (e.g. imposition of price controls or failure of a supplier).

15. Deficiencies of budget control. The following dangers must be recognised:

(*a*) *Unduly detailed budgeting.* This may prove to be more expensive than the savings consequent upon control.

(*b*) *Inflexibility.* Too much emphasis must not be placed upon target figures. Often an increase in costs beyond the standard is justified if advantage is to be taken of a favourable market which will allow for higher profits.

(*c*) *Viability of cost figures.* A cost figure agreed for one budget may be automatically repeated for a subsequent period, although, in fact, costs could possibly be reduced.

Also, managers tend to claim costs higher than justified in anticipation that the figures will be reduced by the budget committee.

16. Functional budgets. The following are summaries of the more common budgets specific to functional areas. A common factor is that all functional budgets must operate within the overall policy of the organisation. Functions are inter-related and each budget must be planned in conjunction with other budgets in related functions.

(a) *Sales budget.* This is a forecast of sales, analysed into areas and products. It must be related to the availability of supplies or the rate of production. Calculations will be based on existing data and estimates made as a result of market research. It must be capable of variation because of such unknown factors as the strength of competition, market demand, etc.

(b) *Sales and distribution costs budget.* This will not necessarily relate directly to the volume of sales over a short period. Advertising, for example, will be a fairly long-term project with possibly little immediate effect on sales. Data will include administration costs, salaries of salesmen, distribution expenses, etc.

(c) *Production and production cost budgets.* The first refers to the amount of production required to meet the sales anticipated in the sales budget. The second translates the figures into monetary terms.

(d) *Purchases and materials cost budgets.* The first is concerned with the physical purchases and the second is related to the costs. Both are related to the sales budget mentioned in (c) above.

(e) *Administrative cost budget.* This relates to all overheads relevant to administration. It includes salaries, office expenses, heating and lighting, etc. It is frequently subdivided into departmental budgets.

(f) *Capital expenditure budget.* This budget is a form of long-term forecasting of expenditure on fixed assets. It is therefore relevant to major policy decisions concerning future development as well as to routine current capital expenditure.

(g) *Cash budget.* The cash budget is a method of forecasting the in-flow and out-flow of cash (*see* VI, **5**).

DECISION ACCOUNTING

17. Application. Decision accounting is not a technique in itself. The term signifies recognition that a major function of accounting is to provide information necessary for decisions to be made. Examples of the problems which accounting can help to solve are as follows:

(a) In an exercise on rationalisation, what would be the effect of closing a particular department?

(b) Should a certain component be purchased or produced within the business?

(c) What is the better choice between two forms of investment?

(d) What is the most advantageous method of raising capital?

18. Evaluating project profitability. Various methods can be used to ascertain the true profitability of a project or to determine the most advantageous of several possible projects.

(a) *Pay-back method.* This attempts to equate the costs and the revenue relevant to a project over a period of time. Broadly, it aims to determine the number of years a project is providing revenue before it "pays for itself". For example, a machine costing £5,000 and providing revenue of £1,000 per annum would have a pay-back period of five years.

(b) *Rate of return.* This relates the average annual return from a project (the total return over the life of the investment divided by the number of years it produces income) to the initial outlay.

(c) *Discounted cash flow (DCF).* The concept of rate of return mentioned above does not take account of the fact that future income is worth less than current income of the same amount. For example, if X lends Z £100 on the agreement that Z will repay £105 in one year's time, it follows that £100 now is agreed to be equal to £105 one year hence. If the term was for two years, the value of £1 at present, assuming compound interest of 5 per cent, would become £1.1025 at the end of two years. The principle involved in DCF is to reverse the process and to say that £1.1025 received two years hence is equivalent to a present value of £1. If all income from a project is discounted by this method it will be seen that the later the income is produced the lower is the present valuation.

Thus, DCF recognises the influence of the timing of cash flows and gives a more accurate assessment than in (*b*) above.

(*d*) *Net present value* (*NPV*). This method relates the rate of return to the cost of the financing—that is, the interest payable for the money invested in the project. Thus, if the interest rate is 10 per cent and the return will not materialise for five years, the cost of the capital will be 10 per cent compounded for five years. If the project cash flow is discounted at the same rate as the capital rate, the resulting present value of future cash flows can be compared with the cost of the project.

(*e*) *Rate of yield*. This method uses the discounting principle but for a different purpose. The objective is to determine the cost at which discounted earnings will be equal to the present value of the invested capital. This will establish a break-even point at which there would be neither a deficit or a surplus. The method is particularly useful in comparing alternative projects.

COST ACCOUNTING

19. Management accounting. *Financial accounting* cannot provide adequately the information necessary for planning. The necessity for information of an analytical nature to be available to management gave rise to the concept of *cost accounting*. Because it is a direct management aid it is now more usually referred to as *management accounting*.

20. A service to management. The costing department provides a service to management in that it provides analytical data on which decisions can be made. The measurement of business efficiency is profit. A major factor in the achievement of profit is cost. Pre-determination and control of costs is therefore vital.

In designing a costing system, the aim should be to provide the information required by management and to not merely carry out accounting exercises. A costing department is unproductive in itself; it contributes to profitability only as a service. The aims of the department should, therefore, be determined by *management* and not by the department itself.

21. Contributions to management. Contributions to management by an efficient costing department are as follows:

(a) *Budgetary control.*

(*i*) It provides actual cost figures for comparison with budgets.

(*ii*) It facilitates the establishment of target costs for ensuing budget periods.

(b) *Control.* The system enables forms of check and control to operate.

(c) *Allocation of costs.* Costs relevant to more than one function (e.g. administration, heating and lighting) can be allocated between functions.

(d) *Planning.* The compiling of statistics can facilitate planning and the selection of the most advantageous of more than one proposal.

(e) *Disclosure of deficiencies.* The system can identify and quantify areas of wastage (e.g. the amount of production scrap) and diseconomies of methods (e.g. the buying of components which could be self-produced more cheaply).

(*f*) *Price determination.* This is made easier when costs at different production levels can be calculated. Forecasted costs can thus be related to the prices which would be acceptable to the market. It can also make tendering more efficient.

(g) *Level of production.* The optimum level of production where profits are highest can be determined with the aid of costing data related to the different levels.

22. Elements of cost. The broad categories of the constituents of cost are *materials, labour* and *services (or expenses).*

These are subdivided according to whether the cost item is incurred *directly* in relation to the product or is an *indirect* item.

Direct materials (used in manufacture).
Direct labour (wages of those in production or in providing a service).
Direct expenses (incurred directly relevant to production or the provision of a service).

     Prime cost

Indirect materials (not directly related to production, e.g. cleaning materials).
Indirect labour (wages which cannot be related directly to production, e.g. office salaries).
Indirect expenses (with general relevance, e.g. office expenses).

     Overhead cost

TOTAL COST

23. Standard costing. This is a technique involving the following points:

(a) The method of production is pre-determined.

(b) It establishes what the cost *should be* and not what it is *expected to be*.

(c) The estimate is made on the assumption of a particular level of production and the existence of "standard" conditions.

(d) Comparisons of the actual and the estimated costs are made to determine variances.

(e) Variances are analysed to establish the causes.

(f) In general, it can be applied only to standardised methods and products.

24. Setting standard costs. The general principles are as follows:

(a) *Direct materials.* These relate firstly to prevailing purchases prices relevant to the volume of materials to be purchased. They may be adjusted for possible changes in price during the period of purchase. Allowance may have to be made for wastage, e.g. losses in cutting.

(b) *Direct labour.* These costs may be based on work study which will calculate the labour time per unit or operation, the wage rates according to the grades of labour employed, and any allowances for overtime and/or bonus rates.

(c) *Overhead costs.* The total anticipated costs will be allocated according to their relevance to the process.

25. Advantages of standard costing.

(a) *Efficiency standards* will be achieved, for if only actual costs are used there is no method of testing the efficiency of the performance. Comparisons with standards, however, provide a form of measurement.

(b) *Variances will indicate degrees of efficiency* in specific areas.

(c) *The exception principle* allows management to concentrate on deviations without having to be concerned with the overall performance.

(d) *Control* can be exercised at every stage.

(e) *Comparisons of methods* is facilitated by the degrees of efficiency achieved, thus making easier the choice of methods.

(f) *Targets are personal to those concerned,* giving an incentive to efficiency.

(g) *Incentive schemes* can be superimposed on the system.

26. Marginal costing. This is a technique which recognises that a change in the amount of output may result in a change in cost per unit.

(a) *The cost behaviour concept.* Obviously, costs will rise as production increases but not necessarily at the same rate. Thus, if output doubles it is probable that there will be a less than 100 per cent increase in costs.

(b) *Variable costs* are those which tend to alter with changes in output and are referred to as *marginal costs* (e.g. materials used).

(c) *Fixed costs* are those which tend to remain constant irrespective of the amount of output (e.g. rent). These do not form part of the marginal cost and are disregarded. Instead, the total fixed costs are allocated to appropriate cost areas to be met from the difference between sales income and marginal costs (known as the *contribution*).

27. Break-even analysis. The marginal costing technique makes possible the drafting of "break-even charts".

A horizontal line indicates the amount of fixed costs at any level of production. In Fig. 7 these amount to £20,000.

The chart is based on a sale price of £2 per unit. The marginal costs are £1 per unit and the resulting figures are charted above the fixed-cost line to give the total-cost line. Where the total-cost line and the sales line meet is the "break-even point", that is, the point where neither a profit or a loss is made. In Fig. 7 it will be seen that up to 20,000 unit sales, losses are sustained and that beyond that figure profits accrue at an increasing rate.

The proportion of sales above the break-even point is known as *the margin of safety,* as this indicates the extent to which sales can fall before the business reaches a loss position.

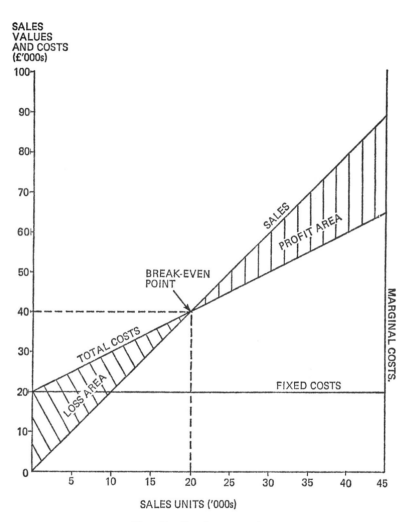

FIG. 7—*Break-even point.*

PROGRESS TEST 14

1. What sort of data does the accounting function provide management? (1)

2. Distinguish between financial accounting and cost accounting. (2)

3. What objectives are achieved in providing financial summaries in published-account form? (3)

4. To what extent is the effectiveness of financial accounting limited? (4)

5. What is the principle in calculating ratios? (5)

6. Define: (a) return on capital employed; (b) liquidity ratio. (5)

7. Define: (a) budget; (b) budgetary control. (6, 8)

8. What is the organisation framework for the working of a control budget? (9)

9. What are the functions of a budget officer? (10)

10. Distinguish between appropriation budgets, fixed budgets and flexible budgets. (11)

11. Distinguish between the following in relation to profits: (a) minimum rate; (b) normal rate; (c) target profit. (12)

12. What are the advantages of budgetary control? (13)

13. What is "the principle of exception"? (13, 25)

14. In respect of budgetary control, distinguish between routine and special reports. (14)

15. What could be the deficiencies of a budget control? (15)

16. What are: (a) the pay-back method; (b) rate of return method? (18)

17. Compare: (a) discounted cash flow; (b) net present value; (c) rate of yield. (18)

18. In what ways does management accounting contribute to management? (21)

19. What are the elements of cost? What are direct costs and indirect costs? (22)

20. What are the features of standard costing? (23)

21. What are the advantages of standard costing? (25)

22. What is marginal costing? Distinguish between marginal costs and fixed costs. (26)

23. What is the principle of break-even analysis? (27)

CHAPTER XV

THE OFFICE

THE OFFICE FUNCTION

1. Office management. Office management has been defined by the Institute of Administrative Management as: "that branch of management which is concerned with the services of obtaining, recording and analysing information, of planning and of communicating, by means of which the management of a business safeguards its assets, promotes its affairs and achieves its objectives".

2. The office as a service. The above definition stresses that the function of the office is to provide services to the organisation generally. These services may be described in more detail as:

(*a*) *obtaining information.* This may flow in:

(*i*) from outside the organisation as part of the normal process of the business;
(*ii*) from other parts of the organisation in accordance with prescribed procedures;
(*iii*) as a result of the office seeking the information.

The methods include letters, reports, forms, etc.;

(*b*) *recording information.* This includes all information required by management and must be in a form acceptable to management. Other information is recorded because of legal requirements so to do (e.g. that required by the Companies Acts);

(*c*) *analysing information.* This implies the rearranging of information into a form required by the organisation. It could include the collating of data from different sources, the making of calculations from information received, and the making of reports, statements, etc.;

(*d*) *providing information.* Information, analysed and/or

rearranged as required, is passed on to the appropriate departments as part of a procedure or upon specific request.

3. Effectiveness of office services. The extent to which the office contributes to the overall efficiency of the business will depend upon factors including the following:

(*a*) *Organisation structure.* The structure must be such that clerical centres are positioned so as to provide rapid and effective communication with their related function areas.

(*b*) *Office organisation.* The office must be organised to operate swiftly and efficiently. This will entail considerations concerning planning, machines and equipment, and staffing.

(*c*) *Servicing status.* The office must be designed *to serve,* it must not become the master. The office must be ready to change its methods to suit the convenience of the functional areas it serves. The reverse should not apply.

(*d*) *Cost-effectiveness.* The office should be economic in carrying out its own functions. It should also act so that, where possible, it does not increase costs outside the office.

(*e*) *Recognition of its importance.* Office management must be recognised by top management as a specialist function and one in which efficiency is vital to the business. Other functional managers must recognise its importance and, therefore, provide full consultation and co-operation.

4. Specialist or non-specialist function. Control of clerical functions may rest with the heads of departments who have clerical staff.

Responsibility for all clerical work does, however, frequently belong to a specialist manager. He may be known as, for example, the office manager or the office services manager. The centralising of such authority should not mean all clerical work would be centralised. Office staff would continue to work in those departments they service, but the office services manager should be responsible for the staff and the organisation of all areas of clerical work.

5. Scope for centralisation of office services.

(*a*) To some extent, the *clerical work of each department must be specific to that department,* e.g. invoicing in the sales department or calculating of wages in the wages department. Thus, absolute centralisation would not be possible.

(b) *Some clerical functions*, however, *will be common to all departments*. It may be possible for all or a major part of the work to be performed in a centralised specialist department. Common examples are typing, filing, duplicating and mailing.

(c) *Other services* may not be in frequent use by all departments but may be *required by most of them from time to time*. In such cases, centralised services could be made available. Examples are office printing, statistical services and mechanised addressing.

6. Advantages of centralised services.

(a) *Economy of staffing*. Because of flexibility, fewer staff would be required. For example, "peaks" of work in one department may be compensated by "troughs" in others.

(b) *Reduced costs of machines and equipment*. Costs would be reduced because machines and equipment would be more fully employed.

(c) *Specialised working conditions*. As the room would be used solely for one purpose, it could be designed and equipped specifically for that purpose, e.g. mailing, typing.

(d) *Uniformity of methods*. This would be possible, and could include such things as the standardisation of the style of typed letters.

(e) *Specialist staff*. Increased efficiency would result from the use of specialist staff, particularly as the supervisors would also be specialists.

(f) *Work standards*. Control in maintaining standards of work would be facilitated because of better supervision and training.

7. Disadvantages of centralised services.

(a) *Delays can occur*. Because of physical remoteness, files, etc., would not be immediately available.

(b) *Unsuitability for confidential work*. Papers of a confidential nature must have limited accessibility and therefore should not be away from the office responsible for the confidentiality.

(c) *Loss of personal interest*. Staff in centralised departments may have little or no interest in the work they are doing for other departments.

(*d*) *Increased possibility of errors.* Because centralised staff have little understanding of many of the documents they handle, the danger of errors being committed is increased.

(*e*) *Conflict of priorities.* Work from more than one department to be carried out by a centralised department may have equal claims for priority on the grounds of urgency. The allocation of priority between them in times of pressure may cause discord and inefficiency.

OFFICE ORGANISATION

8. An aspect of management. The principles applicable to management generally are also relevant to office management. In particular, the following are pertinent:

(*a*) *Simplicity of operations.* Basically, all clerical processes consist of simple operations. Efficiency requires extensive simplification and standardisation.

(*b*) *Planning.* An element of planning exists in even the simplest clerical operation, but the planning is of particular importance in the assembling of numerous simple operations into a comprehensive whole.

(*c*) *Co-ordination.* This is part of the implementation of planning, being concerned with the flow of work from one stage to another and relating it to other work processes. Thus, there must be co-ordination *within* a department and *externally* to related areas.

(*d*) *Specialisation of labour.* The different stages in a work process may be the responsibility of different persons. There must therefore be co-ordination of persons as well as of functional stages.

(*e*) *Objectivity of functions.* The organisation must be geared specifically to meet the requirements of those being serviced. Frequently, the same material must be presented to different departments, often in forms specific to each serviced department.

(*f*) *Control.* The office must be so organised as to enable the efficiency of the procedures to be checked and, if necessary, amendments made.

9. Organisation and methods (O. & M.). In an organisation of a reasonable size, the extent and complexity of clerical work may be such as to warrant the appointment of specialist staff to undertake scientific study of the problems, with the aim of increasing efficiency. The nature of this expertise is indicated by its alternative title of *work simplification*.

10. The O. & M. department. The O. & M. department has the following characteristics:

(*a*) It consists of *specialists*.

(*b*) It is *independent* and provides a service to all departments.

(*c*) Basically, its *services are advisory*.

    (*i*) These may be offered to any department requesting them.

    (*ii*) It may be assigned to carry out investigations.

    (*iii*) It may carry out a continuous survey.

(*d*) Its advice is given in the form of *reports*, often to top management.

(*e*) It may be required to *implement and control* those procedures it recommends.

11. Activities of the O. & M. department.

(*a*) *Planning new departments or functions.* The establishment of a new department or the addition of a new function can be complex, particularly its integration into the existing total structure.

(*b*) *Surveying existing systems.* This is done with a view to improvement.

(*c*) *Solving problems.* Difficulties may have arisen which may call for changed methods. Examples are delays in dispatching monthly statements to debtors and an unreasonable amount of errors in one section.

(*d*) *Machinery and equipment.* The department should advise on the choice of office machinery and equipment, bearing in mind the particular requirements of the organisation and the importance of true economy.

(*e*) *Forms control.* The department would advise or, more probably, actually design and control forms used in the office (*see* **24** below).

(*f*) *Advising on staffing.* The department may be consulted about the appointment of new staff, transferring staff and training staff, because of its specialist knowledge of the requirements of clerical jobs. Also, changes in organisation proposed by the department may entail relocation of staff.

12. O. & M. assignments. The stages in carrying out an assignment are broadly as follows:

(*a*) *Briefing.* This would entail a discussion with those commissioning the assignment to reach agreement on the purpose and extent of the investigation and any constraints concerning cost, etc.

(*b*) *Preliminary survey.* This would involve establishing basic facts concerning the department or procedure to be investigated, such as:

(*i*) the relationship of the department or procedure to adjacent ones;

(*ii*) the stated purpose of the department or procedure;

(*iii*) the number and grades of staff involved;

(*iv*) the machines and equipment available.

(*c*) *Detailed investigation and analysis.*

(*d*) *Design of new procedures for comparative purposes.*

(*e*) *Report to the commissioning body.*

(*f*) *Draft the new procedure.*

(*g*) *Install and check.*

13. O. & M. investigation. Having established the basic facts, a detailed investigation of the existing system must be carried out. The results of each aspect of the enquiry should, where possible, be expressed on specially designed forms and charts. A summary of the areas of enquiry is as follows:

(*a*) *Concerning the department or procedure generally.*

(*i*) The object or purpose.

(*ii*) An analysis of the staff, indicating the functions of each member.

(*iii*) The time factor for completing a cycle of work, and any constraints on time (e.g. dispatch of statements within two days of the month-end).

(*iv*) The work-load, i.e. the volume of output and any regular variations in the output.

(*v*) The sequence of operations within the overall procedure.

(*vi*) Any features specific to the department or procedure.

(*b*) *Concerning each operation within the procedure.*

(*i*) Its purpose and relationship with adjacent operations.

(*ii*) The methods employed (including any forms used).

(*iii*) Who does the operation.

(*iv*) Quantification, where possible, e.g. the number of operations in a set period, or the time to complete an operation.

(*c*) *Factors external to the procedure.*

(*i*) The sources and types of information received and the forms used.

(*ii*) The destinations and types of information after processing, and the forms used.

14. Designing a new procedure.

(*a*) *Assemble the information obtained from the investigation.* Where possible, this should be in diagrammatic form and be quantitative.

(*b*) *Determine the objective.* The natural development of a procedure over a period of time may tend to blur the objective. It may be found that it no longer provides all the information required, or that the requirements may have changed, so that the objective is now different. It may provide more than is now required.

(*c*) *Devise new methods.* These could include the following:

(*i*) Eliminating duplicated work, e.g. two clerks coincidentally producing the same information.

(*ii*) Simplifying, eliminating and/or combining forms.

(*iii*) Rerouting the flow of documents.

(*iv*) Eliminating stages and documents no longer required.

(*v*) Combining operations into single operations.

(*vi*) Reducing the scope of operations as a method of simplification (e.g. to introduce two operations in place of one).

(*vii*) Redeploying staff duties.

(*d*) *Compare original and new methods.* Any quantification of the original procedure can be measured against that relative to new methods being considered. Quantifiable data could include:

(*i*) number of operations in a sequence;

(*ii*) production rate or completion time for a sequence;

(*iii*) staff required and cost (machine operators may replace manual staff);

(*iv*) stationery costs;

(*v*) office space occupied;

(*vi*) initial and running costs of machines.

(*e*) *Select the most advantageous method.*

15. The objectives of O. & M. These may be summarised as follows:

(a) To reduce costs, subject to the maintenance of efficiency.

(b) To increase output or reduce time spent.

(c) To reduce errors.

(d) To improve service to management.

OFFICE MANAGEMENT TECHNIQUES

16. Procedure analysis (or process chart) This lists and describes all the operations within a procedure. Symbols are used to indicate the type of each operation, i.e. hand or machine, sequence movement, storage or waiting, action terminated, and check or verification.

The chart indicates the sequence of operations. If the operations are capable of timing, the total time can be shown on the chart—or the quantification may be of the amount of production.

17. Procedure flow chart. This indicates the routing of documents between departments or sections. It is particularly appropriate in illustrating the distribution of multi-copy forms.

18. Work schedule. This is a programme of job stages for the completion of an operation, reference being made to a time-table. It may refer to a regular exercise, such as the monthly dispatch of statements; it may be a less frequent operation, such as annual stock-taking; or it may refer to a rare operation, such as moving to another office or introducing a new procedure.

The timetable is designed to ensure that:

(a) each stage and the whole operation is completed by predetermined dates;

(b) staff and equipment are made available when, and to the extent, required;

(c) the sequence of stages is logical so that the exercise proceeds smoothly.

19. Movement chart (or string diagram). This technique for planning the flow of work can be applied to the office as well as to the factory (*see* X, **34**).

20. Quantity control. This may be effected if the following apply:

(*a*) *The output must be capable of measurement.* It would therefore not be applicable to non-routine jobs.

(*b*) *Standards must be set and be reasonable.*

(*c*) *Time cycles must be recognised.* That is, allowance must be made for peaks and troughs of work-load. These may be on a daily, weekly or monthly basis and would occur predictably. For example, in a weekly payroll procedure, the clerical work involved would not be at the same level throughout the week, but the pattern of one week would be similar to that of another.

21. Quality Control. This refers to attempts to reduce the incidence of errors. The principle is to:

(*a*) *check work to identify personal inefficiences.* This may indicate poor selection and/or training;

(*b*) *analyse areas of errors.* This may indicate that a high frequency of error in certain operations is largely due to the procedure adopted. Determination of the cause of the errors thus allows for the procedure to be improved;

(*c*) *recognise the true cost of errors.* This includes the time spent in correcting the error (which may be lengthy if the error is mathematical), spoiled work and loss of customer goodwill;

(*d*) *recognise the cost of control.* A 100 per cent check would probably cost more than the resulting savings. The "exception principle" should be used and be geared to a reasonable level of cost and effectiveness.

FORMS DESIGN AND CONTROL

22. The benefits from using forms.

(*a*) *Objectivity.* A form is designed to meet the requirements of the person(s) requesting the information.

(*b*) *Positive answers.* A form contains questions which must be answered. Accordingly, the person completing the form cannot withhold information.

(*c*) *Analysis.* As the data is standardised, it is possible to quantify all the information from a collection of forms, analysed according to the questions.

(d) *Clarity.* Essay type reports may suffer from inadequate expression. Forms obviate that possibility.

23. Form design. The following rules are relevant to the design of forms:

(a) *Identification.* The form must have:

(i) a title, indicative of the purpose of the form;
(ii) a code, for reference purposes.

(b) *Appearance.*

(i) The layout should be neat and balanced;
(ii) The typeface should be clear. A variety of typefaces may be used where necessary but an undue number of variations may provide a confusing and unbalanced layout.

(c) *Sequence of items.*

(i) Items should be in logical order.
(ii) They should, where appropriate, be numbered for ease of reference.

(d) *Answer spaces.*

(i) Spaces must be adequate to hold the information required.
(ii) If the answers are to be typed, the answer areas must accord with typewriter spacing.

(e) *Paper.*

(i) The standard of durability will be determined by the amount of handling anticipated.
(ii) Provision must be made for filing (e.g. suitable margins and punched holes).
(iii) The surface must be suitable for handwriting if that is to be the method used when completing it.

(f) *Distribution.* The addressees must be clearly indicated. Duplicate forms (preferably in distinctive colours) should be used if there is more than one addressee.

(g) *Instructions* for completing the form should be included if necessary.

24. Forms control. Forms control is a system whereby one person (or group) is responsible for initiating and designing all forms. The necessity for this arises from the following;

(a) *Dangers of proliferation.* If every department (and, as sometimes prevails, every person) is allowed to invent forms, a superabundance of forms will result.

(*b*) *Specialisation*. Designing forms requires a particular expertise and it is therefore advantageous for it to be done by a specialist.

(*c*) *Co-ordination*. The forms control officer will look at the organisation as a whole and design forms accordingly. This will avoid the waste of each department using forms specific only to itself, and the consequent duplication and possible confusion.

(*d*) *Obsolescence*. Unless forms are constantly reviewed in conditions of change, some forms will continue to be used when the information is no longer required or when it is already available on another form or forms.

(*e*) *Economy*. Purchasing costs will be reduced if all printing is ordered by one section. Further savings will result from control of the issue of forms to those who are to use them. These savings are additional to the savings resulting from the major advantage of control—the fact that fewer forms will be in circulation.

MECHANISATION

25. Purposes of mechanisation.

(*a*) *Speed*. A machine can calculate and produce records of a routine nature more quickly than is possible manually, and can often carry out several operations simultaneously (e.g. post sales ledger, personal account, invoice, etc.).

(*b*) *Labour costs*. The amount of labour is reduced as a result of mechanisation. The reduction in wages may not be proportionate, however, because of the high wage-cost of some specialist staff.

(*c*) *Accuracy and control*. Provided any manual input is correct, it is generally safe to assume the accuracy of a machine. Frequently, a process of self-checking is incorporated.

(*d*) *Uniformity and legibility*. Records will be standardised and legible, benefiting the firm and improving customer relations.

26. Other results of mechanisation. In addition to those mentioned above, the following results may also accrue:

(*a*) *Staff work-content.* The more tedious manual jobs will be eliminated, enabling many staff to commence at a more interesting level of work. Against this is the fact that mechanisation results in the creation of many new jobs of a routine nature, e.g. punched-card operators.

(*b*) *"Dehumanisation".* There can be a loss of personal interest and pride in work when mechanisation reaches advanced proportions. Offices can acquire a "factory-like" atmosphere.

27. Reservations concerning mechanisation. Office mechanisation must not be an end in itself. It must be justified by its cost-effectiveness and its effects on the organisation generally. The following possible disadvantages must be considered:

(*a*) *Cost.* The true cost must include the following as additions to the capital cost:

(*i*) Special stationery which may be required.
(*ii*) Depreciation charges (which are frequently heavy).
(*iii*) Wage costs of operators, programmers, etc.

(*b*) *Economic justification.* To justify the above costs, a machine must be employed for a certain minimum number of hours. Below a certain level of usage a machine is uneconomic.

(*c*) *Installation disruption.* Mechanisation often involves a change in existing office systems. The expense and the disruption (including, often, human problems) may be considerable.

(*d*) *Inflexibility.* A machine should be capable of adaption so that it could cope if it was later required to produce more data or produce it in different forms. If the machine was leased instead of purchased, it could be surrendered in favour of a more sophisticated machine, but a purchased machine which is inflexible may become obsolete at an uneconomically early age.

(*e*) *Absolute commitment.* A business which has changed to mechanised methods is committed and cannot revert to manual methods, even for a short crisis period. The inherent dangers in this respect are:

(*i*) staff. Operators and specialists are not always available;
(*ii*) power failure or machine breakdown which will halt all operations.

COMPUTERS

28. Functions. The basic functions of a computer are:

(*a*) *to receive data* from one or more sources;

(*b*) *to process data* according to instructions by:

    (*i*) storing and processing at required stages;

    (*ii*) selecting, rejecting and analysing;

    (*iii*) calculating;

(*c*) *to produce visual results* at pre-determined interim stages and the final stage;

(*d*) *to employ checks* on data received and produced;

(*e*) *to store data for future use.*

29. The processing stages.

(*a*) *Program compiled and fed in.* The program constitutes the instructions given to the computer as determined by the objective of the operation. The use of programs makes a computer capable of numerous different tasks and it may thus be regarded as a multi-purpose machine. The program can be designed to bring in other programs at predetermined stages or upon the happening of a specified event during processing.

The term *"soft-ware"* is used to describe programs, which may be compiled by the user or purchased as "packages" capable of doing standard jobs (e.g. pay roll, stock control).

(*b*) *Input data recorded and fed in.* The data to be processed must be in a form capable of being read by the computer (the forms used are shown in Fig. 8).

(*c*) *Data and program stored in computer language.* This is known as the "memory" and will include standing information (e.g. standard deductions in calculating pay).

(*d*) *Processing.* This involves feeding in data at the required stages, together with existing data from storage; calculating as prescribed by the program; and passing the results to the output stage.

(*e*) *Presentation of processed data.* This consists of translating the computer language version of the results into a usable form, i.e. a printed or screened record, or stored for future use.

30. Advantages of computers.

(*a*) *Speed.* Computers are extremely fast in processing and producing information.

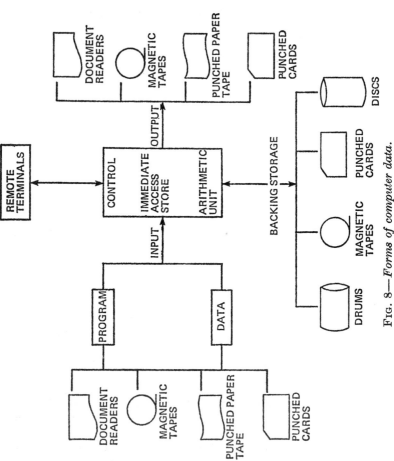

Fig. 8—*Forms of computer data.*

(b) *Improved labour performance.* Much repetitive routine clerical work is avoided; less clerical staff is required.

(c) *Improved accuracy.* Computers have a very high degree of accuracy.

(d) *Multi-purpose.* One machine can carry out a variety of jobs.

(e) *Variety of information.* Computers can produce a wide range of information, much of it incidental to carrying out the main task. It can also make comparisons, select significant information and present data in prescribed forms.

(f) *Managerial aids.* Analyses can be made quickly, mathematical "models" can be compiled to assist decision-making, and mathematical projections can be made.

31. Possible disadvantages of computers.

(a) *Inflexibility.* A computer can work only as it is programmed. Information which is not *normally* required cannot be made available by the machine because it would not be programmed to provide it.

(b) *Program cost.* Writing a program can be a long and expensive operation. Any subsequent necessary changes will add to the expense and delay.

(c) *Capital cost* is high. To this must be added the cost of special stationery, peripheral equipment, special accommodation, etc.

(d) *Data preparation.* Data must be translated into a "machine legible" form (known as *data capture*) and the cost of doing so can be high. There must be a form of checking (which adds to the cost) because errors in input will be continued in the processing.

32. Mini-computers.

The development of integrated circuits and micro-miniaturised techniques has led to a considerable increase in the use of small computers. There has been a decline in the use of "main frame" computer complexes with their bulky equipment because it is now possible to carry out standard procedures by using small models. This provides the following advantages.

(a) Units no longer require special rooms. Mini-computers are part of the normal office equipment, many of them being desk-top models.

(b) Rapidly improving techniques and competition between suppliers make them comparatively inexpensive.

(c) They are simple to operate, so that little training is necessary.

(d) Most machines have built-in programs because they carry out only one main operation (e.g. cash registers which automatically control stock).

Thus, in more and more instances many of the disadvantages of computers no longer exist.

PROGRESS TEST 15

1. Summarise the functions of the office in obtaining and processing information. (2)

2. Why is the office essentially a *servicing* department? (3)

3. Why must the importance of the office be generally recognised? (3)

4. Under what conditions may office organisation be a specialist function? (4)

5. To what extent may aspects of clerical work be centralised? What services may be centralised? (5)

6. How do the following principles of organisation apply in respect to office management: simplification, specialisation, planning, control? (8)

7. What part does co-ordination play in office organisation? (8)

8. Why is the science of Organisation and Methods also known as "work simplification"? (9)

9. What areas of activity may be covered by an O. & M. department? (11)

10. What are the stages in an O. & M. assignment? (12)

11. What aspects would be covered in an O. & M. investigation? Which of them could be quantified? (13)

12. Why is determination of the objective important in designing a procedure? (14)

13. In what forms may the re-designing of a procedure take? (14)

14. Consider the value of quantifying the improvements following the redesigning of a procedure. (14)

15. What is meant by procedure analysis? (16)

16. Define: (a) procedure flow chart; (b) movement chart. (17, 19)

17. What is a work schedule? Give examples of its use. (18)

18. What are the requirements for the establishing of a form of quantity control? (20)

19. What is quality control? Consider the cost of errors and the cost of control. (21)

20. List the rules relating to the design of forms. (23)

21. What is meant by forms control and what is its value? (24)

22. What, in general, are the advantages of mechanisation in the office? (25, 26)

23. Define the following terms relevant to computers: (a) software; (b) program; (c) input; (d) memory; (e) output; (f) computer language. (29)

24. Why has the development of microtechnology increased the use of computers? (32)

EXAMINATION TECHNIQUE

1. The necessity for technique. A candidate who is inadequately prepared cannot expect to succeed in an examination—nor does he deserve to succeed. It is an unhappy fact, however, that a conscientious candidate may fail only because of the manner in which he tackles a paper. It is therefore essential that a candidate takes steps to ensure that his performance is truly indicative of his ability. It must be remembered that an assessment by an examiner can be based only on the written answers supplied by the candidate; he has no personal knowledge of the student. The manner in which those answers are prepared and presented is therefore of considerable importance.

2. Past papers. Papers set in earlier examinations should be studied in order to establish the *style* of questions set. Thus, some papers have a tradition of "discussion questions"; others tend to ask factual questions.

Little or no information on the *subject-matter* in a forthcoming paper can be gained from studying past papers. Almost certainly, a detailed aspect of the syllabus in the last paper will not be repeated in the next one. It will usually be found, however, that the examination topics are spread fairly evenly over the syllabus and that in the space of a few examinations the total syllabus will be covered. It can also sometimes be possible to see one or more broad areas covered in almost every examination. For example, a paper on office management will very probably contain a question relating to some aspect of mechanisation.

A study of past papers will also show the *framework* of such papers. It would not be safe to assume the same pattern would always be followed but such would be the case in most instances. Thus, a paper with a tradition of containing two parts and requiring the candidate to answer a minimum number of questions from each part, is *likely* to be in that form in the next examination.

3. Approaching the examination. Be sure to allow yourself adequate time to reach the examination centre. If you have not done the journey before, have a "trial run" before the examination. A

candidate arriving in a flustered state because of misjudgment of
a bus service—or even because he was lost—is not improving his
chances!

Make certain you are fully equipped. Ball-point pens can fail
at critical moments; see you have a refill or spare pen.

4. Preliminaries in the examination room.

(a) If the system so prescribes, occupy the desk carrying your
entry number. If the desk or chair is faulty (candidates *have*
been known to be provided with unsatisfactory furniture!) tell
the invigilator about it *immediately*; you will not be popular if
you disturb the other candidates after the examination has
commenced. (If, after the examination commences, you wish to
ask the invigilator something, e.g. for more paper, raise your
hand; do *not* leave your desk.)

(b) Read carefully your instructions on the answer book.
Complete the information required. If you have to quote your
entry number, do *not* give your name instead. Write the title
of the subject exactly as it appears on the question paper.

(c) Note any other instructions, such as "write on both sides
of the paper"..."commence each answer on a new sheet"...
"number the questions in the book and on the cover (or fly-
leaf)".

5. Planning the answers.
This is the most vital stage. Time
must be taken to assimilate the paper and then to plan. A candidate who commences to write his answers immediately is most
likely to fail.

(a) *Read the whole paper thoroughly.* An attempt must be
made to identify the principle involved in each question. This
is not always possible on the first review. Take the opportunity
of allowing your mind to "settle down". Once you have familiar-
ised yourself with the paper and with your circumstances, it
will be easier to make a truer appreciation of the requirements
of each question.

(b) *Decide the questions to be answered.* Whether or not any
compulsory question is answered first must be decided by the
candidate. As such a question may carry a higher mark, however, time must be allowed to deal with it adequately.

(c) *Review the chosen questions.* Many candidates have
found it valuable to make notes on a spare piece of paper of
points to be brought out in the answer. They do this for *all*
the chosen questions before writing *any* answers. They have
found that by going over the questions more than once, the
physical action of making notes promotes thought, which, in
turn, allows other thoughts to "surface" from the memory.

Thus, a system of notes is built up and forms a framework of the answer paper.

All this takes time, of course, but it is time well spent if it produces an adequate set of notes. This is the major "thinking part" of the examination; the remaining time is largely spent in the physical process of writing out the answers.

Such a stage also allows the mind to become calmer. The orderly build up of the notes gives a sense of achievement. Most importantly, however, it permits the logical arrangement of points to be presented in the answers. Failure to do this can result in a suddenly remembered point being tacked on to the end of the answer and so be out of logical sequence; or the point may be forgotten entirely!

(The notes must be clearly marked as "Rough Notes" and/or scored through. They *must* be left in the answer book; on no account must any attempt be made to take them with you on leaving. This is very important because otherwise it may lead to a suspicion that they are, in fact, a crib.)

(d) *Plan the timing.* According to the time remaining, allow a certain period for each answer (including extra time for any carrying higher marks). *Every answer must be commenced*, even if time does not allow for completion of all the answers. A candidate who, because of the pressure of time, enters only four answers when five are required, cannot hope for a total of more than 80 per cent. Five good answers may be worth more than four excellent answers. Examiners realise that under the prevailing conditions it is unreasonable to expect perfect answers. The aim must therefore be to answer as well as you can for the full number of questions required in the time available. Time spent in "polishing" an answer (or looking for a small error in a mathematical question) may result in a few marks being added but at the cost of a larger number lost if, as a consequence, there is no opportunity to write all you wish to write.

6. Answering the questions.

(a) *Answer the question set.* This may appear to be an obvious statement, but a considerable number of candidates give the answer they want to provide and not the one the examiner requires. Frequently, this is because they have not studied the question thoroughly. This can arise because the candidate *thinks* the question is one he is very familiar with and, in a burst of gratitude, gives an excellent answer which, unfortunately, does not fit the question. The following is a typical example: "Your directors have asked you, as chief accountant, to report on the advisability of employing a computer bureau to process the payroll". The question does *not* want a list of the advantages and disadvantages of computers. The question relates to a comparison between employing a bureau and doing the work in the company's own office; and it requires an answer in the form of a report.

(b) *Make your answer objective.* This means giving *all* the relevant information and *no more.* Straying from the point earns no marks and may give rise to a charge of "padding". If your answer appears to be unduly short, it may be that it shouldn't be anything else. A question on law, for instance, may possibly be answered in a few sentences. Provided they contain the correct information and no other facts can be presented, a short answer would be a successful one.

Open by explaining the objective of the answer if the question lends itself to doing so. This can sometimes be done by transposing the words in the question. For example, a question beginning "What factors should be borne in mind when . . .", can give rise to an answer commencing "The factors to be borne in mind when . . .". At least this would restrict the candidate to the confines of the question.

(c) *Factual questions and discussion questions.* Factual questions require precise answers. A point of law, an economic principle, etc., must be given clearly and adequately.

Discussion questions usually demand a statement of the pros and cons. Questions may be worded as "Give your view on the contention that . . ." or "Comment on the statement that . . .", for example. In such instances, the requirement is to give views for and against. In general, one should not give a firm conclusion; almost certainly it would be unsafe to be dogmatic. For example, one could make various comments about the following statement but no positive conclusion could be expressed: "Mechanisation of the office would lead to increased efficiency and economy".

What the examiner requires is a reasoned discussion—but if a conclusion *is* asked for it must, of course, be given. The fact that the examiner may not agree with your conclusion is immaterial; the important point is the discussion.

If, in drafting your answer, you make an assumption, *say so.* Many questions (including the one quoted above) cannot be answered unless assumptions are made. Thus, one could write "Assuming the business is a large one . . .".

(d) *Answer the required number of questions.* If the candidate answers more questions than is required, the *last one he writes will be deleted.* If you find you can answer another question better than one you have already answered (which would be the result of bad planning and a waste of time!) delete the earlier answer.

Be sure to include any compulsory questions. Where appropriate, be certain you have answered the correct number from each section.

(e) *Help the examiner.* A legible, clearly set out answer makes it easier for the examiner. He cannot be expected to struggle through a maze of disjointed points because you have not taken the trouble to present them clearly.

If the question is in parts, such as (a), (b), (c), your answer *must* be similarly identified.

If you are asked to enumerate, be sure to do so.

Write short paragraphs. A good rule is to use one paragraph for each major point. It leads to clarity of expression and makes the examiner's task easier.

Any deletions must be made neatly and positively. The examiner must be left in no doubt as to what you require to be removed.

EXAMINATION AND EXAMINATION STYLE QUESTIONS

Chapter I.

1. "The policy of the board of directors in a public company should be concerned primarily with the earning of maximum profits for the benefit of the shareholders". Discuss this statement. (*A.C.A.*)

2. Discuss the social responsibilities of management. (*I.C.S.A.*)

3. Discuss the "trusteeship" function of the board of directors of a public company. How far do you consider it is proper to enlarge this concept of trusteeship to include the interests of employees, the customers, and the general public? Detail those major objectives of a business whose determination is essentially the responsibility of the board; comment where you consider necessary. (*I.C.S.A.*)

4. Explain how different industries would be affected in the following circumstances: (*a*) upon the collapse of a motor manufacturer; (*b*) where the Government makes a severe cutback in the Defence Estimates; (*c*) where a major road-building plan is approved; (*d*) where there is a steep rise in the price of houses.

5. What different attitudes to profits may prevail between: (*a*) ordinary shareholders; (*b*) managers; and (*c*) factory-floor workers?

6. Consider how the policies of a limited company may be influenced directly or indirectly by shareholders, employees and customers. (*A.C.A.*)

7. "The health of the economy is still measured in terms of the efficiency with which it can produce large quantities of consumer goods. A second measure—and concern—is needed: one which considers the contribution work is making to the quality of life and growth and happiness of the worker" (Department of Employment Report 1973).

Do you consider a manager has a responsibility for the quality of working life of his staff, and if so what are some specific actions he can take to improve it? (*I.C.S.A.*)

Chapter II.

1. Mr. *A* contemplates opening a business which will require a capital of £10,000. What factors should be considered in choosing between: (*a*) investing £6,000 of his own money and borrowing the balance; and (*b*) making a personal investment of £6,000 and having two friends join him as partners investing £2,000 each?

2. What factors should be considered in deciding whether to trade as a private company or a public company when establishing a business? (*I.C.S.A.*)

3. Compare the possible consequences of a partner withdrawing from a partnership and a shareholder ceasing to be a member.

4. What is the significance of *XYZ* Ltd. and Mr. *X* and Mr. *Y* (shareholders in *XYZ* Ltd.) each being a legal entity?

5. "The directors of a company are both agent and trustee in relation to that company". Discuss. (*I.C.S.A.*)

Chapter III.

1. Account for the decline in the number of independent wholesalers.

2. Show how the operations of grocers have changed in recent years. Are there any social causes of such changes?

3. Is it correct to say that a sharp distinction can still be made between departmental stores, multiples and variety chains?

4. Account for the growth of mail order retailing and explain the problems specific to such businesses.

5. Discuss the independence of sole traders in the retail trade who: (*a*) are members of a voluntary retail chain; and (*b*) have a franchise.

6. A shopper is looking for a particular article.

(*a*) Why may he find exactly the same articles in shops of different types?

(*b*) Why may he find it difficult to obtain one particular article amongst a number of closely similar ones?

Chapter IV.

1. Discuss the conflict between the requirement of a nationalised industry to be financially viable over a period and the provision of an economically priced service to the public.

2. To what extent and to whom are nationalised industries accountable? (*I.C.S.A.*)

3. What characteristics serve to distinguish local authorities from other organs of government? (*I.C.S.A.*)

4. What factors are relevant in determining whether a public service is best administered by a local authority, a public corporation or a government department? (*I.C.S.A.*)

5. Compare the functions and structure of the Trades Union Congress with those of the Confederation of British Industry.

Chapter V.

1. Briefly describe both horizontal and vertical integration, and consider the advantages and disadvantages of increasing the size of a particular business by: (*i*) horizontal integration; (*ii*) vertical integration; (*iii*) merger. (*A.I.A.*)

2. As a form of diversification, a company owning a number of hotels decides to acquire a chain of wine and spirit stores. What advantages could this provide and what could be some of the problems it produces?

3. "There must be a point in an expansionist situation at which the diseconomies of size become apparent". Discuss.

4. Explain why some firms must grow in order to survive, whereas others can continue to exist only if they remain small.

5. A motor manufacturing company wishes to produce vehicles in certain overseas countries. What could be the reasons for this? In what forms could central control of overseas functions take?

Chapter VI.

1. The directors of a company seek your advice as to the relative merits of preference and ordinary shares as a means of raising capital. What are the general considerations involved? (*I.C.S.A.*)

2. The engineering company of which you are the secretary is about to modernise and extend its plant. It is expected that some four years or so will elapse before completion of the work. As the scheme cannot be financed from the company's present resources, the directors are considering the available methods of borrowing or raising fresh capital. You are required to report to them on the relative merits, in the circumstances, of: (*a*) a bank loan or overdraft; (*b*) the issue of debentures; and (*c*) the issue of redeemable preference shares. (*I.C.S.A.*)

3. What service does the Stock Exchange give to the business and industrial community? (*I.C.S.A.*)

4. Your company is considering a further expansion of the business in the near future which will necessitate finding additional capital over a period of several years. You have to advise the board on possible sources of funds. Write a short report and mention factors which might influence the decision as to which additional sources of capital should be sought. (*A.C.A.*)

5. Sales forecasting has been described as the first stage in management. Do you agree? If you agree or disagree, state why. (*A.C.A.*)

6. Comment briefly on the usual rights of holders of preference

shares as to dividends, return of capital and participation in the distribution of surplus assets. (*I.C.S.A.*)

7. Describe the different types of shares and securities which might be issued by a listed company and explain their impact upon its cost of capital. (*I.C.S.A.*)

8. What are the usual features of a debenture? In what respects, if any, might the issuing company make debentures more attractive than other securities? (*I.C.S.A.*)

Chapter VII.

1. The terms *administration* and *management* are often used synonymously. What is the distinction between the two terms? To what extent is the secretary of a large organisation likely to be concerned with: (*a*) administration; (*b*) management? (*I.C.S.A.*)

2. Henry Fayol said that management consisted of six main activities: forecasting, planning, organising, commanding, co-ordinating and controlling. Comment briefly on the nature of each of these functions. (*I.C.M.A.*)

3. Show how the policy of an organisation of your own selection may be clearly defined and communicated to the different levels of management. (*A.C.A.*)

4. A non-executive director has made a suggestion which involves a major change in a company's selling policy. Illustrate the procedures leading to final implementation of the suggestion. (*I.C.M.A.*)

5. Many businesses are engaged in long-range planning of their production and marketing efforts. Why are they conscious of the need for long-range planning? What benefits can be anticipated from such planning? (*I.C.M.A.*)

6. A works manager in a car plant, a bank manager, a data processing manager and a colliery manager are responsible for widely differing work, but all have the word "manager" in their job title. What are the common elements in managerial work and have they changed over the last 70 years? (*I.C.S.A.*)

7. What activities are likely to be carried out in a corporate planning department and why have such departments become a more frequent feature of business organisation? (*I.C.S.A.*)

8. Effective corporate planning depends on the prior formulation of a business policy with long-term objectives for the company which will lead to a co-ordination of all the various activities and their orientation towards the corporate objective. Discuss the factors which need to be considered in defining the corporate objective. (*I.C.M.A.*)

Chapter VIII.

1. What do you understand by "organisation"? List the rules which ought to be applied to ensure that it is effective. What are the chief forms of organisation found in commercial undertakings? (*I.C.S.A.*)

2. Write an essay, not exceeding 300 words, on the seeming conflict between "delegation" and "control" in business administration. Suggest how you think a business could realise the advantages of delegation and at the same time maintain centralised control. (*A.C.A.*)

3. You are the company secretary of a large manufacturing organisation which has four factories, each employing about 1,000 people, in Manchester, Bristol, Newcastle and Coventry. The Bristol factory is also the head office (which is where you are based) and offers the full range of central services to the rest of the organisation. However, there is much evidence of inefficiency and delays in these central services and their cost-benefit is being questioned by senior management. The Managing Director has asked you for definite proposals for restructuring the organisation to overcome these problems. What advice would you give him? Use organisation charts to support your answer. (*I.C.S.A.*)

4. Classify the various types of committee and consider their use as an effective means of co-ordination of management policy. (*A.C.A.*)

5. In recent years the amount of time required to be spent in committee work by senior staffs in industrial and other organisations has increased considerably. State briefly the purposes for which committees may be formed and consider the importance of the rationalisation of procedures and of sound administrative arrangements for the expeditious and efficient conduct of business in committee meetings. (*A.C.A.*)

6. "A logical structure (for organisations) is better for efficiency and morale than one allowed to develop around personalities". (Colonel Urwick.) What would be your reasons for agreeing or disagreeing with this statement? (*I.C.S.A.*)

7. What are the responsibilities normally undertaken by a board of directors? State the particular functions of the managing director and his relationship to the rest of the board. What are executive directors? (*I.C.M.A.*)

8. In what sense does a board of directors "manage" a business? What grades of executive do you consider the board should be responsible for appointing, and why? To what extent should the board supervise the financial and other results of a business, and by what means? (*I.C.S.A.*)

Chapter IX.

1. In constructing a table of statistics, (*a*) what decisions should be taken before its preparation; and (*b*) what considerations should you observe in its construction? In your answer, state which form of statistical table you have in mind. (*I.C.S.A.*)

2. "Management must be made aware of the increasing importance of maintaining good communications, both internal and external". Why are good communications so important, and, what oral, written and visual methods of communication are available to those responsible for management? (*I.C.S.A.*)

3. The directors of a company in the light engineering industry with about 2,000 employees are concerned about the high rate of labour turnover within the organisation. They request you to draft a report listing the probable causes and suggesting ways in which a significant reduction in this turnover may be brought about. (*A.C.A.*)

4. Outline the basic requirements of network analysis in office management and state the benefits likely to accrue from a well-organised analysis. (*A.C.A.*)

5. Explain the purpose of a break-even chart. Prepare a simple chart to illustrate your answer and indicate what conclusions might be drawn from it. (*I.C.S.A.*)

6. There have been several letters in your local press urging a ban on smoking on your company's double decker buses. As Public Relations Officer, write a reply explaining your company's attitude. (*I.C.S.A.*)

7. Describe how you would use: (*a*) printed material; (*b*) films; (*c*) tape recorders, on an induction course for 16-year-old recruits. (*I.C.S.A.*)

8. "If we accept the view that the essential job of a manager is to get work done through other people, it follows that his effectiveness as a manager must depend on his ability to communicate with his working groups and of their ability to communicate with him". (Noel Branton.) Discuss the problem of communication "upwards" and "downwards" within the business, and outwards to the public. (*I.C.S.A.*)

9. "Staff morale depends largely upon the communication of information". Discuss this dictum and indicate ways in which the communication of information can be made to maintain a high level of morale in a large industrial or commercial organisation. (*I.C.S.A.*)

10. What would you say are the main advantages of the spoken word over all other forms of communication? (*A.I.A.*)

11. Illustrate and state the purpose(s) for which each of the following are used: (*a*) pictogram; (*b*) cartogram; (*c*) pie chart; (*d*) ratio scale graph. (*I.A.A.*)

12. Give a concise description of the technique of critical path analysis and show its value to management. (*A.I.A.*)

13. As a secretary of an organisation, prepare a memorandum on the dissemination of management-employee information. (*I.C.S.A.*)

Chapter X.

1. Describe how a good plant layout may reduce manufacturing costs and increase efficiency. State briefly the steps you would take when planning a new plant layout. (*I.C.M.A.*)

2. Summarise the functions of production planning, progressing and control. Start with the assumption that the sales forecast has been completed. (*I.C.S.A.*)

3. What is meant by diversification of a product line? Why should a company undertake diversification? (*I.C.M.A.*)

4. State the advantages you think would arise to (*a*) manufacturers, (*b*) distributors, (*c*) consumers, from specialisation, simplification and standardisation in the production of a commodity. (*A.C.A.*)

5. In order that the function of inspection shall not be negative only, it is essential to recognise that "the task of inspection is to control the quality of production". Referring to the above statement, outline the basic features which should be included in a system of quality control by inspection. (*A.C.A.*)

6. A designer must take into consideration a number of points in the design of a successful article. Enumerate these as they might apply to products generally and not to one particular item. (*I.C.M.A.*)

7. Distinguish between method study and work measurement and indicate what each sets out to achieve. What arguments would you advance to persuade critics that the successful application of these techniques is worthwhile? (*I.C.S.A.*)

8. Consider the advantages and disadvantages of a full order book, from the point of view of economy and efficiency in manufacturing, and comment on the importance of balanced use of factory capacity. (*I.C.S.A.*)

9. What benefits are likely to be derived by an industrial organisation where great importance is attached to good housekeeping in the factory (that is, maintaining a high standard of order, neatness and cleanliness)? (*A.C.A.*)

Chapter XI.

1. The purchasing officer must exercise skill and judgment when buying materials. Give examples of his duties to support this statement. State briefly the main items of information which should appear on the purchase order. (*I.C.M.A.*)

2. What procedure would you introduce to control the purchase of replacement and additional capital equipment? (*I.C.M.A.*)

3. Describe the organisation of the purchasing department of a manufacturing business. Reference to purchasing procedures and policy may be made but it is not necessary to go into the detail of purchasing records. (*I.C.S.A.*)

4. Should the purchasing department in a large undertaking be a completely separate department or part of the administrative department? How far should purchasing staff be permitted to challenge or enquire about requisitions that reach them? (*I.C.S.A.*)

5. Set out the duties of a head storekeeper. What principles would he adopt when arranging the location of materials in his store? (*I.C.M.A.*)

6. What preliminary arrangements would you make for the taking of stock at the year-end? Presume that you will have stock at the works, in bond and on consignment. (*I.C.S.A.*)

7. The management have noted a significant increase in the level of stocks held and ask you to carry out an investigation. Set out the possible reasons to which you consider this increase might be attributed. (*I.C.M.A.*)

8. What are the major differences which are to be expected between the stock control systems of two industrial firms, one of which has a seasonal demand for its products and the other a seasonal supply of raw materials? (*A.C.A.*)

Chapter XII.

1. In your opinion, does advertising help to decrease or increase the cost of goods to the ultimate customer? Give reasons for your answer. (*A.C.A.*)

2. Draft a report outlining the scope, purpose, method and justification for market research. (*I.C.S.A.*)

3. Describe briefly: (*a*) the main functions of the export department within the home organisation of an exporter; (*b*) the channels of distribution of goods available to an exporter. (*A.C.A.*)

4. "There is a general lack of understanding of the functions of the modern retailer and of the fact that marketing . . . is essentially a continuous process from the factory floor to the store counter"—Chairman, Marks & Spencer Ltd. Comment. (*I.C.S.A.*)

5. What are the purposes of sales forecasting? State the factors influencing the level of sales in any company, distinguishing between controllable factors and uncontrollable factors. (*I.C.M.A.*)

6. In what ways can a manufacturer keep himself informed about the state of the market for a new product both before and after its introduction? (*I.C.M.A.*)

7. How would you establish an efficient and comprehensive

after-sales service for a manufacturer of mechanised equipment? (*I.C.M.A.*)

8. The board of a raincoat manufacturing company, with capital employed of about £250,000, has discussed the possibility of increasing the company sales by entering the export field. You are required to advise the board about the information necessary to enable a decision to be made whether to export or not, and to state the sources from which advisory information for exporters may be obtained. (*A.C.A.*)

9. Describe any of the usual credit control methods adopted in any business known to you. Do you consider that credit insurance should be regarded as an alternative to, or complementary with, the usual credit control methods? (*I.C.S.A.*)

Chapter XIII.

1. State the essentials of good company-employee relationship and welfare services. (*I.C.M.A.*)

2. What steps would a personnel officer take to ensure that the staff selection procedure operated by his department is efficient and effective? (*I.C.M.A.*)

3. What are the essentials of a sound policy for the training of supervisors? How would a training scheme for senior management differ from that for supervisors? (*A.C.A.*)

4. Discuss the growing importance of the personnel officer, and justify the statement that "the existence of a personnel department is by itself no guarantee of good relations within an organisation". (*I.C.S.A.*)

5. Describe the records to be kept in a large organisation to ensure that salary increments are granted only when deserved and that promotion is the reward of merit alone. (*I.C.M.A.*)

6. You have been retained by a company which foresees that a number of its employees will become redundant in the near future. You are required to outline the basic principles to be taken into account in the design of a redundancy scheme, indicating any practical features which may operate as a modification to such a scheme. Details of the *Redundancy Payments Act* 1965 are not required. (*A.C.A.*)

7. The directors of a company in the light engineering industry with about 2,000 employees, are concerned about the high rate of labour turnover within the organisation. They request you draft a report listing the probable causes and suggesting ways in which a significant reduction in this turnover may be brought about. (*A.C.A.*)

8. "Joint consultation is not concerned with pay or conditions of service". Assuming this is true, what other matters might be dealt with by joint consultation? In the capacity of secretary in a

large trading concern, what part would you play, and what methods would you suggest should be used for achieving the best results from joint consultation? (*I.C.S.A.*)

9. You are required to draft an advertisement, for insertion in a professional journal, for the appointment of a group personnel officer. In addition, you should prepare, in summary form, a schedule of the responsibilities of this officer. (*A.C.A.*)

Chapter XIV.

1. Explain the control element in a system of budgetary control, and describe how standards for labour, materials and overheads are established in a system of standard costs. (*A.I.A.*)

2. "Scientific management is more concerned with future developments than historical facts". Discuss, and state how, in your opinion, an efficient costing system can assist management in formulating a forward-looking business policy. (*I.C.S.A.*)

3. The main function of accounting is to record, summarise and report various business facts. To do this requires a measurement of these facts and an accounting measurement, like most others, is an approximation. Why are accounting figures approximations? Give examples of three items which appear in the published accounts of a limited company and which are approximations. What basic requirements of a management accounting system add to the degree of approximation in accounting figures? (*A.C.A.*)

4. "Costing is an instrument of management control". "Costing is nothing more than a detailed analysis of expenditure". Reconcile these two statements, quoting examples to illustrate the truth of each. (*A.C.A.*)

5. "The management accountant must be able to communicate his findings effectively to all levels of management". Discuss this statement and explain the general principles you would observe in the design and presentation of management accounting reports. (*I.C.S.A.*)

6. Your organisation has decided to introduce a comprehensive system of budgetary control. As a first step it has been decided to form a budget committee, and you have been requested to prepare a report for your managing director on the functions of such a committee within the system of budgetary control and who should serve on it. (*A.C.A.*)

7. Explain what you understand by "contribution", in a cost accounting sense. How is it related to profit? List three benefits that management can obtain from knowing the contribution from its cost units. (*I.C.M.A.*)

8. "A knowledge both of the detailed make-up of overheads and of the general relationship between overheads and volume of production can often be a key to higher profits". Explain and discuss. (*I.C.S.A.*)

Chapter XV.

1. What do you understand by the statement that management of the office is a specialist function? Explain how recognition of this fact affects the general organisation of a business. (*I.C.M.A.*)

2. What are the tests to be applied in assessing office efficiency? If an office is shown to be inefficient, can it necessarily be made more efficient by mechanisation? Discuss. (*I.C.S.A.*)

3. List and briefly discuss at least four advantages likely to be obtained by introducing mechanised accounting in place of manual methods. To what particular points would regard be paid when deciding whether to make such a change? (*I.C.S.A.*)

4. What factors make work measurement in the office difficult and in what ways have the problems been surmounted? Refer in your answer to contemporary approaches to the problem. (*I.C.S.A.*)

5. Describe the benefits which may be expected from the formation of an office methods department in an organisation of your choice. (*A.C.A.*)

6. An office which is primarily engaged on work of a technical nature is staffed by ten technical officers, each of whom has the assistance of a non-technical clerk. It is proposed to place the clerks under the control of a senior clerk, who would be responsible for providing a clerical service to all the technical officers. What are the likely merits and demerits of such a plan? (*I.C.M.A.*)

7. Enumerate the factors to be taken into consideration when a form is being designed. (*I.C.M.A.*)

8. Discuss the means of reducing paper-work without loss of efficiency in a group of companies in the retail trade with about 100 multiple branches. (*A.C.A.*)

9. In carrying out a work-study programme, a team working under your supervision has discovered that there is a great deal to criticise on the subject of your employer's methods of written communication. Report to your board of management, summarising your team's findings, and submitting their proposals for setting up a system of forms control, which would result in improved methods of written communication, both internal and external. (*I.C.S.A.*)

INDEX

Ability tests, 173
Accounting, 192 *et seq.*
  budgetary control, 195-9
  ratios, 194
Activity sampling, 116
Administration, 58
  cost budget, 199
Advertising, 137, 147-51
After-sales service, 153
Analytical estimating, 116
Appraisals, staff, 166, 177
Aptitude tests, 173
Articles of Association, 16
Assembly-line system, 104
Assurance companies, 52
Attitude surveys, 139
Authority and responsibility, 70-3
Automatic control, 112
Automatic vending, 25

Band curve charts, 97
Banks, 52
Bar charts, 97
Batch production, 103
Bonus schemes, 180
Borrowing, 44
Break-even analysis, 204
Break-even chart, 98, 204
Budget, 195-9
  administration cost, 199
  capital expenditure, 199
  cash, 47, 199
  centre, 197
  classifications, 196
  committee, 196
  materials, 199
  officer, 196
  plant, 117
  production, 199
  purchasing, 199
  sales, 199

Budgetary control, 195-9
Buildings, factory, 106
Bureaucracy, 36, 79
Business
  attitudes, 6
  classifications of, 2, 4, 6, 9
  control and ownership, 55
  expansion, 33 *et seq.*
  objectives, 6
  units, 10 *et seq.*
Buying methods, 124

Capital, 18, 44 *et seq.*
  company, 48-51
  expenditure budget, 199
  gearing, 51
  return on, 194
Capitalisation, under-, 48
Cash budget, 47, 199
Centralisation, 78
  office services, 208
  purchasing department, 125
Chain of command, 81
Chain stores, 23
Chambers of Commerce, 31
Channels of communication, 88
Charts, 97
Collective bargaining, 186
Collective organisations, 29-31
Committees, 77
Communication, 86 *et seq.*, 163
  barriers to, 87
  channels of, 88
  external, 89
  management information, 95
  public delivery, 91
  reports, 93
  verbal, 90
  visual aids, 92
Companies, *see* Limited com-
  panies